American Commonwealths.

VOLUME 11

MISSOURI

AMS PRESS
NEW YORK

American Commonwealths

MISSOURI

A BONE OF CONTENTION

BY

LUCIEN CARR

BOSTON AND NEW YORK
HOUGHTON, MIFFLIN AND COMPANY
The Riverside Press, Cambridge

Library of Congress Cataloging in Publication Data

Carr, Lucien, 1829-1915.
    Missouri: a bone of contention.

    Original ed. issued as v. 11 of American
commonwealths.
    1. Missouri--History. I. Title.
II. Series: American commonwealths, v. 11.
F466.C33 1973   977.8   72-3761
ISBN 0-404-57211-1

Reprinted from the edition of 1888, Boston and New York
First AMS edition published, 1973
Manufactured in the United States of America

International Standard Book Number:
Complete Series: 0-404-57200-6
Volume 11: 0-404-57211-1

AMS PRESS, INC.
New York, N.Y.   10003

PREFATORY NOTE.

————◆————

IN the preparation of this volume the following works have been found of service, though it is proper to add that the list is by no means complete, and that it does not include any of the authoritative publications that have found their way into the newspapers and magazines of the day.

BANCROFT, H. H. History of the Pacific States. San Francisco.

BARBÉ-MARBOIS. Histoire de la Louisiane. Paris, 1829.

BARNES, C. R., editor. Commonwealth of Missouri. St. Louis, 1877.

BENTON, THOMAS H. Thirty Years in the Senate of the United States. New York, 1856. Abridgment of the Debates in Congress, from 1789 to 1856. New York.

BEVIER, R. S. History of the 1st and 2d Missouri Confederate Brigades. From Wakarusa to Appomattox. St. Louis, 1879.

BILLON, F. L. Annals of St. Louis. St. Louis, 1886.

BRACKENRIDGE, H. M. Views of Louisiana. Pittsburgh, 1814. Recollections of the West, 2d edition. Philadelphia, 1868.

BROWN, G. W. Reminiscences of Old John Brown. Rockford, Ill., 1880.

Buchanan's Administration. New York, 1866.

COOKE, P. ST. GEORGE. Conquest of California and New Mexico. New York, 1878.

DAVIS and DURRIE. History of Missouri. Cincinnati, 1876.

EDWARDS, RICHARD, and M. HOPEWELL. The Great West. St. Louis, 1860.

FLINT, TIMOTHY. Travels. Boston, 1826.

GAYARRÉ, CHARLES. History of Louisiana. New Orleans, 1885.

HUGHES, JOHN T. Doniphan's Expedition. Cincinnati, 1848.

Laws of the United States.

Laws of the State of Missouri.

LUNT, GEORGE. Origin of the Late War. New York, 1866.

MARGRY, PIERRE. Découverte de l'Amérique Septentrionale. Paris.

MARTIN, F. X. History of Louisiana. New Orleans, 1827.

NILES' Register.

Official Records of the Rebellion. Washington.

PARKMAN, FRANCIS. Discovery of the Great West. Boston, 1869.

PECKHAM, JAMES. General Nathaniel Lyon. New York, 1866.

Proceedings of Congress.

Proceedings of the Legislature of Missouri.

Proceedings of Missouri State Conventions, 1861 and 1865.

SANBORN, F. B. Life and Letters of John Brown. Boston, 1885.

SCHARF, J. T. History of St. Louis. Philadelphia, 1883.

SHEA, JOHN G. Discovery and Exploration of the Mississippi. New York, 1852.

SNEAD, THOMAS L. The Fight for Missouri. New York, 1886.

STODDARD, MAJOR AMOS. Sketches of Louisiana. Philadelphia, 1812.

VON HOLST. Constitutional History of the United States. Chicago.

WILKINSON, GENERAL JAMES. Memoirs of my own Times. Philadelphia, 1816.

WINSOR, JUSTIN, Editor. Narrative and Critical History of America. Boston.

The writer desires also to acknowledge his obligations to Messrs. Oscar W. Collet, of the Missouri Historical Society, John N. Dyer, of the Mercantile Library of St. Louis, General James Harding, Railroad Commissioner of the State, and to Alfred Carr, of the Insurance Department; to Ex-Governors Thomas C. Fletcher and Charles H. Hardin, General D. M. Frost of the Confederate service, and to Messrs. James O. Broadhead and Thomas T. Gantt, who as members of the Constitutional Convention, and in other capacities, did good service for the Union. To Mr. R. J. Holcombe of Chillicothe, Missouri, Andrew McF. Davis of Cambridge, Mass., and John Henry Brown of Dallas, Texas, the friend and aid-de-camp of General McCulloch, he is especially indebted for friendly counsel and assistance.

CAMBRIDGE, MASS., May 1, 1888.

CONTENTS.

———◆———

CHAPTER I.

CHAPTER II.

CHAPTER III.

CHAPTER IV.

CHAPTER V.

CHAPTER VI.

CHAPTER VII.

CHAPTER VIII.

MISSOURI.

CHAPTER I.

DISCOVERY AND EXPLORATION OF THE MISSISSIPPI.

ALTHOUGH the French were the first to explore the Mississippi, to map out its course, and to establish permanent settlements upon its banks, they were not its discoverers; neither were they the first to float upon its waters. That honor, if the term can be applied to what was but a lucky incident in a mad search after gold, belongs to the Spaniards, and is usually ascribed to Hernando de Soto, though upon what are believed to be insufficient grounds. Without stopping, however, to discuss the point, it is sufficient to say that almost a century and a half before the French explorers launched their frail canoes upon the stream, he stood upon its banks; and whilst it is not possible to make out, with any degree of accuracy, the itinerary of his journey, there is but little hazard in asserting that the spot from which he first gazed upon its turbid waters must have been at or near the place where the city of Memphis now stands.

Whether in the course of his wanderings he reached the confines of what is now known as the State of Missouri is a question that cannot be definitively settled.

The course and length of the journey which he is said
to have made, after crossing the river, in order to reach
the country of the Capahas, or, as they are now called,
the Quapaws, would seem to indicate that he did; the
mounds and embankments, too, to say nothing of the
other evidences of prehistoric life that are found in such
profusion in the southeastern portion of the State, answer, with singular fidelity, to the descriptions which are
given of the houses and villages of these people, as well
as of their implements and ornaments; and if to this be
added the fact that, a hundred and fifty years later,
they were living in the same region, though not, perhaps,
in the identical localities, it will be seen that a strong
presumptive case can be made out in favor of the truth
of the theory.   However, be this as it may, it is not a
point upon which we care to insist, for even if the fact
be admitted, it was not followed by any practical results.
Like Cortes, Pizarro, and the rest of the Spanish con-
querors, De Soto and his followers were primarily, not
colonists, but adventurers in search of gold, and being
disappointed in their object, they had no thought but to
quit a country which had ceased to be attractive.   Accordingly in 1543, after two years more of wearisome
marching and useless fighting, the survivors of the expedition, reduced in numbers, and with their leader
dead, found their way back to the banks of the river,
and down it they sailed in hastily constructed brigan-
tines, glad enough to escape from a region in which,
instead of wealth and ease, they had met with nothing
but privation and hardship, sickness and death.

  With the failure of this expedition, efforts to explore
the Mississippi valley were, for the time being, brought
to a close; and it was not until after the lapse of a hun-

dred and thirty years that the work was again taken up and carried to a successful conclusion. In the mean time, the Atlantic coast, from Florida to Canada, had been dotted with colonies. Of these, some were comparatively short lived, as, for instance, the settlements of the Dutch and Swedes in New York and New Jersey respectively; others, like the establishments of the Spaniards in Florida, appear to have been always in a moribund condition, and owed what little success they had to the rivalry of their neighbors, rather than to any strength of their own : so that by the close of the seventeenth century, the whole of the vast domain that lies east of the Mississippi and south of Hudson's Bay, except, perhaps, the peninsula of Florida, was in the hands of the English and French.

These nations, enemies and rivals here, as they had been for generations on the other side of the water, were among the earliest to engage in the work of colonization. At first, their efforts met with but little success, and it was not until after repeated failures that they succeeded, in the first decade of the seventeenth century, in effecting permanent settlements at Jamestown and Quebec. Other points were gradually occupied, and as both nations claimed the whole of this region, and did not hesitate, when opportunity offered, to treat their rivals as interlopers, it soon brought on that long and bloody struggle which, beginning with Argall's destruction of the French settlement on the island of Mount Desert in 1613, was only ended, a hundred and fifty years later, by the victory of Wolfe upon the Plains of Abraham.

In watching the course of this struggle, or rather in noting the progress of these colonies, for the struggle

itself interests us but little, we cannot but be struck
with the contrast that exists between the rapid advance
of the French into the interior of the continent and the
slow and steady growth of the English in the same
direction.   As early as 1639, only about thirty years
after Quebec was founded, Nicolet was upon the Wisconsin and within three days' travel of the Mississippi,
or as it was then thought, the ocean; and in 1671, before the Massachusetts colonists had closed in the death
struggle with King Philip, and whilst the spot where
now stands the city of Philadelphia was still a part of
the virgin forest, the Jesuits had completed the circuit
of Lake Superior, and were anxiously waiting for the
word which, two years later, sent Joliet and Marquette
on their voyage down the Mississippi.   Various reasons
are brought forward by way of accounting for the unequal rate at which the colonies of these two nations
moved westward, and, so far as the French are concerned,
there can be no doubt that their progress in this direction was due in great part to religious enthusiasm and
the necessities of the fur-trade.   Unquestionably there
were other causes, as, for instance, the facility of intercommunication and the hostility of the Iroquois, which
contributed either to hasten or retard the movement;
but after all, in its last analysis, it was to the activity of
the fur-trader and the zeal of the missionary that the
French were indebted for their early acquaintance with
all this region.

To appreciate the full extent of the influence which
these two classes exerted in bringing about this result, it
is necessary to bear in mind that they had controlled the
destinies of the colony from its very foundation; and
that, no matter how widely they may have differed at

times in their ends and aims, they were always alike in so far as they both depended, for their continued prosperity, upon the extension of French influence among the native tribes. To them, every step in this direction meant an increase in the number of those who looked to Quebec for a market, or who trusted to it for religious instruction, and hence the energy with which they pushed their way into the interior, sought out new alliances, and established posts and missions wherever there was a promise of a commercial or a spiritual harvest.

Urged on by considerations of this character, the Récollet fathers visited the eastern shores of Lake Huron, and established themselves among the people of that name as early as 1615 ; and, by the middle of the century, the Jesuits, who had succeeded to the control of the religious affairs of the colony, had in operation among this same people one of the most flourishing missions that has ever existed among our North American Indians. Unfortunately, however, for the success of the undertaking, the Iroquois war broke out afresh about this time, and those grim warriors, having obtained a supply of firearms from the English and Dutch traders, soon made a desert of all the region that lies between the Ottawa and the lakes. In their insane fury they spared neither missionary nor medicine man, neither Christian convert nor pagan devotee.

Of those who escaped the general ruin, a part fled to the regions west of the Straits of Michilimackinac, and sought refuge along the southern shores of Lake Superior. Hither, in due time, came the traders and the no less venturesome missionaries, and in this distant region they resumed the work which had met with such a bloody interruption. With characteristic energy they established posts and founded missions among the Huron refugees and their neighbors, and began at once that series of explorations which, in the course of the next fifteen years, not only made the French familiar with the geography of the upper lakes, but brought them to the head waters of streams which, flowing towards the southwest, emptied into a river that led they knew not whither, "perhaps into the Sea of Virginia, the Gulf of Mexico, or possibly into the Vermillion Sea" and the Pacific Ocean.

Henceforward the discovery of this river and of the great valley through which it flows was a foregone conclusion. In fact, its existence seems already to have been generally known both to the traders and the missionaries, for there is scarcely a record of the period in which the references to it are not more or less frequent. In 1658 two traders, Radisson and Groseilliers, wintered on the shores of Lake Superior, and brought back stories of the Sioux and of the great river upon which they dwelt. A few years later Father Allouez confirmed their account, and in 1669–70, in the course of his missionary labors, he visited the Mascoutens, who were then living on the Wisconsin, "within six days' sail of the Mississippi." La Salle, too, was not idle; for it was about this time that, taking advantage of a lull in the Iroquois war, he started out in search of the mysterious stream; and, though the evidence is not sufficient to prove that he reached it during the course of this expedition, yet there seems to be no doubt that he discovered the Ohio, and perhaps also the Illinois. Last, but not least, Marquette, in the "Relation of 1670," reports what the Illinois had told him of this river; and, in his far distant station, near the western extremity of

Lake Superior, he was planning a visit to the "nations that inhabit it, in order to open the passage to so many of our fathers, who have long awaited this happiness." Indeed, a mission among the Illinois is said to have been decided on, and he was already studying that language when the station at St. Esprit was broken up by the Sioux, and the unfortunate Hurons were obliged to resume their wanderings. Following his flock as they retraced their steps towards the east, he came with them to the Straits of Michilimackinac, where, tempted by the abundance of fish and the facilities of trade, they halted and fortified themselves. Here he built a log chapel and founded the mission of St. Ignatius, and here he passed the next two years of his life in the faithful discharge of the round of duties that fell to his lot, though his thoughts seem to have been ever turned towards the Mississippi. Even when writing hopefully of his work among the Hurons, as he did in 1672, he avows his willingness "to give it up and go to seek new nations towards the south sea . . . to teach them of our Great God," whenever it should be thought advisable for him to do so.

Fortunately he had not long to wait, for, in the autumn of this year, Frontenac became governor; and as he was a man of ideas as well as of action, he quickly saw the importance of the scheme which he had inherited from Talon for the occupation of the interior of the continent, and he determined to carry out the plan which had already been partially formed for the discovery and exploration of the Mississippi. Joliet, who had been educated for a Jesuit, but who was now a furtrader, and a man of experience, and "had already been near the great river," was chosen for the work, and with him was associated Marquette, the saintly missionary at Point St. Ignatius, or, as it is now called, Mackinaw.

Starting on his journey without any unnecessary delay, Joliet reached the mission at Mackinaw, and on the 8th of December, the festival of the Immaculate Conception, gave Marquette the news that he had been assigned to the expedition, — a coincidence which the good father does not fail to notice. During the next few months, the explorers busied themselves in collecting what information they could as to their route, for they were determined that the enterprise " should not be foolhardy," even if it were hazardous. From the accounts given by the Indians " who had frequented these parts," they were able to trace a map of all the new country, marking down the rivers on which they were to sail, the names of the nations and places through which they were to pass, the course of the great river, and what direction they were to take when they reached it. Everything seems to have been done coolly and systematically, and, so far as it was possible to see into the future, nothing was left to chance. With the return of spring, the final preparations were made for the journey, " the duration of which," we are told, " they could not foresee." This did not take them long, for their outfit was simple, consisting merely of two birch canoes and a supply of Indian corn and dried meat. They also engaged five men to accompany them; and then, having put their voyage under the protection of the Blessed Virgin, they set out on the 17th of May, 1673, " firmly resolved to do all and suffer all for so glorious an enterprise."

Skirting along the shores of Lake Michigan and

Green Bay, they entered Fox River, and followed it up to the water-shed which divides the lakes from the Mississippi. This they crossed, and, launching their canoes upon the Wisconsin, they paddled down stream "for a distance of seventy leagues," when, on the 17th of June, they found themselves upon the broad bosom of the Mississippi.

Descending with the current, they cautiously felt their way along, anchoring at night at some distance from the shores. In a few simple sentences the good father describes the country through which they passed, and the different kinds of animals which they met. Especially was he struck with the size of the fish, and the appearance of the buffaloes. At length, on the 25th, they discovered on the west bank of the river footprints and a beaten path which led into a beautiful prairie. Rightly conjecturing that it was the pathway to an Indian village, they followed it for some two leagues, when they came to a cluster of three villages, which, to their great relief, were inhabited by bands of the Illinois, the very tribe which Marquette had long been anxious to visit. Here they were received with true Indian hospitality. A feast of four courses was duly prepared, during which the several dishes were fed to them as if they were children. They were also treated to the "calumet" dance, and, what was more to the point, one of these mysterious pipes was given to them as a safeguard, for with it "you can march fearlessly among enemies, who, even in the heat of battle, lay down their arms when it is shown."

Resuming their journey, they coasted along the Piasa bluffs, on which were painted two frightful monsters as large as calves, "with horns on the head like a deer, a

fearful look, red eyes, bearded like a tiger, the face somewhat like a man's, the body covered with scales, and the
tail so long that it twice makes the turn of the body, passing over the head and down between the legs, and ending
at last in a fish's tail." These figures were so " high up on
the rock that it must have been difficult to get at them
in order to paint them," and yet the work is said to have
been so well done that " good painters in France would
find it hard to do as well." Green, red, and black were
the colors used, and altogether it seems to have been
a very creditable piece of savage workmanship. Having passed this fearful spot, " on which the boldest Indian dare not gaze long, and whilst still talking about
it," they came to the mouth of the Missouri. From
the description of the scene, it must have been during
the spring freshet, and any one who has ever looked
upon the junction of these two mighty streams at such
a time will not fail to appreciate the dangers to which
our explorers were now exposed. Luckily, however,
they escaped, and holding on their course for a few days
longer they reached the mouth of the Ohio, or Oua-
boukigou, on which the Shawnees are said to have had
thirty-eight villages.

Soon after leaving this point, and whilst floating la-
zily along, scorched by the sun and a prey to the mos-
quitoes, they were startled by seeing on the east bank
of the river a band of Indians, who were armed with
guns, wore cloth clothes, and had hoes, hatchets, beads,
and other things which had evidently been obtained from
the whites. Marquette now displayed the calumet,
which was at once recognized, and he and his party were
invited to land and to partake of a feast, at which they
were served with "wild beef, bear's oil, and white

plums." The next morning they again set out, and after a monotonous journey of some days they came to a village of the Mitchigamea, which was situated eight or ten leagues above the mouth of the Arkansas. Here, for the first time, they met with what promised to be a hostile reception. The war-whoop was sounded, the young warriors crowded to the attack, and one of them threw his war club, which fortunately missed its aim. It was a critical moment, but just at this time some of the old men appeared upon the scene, and, recognizing the peace-pipe which Marquette held aloft, they checked the ardor of the young warriors and put an end to the threatened conflict. The Frenchmen were now invited to land, and after a friendly conference and the usual feast, they passed the night in the cabins of their entertainers, but "not without some uneasiness." Embarking again the next day, they reached the village of the Arkansas ("Akamsea"), which was situated opposite the mouth of the river of that name, in what is now the State of Mississippi. As their coming had been announced, they were received with every mark of honor. A feast was given them which seems to have lasted all day, and at night the chief danced the calumet as a mark of perfect assurance, and then, to remove all fears, he presented one of these pipes to Marquette.

From these Indians they learned that they were ten days' journey from the sea, and that the lower portion of the river was so infested by hostile tribes, armed with guns, that any farther progress in that direction would be attended with great danger. Under these circumstances, the explorers held a council and decided to return. They had gone far enough to satisfy themselves that the Mississippi emptied into the Gulf of Mexico, and they were fearful if they went farther of being captured by the Indians or Spaniards, and thus losing the fruits of their labors. Accordingly on the 17th of July they set out on their homeward voyage. When they reached the mouth of the Illinois they determined to return by that route instead of by the way by which they came. This, we are told, shortened their journey, and brought them without trouble to the lake of the Illinois, or, as it is now called, Michigan. Coasting along its western shores, they reached the mission at the head of Green Bay on the last of September, having been gone just four months and traveled over twenty-five hundred miles.

Leaving Marquette here, to rest and recuperate, Joliet pushed on to Quebec. When near Montreal, and almost in sight of his destination, his canoe was upset, and all his papers were lost. It was a serious accident, but fortunately not irreparable, for Marquette, too, had kept a journal of the voyage; and though Joliet made a short report from memory, yet it is to the narrative of the worthy Jesuit that we are chiefly indebted for what we know of this expedition. In the map which accompanies his " Relation," he has rudely sketched the river system of the valley as far as it was known; and in his speculations as to the length and course of the Missouri, and his familiarity with the names and locations of some of the tribes that dwelt upon its banks, as well as of those that lived upon the Ohio, he gives a very favorable idea of the extent and character of the knowledge which, even at this early day, the French had acquired of the geography of all this region.

Important as were the results of this expedition, there was yet much to be done before the full benefits of the discovery could be reaped. The upper and lower portions of the river were yet to be explored, and when this was done and the course of the great river was known through its entire length, measures would still have to be taken for the occupation of the country through which it flowed. This was a vast undertaking, but it was of a character that was suited to the spirit of that age, and La Salle, who " had obtained the grant of Fort Frontenac, the monopoly of the lake trade, and a patent of nobility," now set out to accomplish it. He was a friend if not a partner of the governor, and he had rich relatives in France who were willing to assist him, so that he was able to command political influence and money, or its equivalent, credit. Besides these essential requisites he was endowed with certain attributes of mind and body, and was possessed of a measure of experience that fitted him for the work. He had already, as has been said, discovered the Ohio, and probably the Illinois too ; and if he did not reach the Mississippi, he certainly knew of its existence, and he may possibly have identified it with the great river of De Soto. At all events, he seems to have had very clear ideas as to where it emptied and of its commercial possibilities, for he had obtained a monopoly of the fur-trade of the valley, and contemplated the erection of forts and the establishment of colonies at such points as would give him the control of this trade in fact as well as in name, and thus enable him to establish his fortunes upon a sure foundation.

In pursuance of this plan, he led an expedition to the Illinois, in the winter of 1679–80, and built a fort on that stream, just below Peoria lake, to which he gave the name of *Crève-cœur*. From this point as a base, he dispatched Father Hennepin to explore the lower Illinois and the upper Mississippi, whilst he himself returned to Fort Frontenac, now Kingston, in order to look after his affairs, which had fallen into confusion.

After some delay, growing out of his unwillingness to undertake the expedition, Hennepin finally set out on the 29th of February, 1680. On the 11th of April, when near the mouth of the Wisconsin, he was captured by a party of Sioux, who adopted him into the tribe. In their company he visited the Falls of St. Anthony, which he named ; and with them he remained until the autumn of that year, when he was rescued by Du Lhut. During the next year, and without having seen La Salle, or made any report to him, the tricky friar sailed for Europe. Soon afterwards he published a narrative of his journey, in which he gave a description of the river above the mouth of the Wisconsin, and an account of the manners and customs of the Sioux. This is the only publication he ever made that is entitled to any credence, and even in this, some of the statements are to be taken with many grains of allowance. In the edition issued some years later, he involves himself in such a net-work of falsehoods and contradictions as to cast discredit upon the work which he really performed.

In the mean time La Salle, having restored his affairs to something like order, returned to the Illinois, only to find that, during the absence of Tonti, his fort had been plundered and destroyed by his own men. This necessitated another trip to Fort Frontenac, which must have been made in 1681, for in December of that year he was, once again, at the head of Lake Michigan, accompanied by Tonti, Father Membré, and some others, who had been faithful to him during his adverse fortunes, and who were now to share with him in the glory of his discovery. Including these faithful friends and followers, the party which he had made up for the descent of the Mississippi consisted of twenty-three Frenchmen and thirty-one Indians, of whom ten were women and three children.

Loading their canoes upon sledges, they dragged them across the portage and down the frozen Illinois to the foot of Peoria lake, where they found open water. Here they embarked, and after a somewhat uneventful voyage they reached the Mississippi on the 6th of February, 1682, and the Gulf on the 9th of the following April. Having found a suitable spot La Salle erected a cross, raised the arms of France, and, in a *procés verbal*, which was duly witnessed, he took possession of all the region watered by the Mississippi and its tributaries, and he named it Louisiana, in honor of his sovereign, Louis XIV., by the grace of God King of France and Navarre.

The work of exploration was now complete, but the more difficult task of occupation still remained, and to this La Salle now devoted all his energies. Returning to the Illinois he dispatched Father Membré to Europe, with the news of his discovery, whilst he himself built a fort on Starved Rock, — a bluff near where the town of Ottawa now stands, — which he intended to serve as a centre of trade and a place of refuge against the inroads of the Iroquois. Around this point he speedily gathered a large colony, consisting of a score of Frenchmen, to whom he made grants of lands, and of some thousands of Indians, belonging to different tribes, who were drawn thither by the prospects of trade, and by the promise of protection which the fort afforded.

Leaving Tonti in command of this motley crowd, La Salle, in the autumn of 1683, sailed for France, where his presence was sadly needed. His friend and partner, Frontenac, was no longer governor, and La Barre, who was now at the head of affairs, had identified himself with his enemies, and did not hesitate at any measures that were necessary to effect his ruin. Fort Frontenac was seized on the ground that he had not complied with the conditions upon which it had been granted to him; his men were prevented from obtaining supplies; the Iroquois were told that they might rob and kill him with impunity; and an officer was sent out to take possession of the fort which he had built on the Illinois. Such was the condition of affairs when he left for Europe, and it must be confessed that the outlook was anything but encouraging. He was in debt, and as all his property had been seized, and much of it wasted, there seemed to be no way by which he could extricate himself. La Salle, however, was not a person to be daunted by difficulties. Proceeding to Paris, he laid his case before the colonial minister, and, fortunately for himself, he found in that officer a warm advocate. Frontenac, too, was again in favor, and by the aid of these two powerful friends he soon succeeded in reestablishing his affairs upon a firm basis. Not only were his forts restored, but La Barre was ordered to make reparation for the injury which had been done him, and means were furnished him for establishing a post and colony near the mouth of the Mississippi.

In a memorial which he prepared at this time for the use of the king, he gave a brief statement of what he had already accomplished; set forth his views and plans at some length; and drew such a flattering picture of the military possibilities of the proposed colony in the event of a war with Spain, that the king granted him all the supplies that were asked for. Soldiers, of whom Father Le Clerc did not have a very high opinion, were recruited for the expedition, as were "three or four mechanics in each trade," who were subsequently found to know nothing at all about their several occupations. Some eight or ten families of good people volunteered to go, as did a number of girls, who were "allured by the prospect of certain marriage." A full complement of priests, too, was added, among whom were La Salle's brother — the Sulpitian, Cavelier — and the Récollet Friars Membré, Douay, and Le Clerc. At length, all things being ready, the expedition sailed from Rochelle on the 24th of July, 1684, and, after a series of misfortunes which seem to have attended them from the beginning of the voyage, they reached the Gulf of Mexico, and sighted land on the 28th of December. By accident, or owing to ignorance, or possibly, as Joutel suggests, to treachery, they passed the mouths of the Mississippi, and coasted along in an aimless sort of way until about the middle of February, 1685, when the colonists were landed on the shores of Matagorda Bay, which La Salle had wrongly supposed to be one of the outlets of the great river. Here he built a fort; and, having satisfied himself that he was too far westward, he started out to find the Mississippi, for he knew well that until it was found, and the colony was safely transferred to its banks, all his expenditure of time, labor, and money had been in vain. The effort, however, was not attended with success, and equally futile was a second attempt made in the following year (1686).

Meanwhile, the affairs of the colony had been going from bad to worse. In addition to other misfortunes, disease and death had been busy among them. " Out of one hundred and eighty colonists less than forty-five remained," and they were weighed down by gloomy forebodings as to the future. It was no longer a question of the success of the expedition, but a matter of life and death to the few colonists who were left. In this extremity, La Salle determined to go to his fort on the Illinois, the nearest point from which he could expect assistance. It was a hazardous undertaking; but it was the best thing that could be done. After a painful parting, " which all felt was to be their last," he set out on the 17th of January, 1687, and, on the 19th of March, he, together with one of his nephews, his servant, and his faithful Shawnee hunter, Nika, was murdered by some of his own men. Upon his death, the murderers took control of the party, and for a while they carried matters with a high hand. In a short time they quarreled over a division of the property, and, by a sort of retributive justice, the two principal criminals were in their turn killed by their accomplices. The party now divided. Joutel, the two Caveliers, and Father Douay, who had all been true to their leader, pushed on, and, at the end of two months, they reached the post which Tonti had established the year previous at the mouth of the Arkansas. From here they proceeded by relatively easy marches to the fort on the Illinois, where they were well cared for by the faithful Tonti, to whom they falsely represented that La Salle was alive and in good health, and from whom they borrowed the money necessary to continue their journey. A few months later he learned the truth about La Salle, whereupon he again descended the river in the hope of being able to render some assistance to the colonists who had been left at the fort on Matagorda Bay. In this generous effort he was doomed to disappointment. When on Red River he was deserted by six out of the eight men who were with him ; and though he kept on for some time longer, he was obliged in the end to give up the undertaking, owing to the accidental loss of all his ammunition, and to the refusal of the Indians, among whom he then was, to furnish him with guides. Under these circumstances he decided to retrace his steps; and, after a journey in which he suffered great hardships, he reached the Arkansas in July, 1689, and the fort on the Illinois in September of the same year.

Disastrous as was this attempt at colonizing the lower Mississippi, it did not long delay that event. The situation was too important, considered either strategically or commercially, to be overlooked ; and, as La Salle had foretold, both the English and Spaniards stood ready to seize it, or to occupy such positions along the coast as would enable them to neutralize any advantage which the French might hope to gain from its possession. Indeed, with this end in view, the Spaniards are said to have fortified Pensacola as early as 1696, and some three years later an English expedition ascended the Mississippi, but was turned back by a stratagem of the French, who had anticipated their arrival by only a few months. These designs on the part of their rivals were well known to the French, and caused them to hasten the preparations they were making for the occupation of the mouth of the river. Accordingly, in 1698, the Canadian, Iberville, was sent out in command of an expedition, and, after a successful voyage, he landed at old Biloxi in February of the following year and built a fort. From this point the neighboring coast and the lower portion of the river were explored ; and it was during one of these expeditions that Bienville was handed the letter which, fourteen years before, Tonti had left for La Salle. Other points were occupied in due time, and soon traders and missionaries began to ascend and descend the river. The journey, however, was not always free from danger, as there were times when, owing to the intrigues of English traders and other causes, tribes, like the Chickasaws and Natchez, dug up the hatchet and " barred " the river. As a rule, though, these occasions were rare ; and the journey was made without other dangers and discomforts than those of the river and climate. By superior management the French were able to counteract the influence of the English with the river tribes, and for fifty years and more — from the settlement in 1699 until the cession to Spain in 1762 — the Mississippi was to all intents and purposes a French river.

CHAPTER II.

DURING the whole of the period that the French held the control of the valley, Missouri, as such, had no separate legal existence and not a single settlement that has proved to be permanent, except, perhaps, Ste. Genevieve. Exactly when the "old" village of this name was founded is a matter that cannot be positively determined; and it is not important that it should be, except in so far as it may serve to throw light upon the time when the French began to familiarize themselves with the resources of the region west of the Mississippi. Upon this point the testimony of Pénicaut is of interest. He arrived in lower Louisiana in 1699, and in 1700 he made one of the party that ascended the river with Le Sueur for the purpose of opening a copper mine which was supposed to be on one of the tributaries of the Minnesota. In the journal which he kept of that expedition, he refers to the salt licks near Ste. Genevieve, and says that they were resorted to by the French and Indians, and that "presently" there was a settlement of the French at that place. He also speaks of a mine situated fifty leagues west of the Mississippi, from which the Indians got their supply of lead, and to which they went by way of the Maramec. These statements are explicit; they are borne out by the facts as they now exist, and if they do not fix the precise date when Ste.

Genevieve was first settled, they at least justify the inference that it was shortly after the arrival of the French at the village of Kaskaskia, on the other side of the river, and hence, that it must have been early in the eighteenth century, and not about the middle, as sometimes supposed. They also indicate, with reasonable certainty, the date when the French began to make use of the mineral and other natural resources in which the region lying between the Mississippi and the Maramec abounded.

From this time forward, the career of the French in " the Illinois," as this portion of the colony was called, can be easily traced. At first, and for a quarter of a century or more, it would seem as if they must have been given over almost altogether to the search after silver and copper. At all events, this is the not unnatural inference from the prominence accorded to this pursuit, in all the official documents. As a matter of fact, however, there are two sides to the shield, though there can be no question that, so far as it was possible for the home authorities to make it so, the search for silver was, for a number of years, the controlling interest in the little colony. As early as 1703, a party of twenty set out to go from Kaskaskia to New Mexico, by way of the Missouri River, for the purpose of . . . " visiting certain mines which were said, by the Indians, to yield a kind of lead that was white and of no account because it did not melt in the fire," as did the true lead found nearer home. Of the fate of this expedition nothing is known, but the feasibility of the journey is placed beyond doubt by the fact that, in 1714, specimens of silver were forwarded to La Mothe Cadillac, at Mobile, and the report that they had been taken from mines near

Kaskaskia brought that official up the river only to find that he had been deceived, and that the specimens had really come from Mexico. In spite of disappointments like these, and of the fact that thus far not a particle of silver had been found in this region, the colonial authorities were satisfied that it would ultimately be discovered, and they ascribed the failure to find it to the want of skill on the part of their agents.

Impressed with this belief, the directors of the Mississippi Company, who had come into the possession of the charter of the colony after its relinquishment by Crozat, in 1717, sent out several parties composed of men who were supposed to be accustomed to this kind of work, though Charlevoix, for reasons that appear to be good and sufficient, doubts their capacity. Among the first to arrive was the Sieur de Lochon, who came out in 1719. He "dug in a place that was showed him, took up a pretty large quantity of the mineral, a pound of which, that took up four days to melt, produced, as they say, two drachms of silver; but some persons suspect that he put in the silver." A few months later he tried for lead, "and from two or three thousand weight of the mineral he extracted fourteen pounds of very bad lead, which cost him 1,400 livres." Disheartened by this failure, he gave up the work and returned to France. Other parties followed in quick succession, but met with no better success. They found no silver, or, if they did, they put it into the melting pots themselves; and though lead was abundant, yet they got but little, for the reason that "they did not know how to construct their furnaces." Finally, in 1720, there came the Sieur Renaud, one of the directors of the company, who is said to have surveyed these Maramec mines very

thoroughly. He fared no better in the search for silver than did his predecessors, and his errand here would
not call for further comment but for the fact that, in
1723, the earliest grants of lands in what is now known
as the State of Missouri were made to him, and because,
either directly or indirectly, he was the means of introducing negro slavery into this portion of the colony.
According to the chronicles of the day, there came with
him "many families who had received concessions of
lands in the neighborhood of Kaskaskia, and who brought
with them a number of negroes, granted to them by
Bienville, for the purpose of cultivating these lands."
After this we hear but little of silver, though as late
as 1744 Vaudreuil forwarded to France certain specimens of copper, which were said to have been found in
the district of the Illinois. The lead mines of this region, however, were steadily worked, and among the
articles sent down the river, lead was not the least important.

But whilst the authorities at New Orleans and Paris
were dreaming of silver mines and squandering large
sums of money in a vain search for them, the colonists
in this district, consisting almost entirely of emigrants
from Canada, were quietly pursuing the even tenor of
their way, and devoting more or less of their attention to the trade in furs, and to the more prosaic but
not less useful business of farming. Besides the expedition up the Missouri, to which reference has already
been made, they explored the Des Moines and the
Osage, and penetrated into Kansas among the Panis,
where Dutigné, in 1719, planted the arms of France.
This steady progress westward excited the jealousy of
the Spaniards, and, in 1720, they fitted out an expedition

for the purpose of taking a position on the Missouri which would enable them to check the advance of the French in this direction, and divert the trade of the Indians from Kaskaskia to Santa Fé. In this they were unsuccessful, as the expedition fell among hostile tribes and was destroyed.

Alarmed by the boldness of this expedition, and with the view of guarding against future danger from this quarter, as well as in the expectation of extending their trade, the French sent a force up the Missouri, and built a fort near a village of the tribe of that name, which they called Fort Orleans.[1] At the date of their arrival here, a general war was raging between the Padoucas on one side, and the Missouris, Osages, Iowas, Pawnees, Ottos, Mahas, etc., on the other. As these last were all friends of the French, and the war interfered very seriously with the trade in "buffalo's wool," it became a matter of the first importance to bring about a peace between these tribes. Accordingly, M. de Bourgmont, the commandant of Fort Orleans, summoned them to meet him at a council which was held in 1724, at a point situated on one of the western tributaries of the Kansas, when and where the pipe was smoked, and a general peace was concluded. Soon after this, Fort Orleans was destroyed and the garrison massacred, probably by the Missouris, though upon this point there is room for doubt. Bossu, however, ascribes it to them, and intimates that the outbreak was due to the frauds practiced upon them in the way of trade, and to the fact that the French debauched their women.

[1] Du Pratz says this fort was on an island opposite the village of the Missouris. There is reason, however, to believe that it may have been on the south side of the river, fifteen or twenty miles above the mouth of Grand River. Margry, vi. p. 393.

These were the only occasions, during the rule of the French, upon which the settlers in this portion of the colony were exposed to serious danger, though they bore their share of the loss entailed by Bienville's unsuccessful war with the Chickasaws, and took a prominent part in the fighting which began about the middle of the century, on the head waters of the Ohio, and ended in the treaty of Paris, February, 1763, and the expulsion of the French from the North American continent.

During all these years the little settlement on the Illinois, left in a great measure to itself, and separated by a thousand miles and more from the intrigues and exactions that prevailed at Quebec and New Orleans, continued to grow slowly but steadily in population and prosperity. Besides the fur-trade which now extended some three or four hundred leagues up the Missouri, and the lead mines of the Maramec from which the yield was, practically, unlimited, the agricultural products of the district began to assume important proportions. From the first arrival of the French in this quarter, they had given more or less of their attention to the cultivation of the soil, and it was owing to this fact that they were exempt from the oft recurring seasons of scarcity to which the inhabitants of New Orleans and the settlers on the Gulf coast were subject. As early as 1721, Charlevoix, writing from Kaskaskia, says that the French in that neighborhood were living " pretty much at their ease." They cultivated wheat and corn, and had domestic cattle and fowls. The Indians, too, whose villages adjoined the settlements of the French, were " very laborious, and cultivated their fields in their own fashion." A few years later, the farm products of this " district " had increased to such an extent that they constituted a regular article of shipment. Le Page du Pratz and Bossu both speak of the amount of flour which was sent to New Orleans, and Vaudreuil who, in 1743, succeeded Bienville as governor, and who was not a partial witness, in a letter to the minister, says that every year, in the latter part of December, there came from "the Illinois" boats loaded with "flour, corn, bacon hams, both of bear and hog, corned pork and wild beef, myrtle and beeswax, cotton, tallow, leather, tobacco, lead, copper, buffalo-wool, venison, poultry, bear's grease, oil, skins, fowls, and hides." Varied as is this list, it is not complete, for Captain Pittman, who traveled up the river soon after the eastern portion of the valley fell into the hands of the English, adds "beer and wines." This is certainly a very creditable showing, and furnishes good grounds for doubting Vaudreuil's sincerity, when he seeks to justify his grant to Deruisseau of the monopoly of the fur-trade of the Missouri, by saying that the only way in which he could make the people in this part of the colony abandon their wandering mode of life and settle down to farm work, was by preventing them from trading with the Indians, and by prohibiting them from acquiring any more negro slaves. The two statements, to say the least, do not harmonize. A wandering life is never compatible with the successful employment of slave labor, and the fact that, in 1745, the negroes in this district were half as many as the whites, is not only conclusive as to the profitable use of this form of labor, but it is equally decisive as to the manner of life of the owners of these slaves, even without the confirmatory evidence of the products which they annually sent down the river.

Notwithstanding the measure of success which attended this corner of the colony, Louisiana, taken as a whole, and regarded, as colonies then were, simply as a mercantile venture, was a decided failure. So far from returning a profit upon the sums expended, there never was a time when it was self-supporting. Under the system of restrictions upon trade and production which prevailed, and which embodied the highest commercial wisdom of the day, the colonists were virtually prohibited from producing anything that could be obtained from the mother country. They were taught to look to France even for their food. As a consequence, on more than one occasion when the supplies failed to arrive, the settlers on the lower Mississippi and along the Gulf coast were reduced to such straits that they were obliged to quarter themselves upon the neighboring Indians, in order to escape starvation. As late as 1741, owing to the destruction by a storm of the warehouse in which their provisions were stored, the inhabitants of Mobile and of some other places in that part of the colony were threatened with a famine ; and the dispatches of that day and even those of a much later date are filled with pitiful appeals to France for aid. Of course, so long as those who held the franchise of the colony, no matter whether it was the state, a company, or an individual, were able and willing to furnish the necessary supplies and make good the yearly deficit in men and money, it was easy enough to counteract the evil effects engendered by the attempt to put into practice the false theories upon which the enterprise was managed. It was even possible, provided the expenditures were upon a sufficiently lavish scale, to give the settlement an appearance of prosperity, as was the case with Louisiana from 1717 to 1731, when the Mississippi

Company held the charter. But when the time came, as sooner or later it did, that the supplies were either cut down or withheld altogether, or when from any cause they became irregular and uncertain, the semblance of prosperity disappeared, and the fatal effects of this false system of management, in the shape of want and its attendant train of evils, began at once to make themselves felt.

Such in brief was the history of Louisiana under French domination. Its most prosperous period was during the fourteen years that the Company of the Indies, or, as it was also called, the Mississippi Company, controlled its destinies, and its prosperity then, as has been already intimated, was not a healthy growth, but was the result of the lavish manner in which supplies of men and money were poured into the colony from abroad. Some idea of the rate at which this was done may be gathered from the fact that, during this time, the expenses of the colony are said to have been upwards of twenty million livres, and that the population was swollen from seven hundred to seven thousand, of which number two thousand were negro slaves.

After the surrender of the charter to the king, in 1731, the regular expenses of the colony were reduced to a fraction of what they had been during the extravagant days of the company, and the population, no longer fed by arrivals from abroad, gradually fell off, until, in 1745, the number of inhabitants was only about six thousand, of whom four thousand were whites. Compared with the previous census, this shows a decrease of one thousand whites, the number of negroes remaining the same. In all probability this loss was afterwards made good, and it is possible that the number of whites may have been slightly increased over what it was in the palmy days of the company, but not to the extent claimed by Redan de Rassac. According to him, Louisiana, in 1763, at the date of the treaty of Paris, contained "three thousand French families." Allowing four persons to each family, — a liberal allowance, if we are to credit the statement as to the age of many of the married women, — it would give a total white population of twelve thousand, which is believed to be much too large, as it is more than twice as many as were living in Spanish Louisiana in 1766,[1] when probably four fifths of all the inhabitants of the colony were on that side of the river.

However, be this as it may, there can be no question that, excluding the years in which the budget was swollen by the payment of obligations incurred in prosecuting the Chickasaw war, there was a marked increase in the regular annual expenses from 1731 until the cession to Spain in 1762. Thus, for instance, in 1740, the expenditures were 310,000 livres; in 1747 they had increased to 539,000 ; and during the years 1754–56 and 1759 the average was at the rate of 800,000 livres per annum. Probably during the whole of the time that Louisiana was a dependency of the crown, it had cost not less than from forty to fifty millions of livres (eight to ten millions of dollars), and this, of course, independent of the amount paid out by Crozat, and of the twenty million livres which the Mississippi Company is said to have wasted.

This was a heavy price to pay for what had thus far

---

[1] "It had . . . in all, five thousand five hundred and fifty-six white inhabitants. The blacks were nearly as numerous." Martin's *History of Louisiana*, vol. i. p. 354. New Orleans, 1827.

proved to be but an empty honor, and, in the present exhausted condition of France, it must soon have become a serious burden. But even if this had not been the case, and the French king had been as able, as he seems to have been willing, to preserve his American possessions, it was no longer possible for him to do so. The fortunes of war were against him. Canada had fallen; and, with Havana in the hands of the English, and their ships riding triumphant on the ocean, Louisiana was at their mercy. Under these circumstances, his most Christian majesty made a virtue of necessity, and, in November, 1762, he transferred the whole of that colony to the king of Spain. It was, at best, a gift of doubtful value, and the Spanish monarch seems to have accepted it somewhat reluctantly, and as a favor to France rather than in the hope of deriving any benefit from it for himself.

For reasons that will readily suggest themselves, this gift and its acceptance were not made public, the king of France continuing to act as if he were still the rightful owner of all that domain. Indeed, in February, 1763, at the treaty of Paris, he ceded to the English all of Louisiana that was east of the Mississippi River, except the city of New Orleans and the island on which it was situated, and this in face of the fact that, less than six months before, he had presented that very same region to his much-loved cousin of Spain. No authoritative explanation has ever been given of this transaction; but the fact that the king of Spain was a party to the treaty, and made no objection to the arrangement by which he was deprived of a good part of the colony which had been so recently presented to him, affords ample grounds for doubting the good faith of the original gift. In all probability it was a mere ruse, under cover of which the French king hoped to retain some portion of his American possessions.[1]

As there were no reasons why the treaty of Paris should be kept secret, and no possibility of keeping it so, even it if had been desired, its provisions were at once made public, and, early in the ensuing spring, the people of Louisiana were officially informed of the dismemberment of the colony. By this act, the district of the Illinois was divided into two unequal parts, all on the east side of the Mississippi River being ceded to the English. Except the village of Ste. Genevieve, all the French settlements in the district were situated within this area, including, of course, Fort Chartres, the *chef-lieu*, or seat of justice.

With the surrender of this important position, "the key to the trade of the upper rivers," it became necessary to select another situation within French, or rather Spanish, territory, to which the government of the district might be removed, and which might serve as a centre from which the different Indian tribes could be furnished with their regular annual supplies. Unfortunately, however, the colonial treasury was at this time

[1] Under date of May 11, 1763, the Spanish minister, the Marquis Grimaldi, wrote to the Spanish ambassador at the court of France as follows: " M. le duc de Praslin (French minister of the marine) se rappellera qu'il y eut des doutes de notre part à l'égard de l'acceptation. Mais, comme les mêmes raisons qui faisaient croire à la France la nécessité de la cession, conseillaient à l'Espagne de l'accepter, le roi le reçut, quoique l'on reconnût parfaitement que nous ne faisions l'acquisition que d'une charge annuelle de deux cent cinquante mille à trois cent mille piastres, en échange d'une utilité négative et éloignée, c'est-à-dire, celle de posséder un pays pour qu'un autre ne le possédât pas." — Gayarré, *Histoire de la Louisiane*, vol. ii. p. 160.

empty. It had neither money nor goods; and as the matter was somewhat urgent, " it was deemed best to grant the exclusive trade of the north and northwestern part of the territory still remaining to a company strong enough to manage it and to supply the wants of the Indians, and which could make the necessary provision for the accommodation of the district government on the west side of the river." [1] This was done, and the firm of Maxent, Laclède & Co., having received the grant, fitted out an expedition, which left New Orleans on the 3d of August, 1763, and wintered at Fort Chartres. Laclède, or, to give him his true name, Pierre Laclède Ligueste, a junior partner in the firm, was placed in charge of the expedition, and in the exercise of the discretion which seems to have been allowed him, he fixed upon the spot where the city of St. Louis now stands as the site for the new post. In February or March — the date is somewhat uncertain — of the ensuing year he sent Auguste Chouteau and a band of workmen to that place with orders to make a clearing, and to begin building cabins for the accommodation of his men and the storage of his goods. In good time a number of French families, unwilling to abandon the white flag, crossed the river and took up their residence at the new post ; and in October, 1765, St. Ange de Bellerive, having formally delivered the region east of the Mississippi to Captain Sterling, the English representative, also removed to that place, and St. Louis became the official residence of the commandant, and the *chef-lieu* of the district.

[1] In this statement I have followed Mr. Oscar W. Collet, whose articles upon the early history of Missouri, in the *Magazine of Western History*, and elsewhere, are models of careful research.

Meanwhile, in October, 1764, the letter of the king to Governor d'Abbadie announcing the gift of Louisiana to Spain had been made public, though it was not until March, 1766, that Ulloa, the Spanish representative, arrived in New Orleans for the purpose of receiving the transfer of the colony. He seems to have been a worthy sort of man, given to literature and science, perhaps, rather than to politics, and to have been actuated by a sincere desire to discharge his disagreeable duties in such a way as to avoid giving offense. In this he was disappointed. The people of New Orleans, or, to speak more correctly, a portion of them, were not to be placated, and they refused to recognize Ulloa's authority, though, with curious inconsistency, they did not object to the payment of all the expenses of the colony by the king whose agent he was.

After a year or two of ill-concealed strife, Ulloa was banished by a decree of the council, dated October 29, 1768; and, singularly enough, one of the main charges brought against him was that he had established posts and "hoisted the flag of Spain at the Balize, at the Illinois," and at some other places. It is difficult, at this late day, to understand how this could have been construed into a crime against either the French or Spanish crown, since it was clearly in the line of his duty to his own sovereign, and was done, if not with the approval, certainly without any objection on the part of the French authorities. It also shows that, outside of New Orleans and some other places in that immediate neighborhood, the objection to the transfer was neither as general nor as inveterate as is sometimes supposed. Indeed, on this point there seems to be no room for doubt, in view of the official recognition of Ulloa's authority by the French governor, and of the fact that the commandants of the different districts solicited and obtained from him a continuation of their respective commands. That St. Ange was one of these is, we think, made clear by the dispatches of Aubry, the *Acte d'accusation,* and by his appointment to a position in the army of his most Catholic majesty ; and thus it was that, although a Frenchman by birth, he became the first commandant of upper Louisiana under the Spanish régime.

CHAPTER III.

A PROCEEDING as revolutionary in its character as was the expulsion of Ulloa could not be quietly passed over. The Spanish king could not forget that he had accepted Louisiana as a favor to France, and that in so doing he had involved himself in a heavy annual outlay without the prospect of any immediate return; and he knew very well that the measures complained of were, to a very great extent, a legacy from the former government, and that the changes that had been made, by which the trade of the colony was transferred from French to Spanish ports, were not intended as acts of oppression, but were in harmony with the received commercial ideas of the day. The hard lesson taught by the revolt of the English and Spanish colonies in America had not yet been administered; and it was not until the next generation that the different European powers were made to understand that the interest, real or supposed, of a colony might conflict with that of the mother country, and that when such was the case, it was the part of a wise political economy to recognize the right of the colonists to freedom of action in trade as well as in politics. Unable to grasp this truth, and conscious alike of the honesty of their own intentions and of the sacrifices which they made in retaining Louisiana, the Spanish cabinet looked upon the conduct of the people of New

Orleans as being doubly criminal, since it was not only revolutionary in its character, but it also savored strongly of ingratitude. As such it was not to be tolerated, and they sent O'Reilly to the colony, with a force large enough to overcome all opposition. On the 18th of August, 1769, he took peaceable possession of New Orleans, having found no occasion for the use of his troops. During the nine or ten months that had elapsed since the banishment of Ulloa, a reaction had taken place in the minds of the people, and those who had been most active in fomenting the insurrection were now among the first to protest their willingness to submit to the orders of the king. They even went so far as to assert that they had never intended any disrespect to him ; and they besought O'Reilly, inasmuch as the revolution was due to the severity of Ulloa, and to the withdrawal of certain privileges which they were pleased to say had been guarantied them by the act of cession, not to look upon the colony in the light of a conquered province. In spite of these protestations, an example was deemed necessary, and twelve of the ringleaders in the conspiracy were tried and condemned. Of these, one is said to have died and five were executed. The others were imprisoned, but only for a short time, as they were pardoned during the ensuing year, — a fact which is not always mentioned by those who have seen proper to comment upon the transaction.

With the execution of these sentences, Spanish justice, or vengeance, as it is more often called, was satisfied, and O'Reilly now turned his attention to the reorganization of the colonial government. Among other changes, he abolished the council, and superseded the French code by a set of regulations, based upon the laws of

Castile and the code of the Indies, which he caused to
be drawn up for the guidance of the judges and other
officials. At the first glance it would seem as if such
a wholesale change as this presaged must have been
productive of no little trouble and inconvenience, but in
practice it was found not to be the case. The jurisprudence of Spain, like that of France, was drawn from
the Roman code, and the two systems approached each
other so closely in those particulars in which they touched
the individual most nearly, that the transition was not
perceived until it became an accomplished fact. Moreover, a wide latitude seems to have been allowed in
the construction and enforcement of these laws. Thus,
for instance, although Spanish was declared to be the
official language of the colony, yet the use of French
was permitted in the judicial and notarial acts of the
commandants of the several districts; and in upper
Louisiana, where the laws of Spain relating to inherit-
ance, dowry, and grants of land had been published
and were in force, the *coûtume de Paris*, or, as Brackenridge calls it, the common law of France, was the system
by which their contracts were governed; and he gives
an instance in which a case, involving the dower right
of a widow, was decided by a United States court in
accordance with that law under the " article of cession,"
which provided that respect should be paid to the usages
and customs which had prevailed in the country.

For the purpose of facilitating the administration of
justice, the colony was divided into a number of districts, in each of which a commandant was appointed,
who was invested with such civil and military powers
as were thought necessary to the discharge of his duties.
These officers were generally taken from the army or

militia, and as they were paid by the crown, and were, as a rule, Frenchmen, it is believed to indicate very clearly the kindly feelings by which the Spanish authorities were animated in their dealings with the colonists.

In making this division, the settlement of the Illinois, or, as we shall now call it, upper Louisiana, was considered of too much importance to be classed any longer with the districts, and it was constituted into a sort of province, separate and distinct from lower Louisiana, but in some respects dependent upon it. At this time (1769) it had a population of 891, confined to the villages of St. Louis and Ste. Genevieve; and after 1799, when New Madrid was added, it embraced all the region west of the Mississippi and north of the latitude of Memphis, once claimed by France. Practically, however, except perhaps Dubuque, the new settlements within the province, during the whole of the Spanish domination, never extended beyond the limits of what is now known as the State of Missouri. A lieutenant-governor was placed in command, who derived his power directly from the crown, though he was obliged to conform to the orders of the governor-general, and also of the intendant, after the reëstablishment of this office in 1794. "As sub-delegate to the latter, he superintended the finances within his jurisdiction, including everything that related to the Indians, to commerce, to the sale and grant of lands, and to the levy and collection of the public revenue. As next in authority to the governor, he commanded the military, and chose the commandants and other officers of the districts" that were within his province. His authority is said to have been without limitation in civil cases, and it extended to all criminal offenses except capital, though his decisions were liable to be reversed on appeal to the governor or to the intendant, each of whom had appellate jurisdiction within his appropriate sphere. Such appeals, however, were not common, — aggravated crimes against the person being so exceedingly rare that but one case of the murder of a white man by a white man is reported in St. Louis during the whole period of Spanish rule; and in civil cases the proceedings were of such a character as effectually to discourage appeals, save when the object was the reversal of erroneous judgments. In case an appeal was taken, the person so appealing was obliged to pay the opposite party the full amount of the sum decreed against him, bond being given to refund the sum thus paid, provided the decree was ultimately reversed. To any one accustomed to our system of jurisprudence, this method of administering justice will appear arbitrary and somewhat summary; but, taking into consideration the times and the character of the population, there is much to be said in its favor. According to Major Stoddard, who was certainly not a partial witness, "it created a much greater degree of punctuality in the payment of debts than is established in any part of the United States." In fact, "the change produced by the operation of the laws of the United States, the dilatory proceedings of our courts, the introduction of the trial by jury, and the expenses of legal contests," are said to have given "a temporary check to trade and to the credit of merchants, particularly in upper Louisiana. Experience had led them to believe that the Spanish mode of decision, grounded on equitable laws, was much the most wise and salutary;

and they murmured at a system calculated to produce delays, and in many instances to create expenses equal in amount to the sums demanded. They preferred the judgment of one man to that of twelve ; and it is but justice to observe that the judicial officers were in most instances upright and impartial in their decisions."

In estimating for the expenses of the colony, and in the measures which they took to provide the funds to meet them, the Spanish government cannot be accused of harshness or illiberality. A duty of six per cent., amounting, in most prosperous times, to an aggregate of one hundred and twenty thousand dollars per annum, was levied upon all goods and other articles exported or imported ; and this, with the six thousand dollars derived from a tax on salaries and legacies and from a license for the sale of spirituous liquors, constituted the whole of the revenue paid by the colony. No other taxes, direct or indirect, were known. Deducting these amounts from the average annual expenditure of about six hundred and fifty thousand ($650,000) dollars, and it will leave in round numbers a deficit of five hundred and twenty-five thousand ($525,000) dollars, which was made up by a charge of four hundred thousand dollars per annum on the Mexican exchequer, and by drafts on the royal treasury for the balance. Compared with the previous expenses of the colony, even during the extravagant days of the Mississippi Company, or with the estimates of the Spanish ministry at the time of the cession in 1762, this amount seems so out of all proportion that it is difficult to understand what became of the money, without giving credence to some of the stories that were current as to the impositions practiced upon the king "by exorbitant charges for useless fortifications, and for supplies that were never furnished."

Under this mild form of despotism, beneficently administered, life in this portion of the colony moved on much as it had done when upper Louisiana formed a part of "the district of the Illinois," and was under the rule of the French. The nationality of the chief executive officer, it is true, was no longer the same ; the *chef-lieu*, too, had been transferred from Fort Chartres to St. Louis, and a number of families had removed from the east side of the river to the west ; but with these exceptions, the cession of this region to Spain had not been productive of change. As has been already intimated, the colonists were almost exclusively French or of French descent, and naturally enough they clung to the customs in which they had been brought up, and persisted in the use of the only language with which they were familiar. Indeed, situated as they were, it is doubtful whether any change could have been effected in these particulars even had it been desirable. Except in a vague sort of way, they knew of no other mode of life than that which they led. Being all related by blood or marriage, there were no such things as social distinctions among them. The wealthy and intelligent received, perhaps, a trifle more consideration, but this was a personal compliment, and carried with it no social preëminence. In their amusements, as in their labor, at church, as at the fireside, they met upon a footing of equality. Moreover, they were separated by a thousand miles of difficult and dangerous travel from their neighbors in Quebec and New Orleans, and this, of course, deprived them of the healthy stimulus which might have come to them from a contrast of their shortcomings with the progress made by others. Under these circumstances, in the little world in which they lived, innovations were rare, and progress was correspondingly slow. " My father did so before me," was regarded as a satisfactory way of accounting for the existence of a custom, no matter how inadequate, and it usually proved a sufficient answer to any suggestions for improvement.

Such a life may have been narrow, and there can be no doubt that, when judged by our standard, these people were illiterate, and except when occasion called for exertion, they may have been lazy; but, on the other hand, the men were honest in their dealings and faithful to their contracts, and the women were, with but few exceptions, good wives and true and efficient helpmeets to their husbands. It may also be urged in their favor that their wants were but few, and as these were easily supplied there was no necessity for their working more than they did; and that whilst they did not, perhaps, know how to read and write, yet they had a reasonably clear idea of the duties and amenities that belonged to their condition in life, and were, withal, so prompt in practicing them as to extort from Stoddard the somewhat unwilling admission that they were " apparently the happiest people on the globe."

In a community so shut in, and leading the simple sort of life that the people here did, the round of occupations was necessarily small. A few of the more wealthy and enterprising of the inhabitants were engaged in the fur-trade and kept small stocks of goods, not displayed on shelves and counters, for as yet " there were no open shops and stores as in the States," but packed away in chests and boxes, to be opened only when the occasion called for it. Others, especially among the young and adventurous, were employed in the lead mines and in boating, and a few held positions under the government; but "by far the greater number were engaged in agriculture." In fact, this may be said "to have been, in some shape, the business of all," for the surplus produce of this portion of the colony was not sufficient to justify such a division of labor as would withdraw any number of persons, be it ever so small, from the production of breadstuffs.

When not engaged with their crops, some of these small farmers "exercised the calling of rough artisans, and became blacksmiths, carpenters, stone-masons," etc., traveling about from village to village, where their services were needed. At first, there were neither tailors nor shoemakers among them, and no baker until about 1775, when Barrère, who seems to have been the first to embark in that business, came from New Orleans and established himself in St. Louis. Flour-mills and sawmills, however, they had at an early day, and under Governor Delassus, liberal grants of land were made for the establishment of distilleries. Of other manufactures they had none. If we may credit Brackenridge, there was not such a thing as a loom or a spinning-wheel then in the province; [1] and the inhabitants had to depend upon Europe, not only for such luxuries as "laces," but for the materials from which were made the "capotes" of the men and the dresses of the women. The linsey, or homespun, of the thrifty Kentucky housewife was unknown, and in its place they had two and even three-point blankets, calamanco, flannels, etc., which they brought, chiefly, from Philadelphia and Baltimore,

[1] Stoddard, however, gives a different account. He says, p. 305, that "the inhabitants generally cultivated a sufficient quantity of cotton for family purposes, and spun and wove it into cloth."

and which did not always pass through the custom house. Even as simple an article as a churn was not in use, and those among them who indulged in the luxury of butter made it either " by beating the cream in a bowl or shaking it up in a bottle."

Of money they had but little — far too little to serve as a medium of exchange, and in its place peltry, at a fixed rate, was made a legal tender in all transactions in which it was not stipulated that payment should be made in Spanish milled dollars. Lead, too, was used in the same way ; in fact, among themselves, all trading was done by barter. Even the salaries which the government paid to the priests, soldiers, and officials were advanced by the traders, generally in foreign goods, in exchange for bills drawn on the colonial treasury at New Orleans. Except the amounts covered by these drafts, all other remittances were made in lead, peltry, and provisions. Of the total amount of this trade but little is known. The value of the peltries exported during the fifteen years next preceding 1804 is said to have been a trifle over two hundred thousand dollars (\$200,000) per annum ; but this could not have been the whole amount, for as early as 1786, the English are said to have " seized upon the richest part of this trade by ingratiating themselves into the favor of the natives that lived on the Des Moines " and elsewhere west of the Mississippi. Of the amount of the other articles exported, nothing definite is known. All that can be said is that the merchants of upper Louisiana sent their furs and peltries to Canada and brought back such goods as were used in the Indian trade ; that they shipped lead and provisions to New Orleans and exchanged them for groceries, and that they obtained their supplies of other articles from Philadelphia and Baltimore in return for lead and salt, which are said to have found their way up the Ohio in large quantities. To speak of such a people as wanting in enterprise, or to call the hardy voyagers on these "wild and wicked" western rivers lazy, as is not unfrequently done, indicates a confusion of ideas and terms that can hardly be reconciled with truth and fairness.

As land had no value unless it was improved, the wealth of the colonists consisted principally in personal property, slaves being regarded as its most desirable form. For the same reason rent was virtually unknown. Every head of a family was entitled to a house-lot in the village proper, to as much of the common field as he could cultivate, and to the right of pasturage on the village common. In return for these advantages, he was required to keep up his part of the "common" fence, to aid in road making, and bear his share of any other improvements which the villagers, at their regular annual town meeting, should order to be made. Under such a system there was no inducement to acquire any more land than was absolutely necessary ; and although concessions, embracing hundreds and even thousands of acres of fertile lands, could be had for the asking, it was not until towards the close of the century, when immigrants from the States began to pour into the province, that land took on a recognized value, and that "the principal inhabitants began to open plantations at some little distance from the town," and to cultivate them after the English-American fashion. "As a consequence, passengers," we are told, "could now go through the streets without danger of being jostled by horses, cows, hogs, and oxen, which formerly crowded them."

Of politics they knew but little and cared less. It was the commandant's business, so they thought, to look after "all that sort of thing," and consequently they did not allow it to trouble them. Neither did they concern themselves, to any extent, about education. As early as 1772, a school was ordered to be established in New Orleans, and a director was sent out, together with three teachers, one of grammar, another of Latin, and a third of reading and writing. The parents, however, were not anxious to secure the benefits "which the magnanimous heart of his Majesty had put within their reach" for their children, and they failed to send them to the school. Not a single pupil, we are told, ever presented himself for the Latin class; and those who came to be taught reading and writing were but few in number and uncertain in their attendance. In 1788, the school-house was burned down, when a certain Don Andres Almonaster, to his honor be it said, offered a small "edifice, containing a room thirteen feet in length by twelve in width, which would suffice for the present," and might be used until he could build another, which he proposed to do at a cost to himself of six thousand dollars. The Ursuline convent at New Orleans was also in receipt of his Majesty's bounty to the amount of six hundred dollars per annum; but in no other part of the colony was there any provision made for what may be termed public education, nor was there any legal ordinance on the subject. In St. Louis and Ste. Genevieve private schools, in which children were taught reading, writing, and a little arithmetic, were occasionally established, but they were usually of short duration, and produced no good or lasting effect in the society at large. The great mass of the people were unable to avail of even these scanty advantages. Numbers of them " could not read or write their names," and yet we are assured, on the authority of educated travelers, that "their manners were easy, their conversation pleasant and often instructive, and many of them manifested extraordinary natural endowments." It is but just to add that some of the more wealthy sent their sons to Canada to be educated, and that there were among them a few graduates from European universities.

But whilst the great majority of the people were thus illiterate, and careless about political and educational matters, they were by no means neglectful of their religious concerns or their amusements. The ceremonies and festivals of the church occupied not a little of their leisure, and they seem to have been much given to cards, billiards, and other games, as well as to balls and assemblies. These latter usually took place on Sunday afternoon, after vespers, and instead of being scenes of frivolity they were " schools of manners," where the children were taught " the essence of politeness and self-denial." When questioned as to what seemed to their Protestant neighbors like a desecration of the day they would answer : " That men were made for happiness, and that the more they are able to enjoy themselves, the more acceptable they are to their Creator. They are of opinion that a sullen countenance, an attention to gloomy subjects, a set form of speech, and a stiff behavior are more indicative of hypocrisy than of religion ; and they have often remarked that those who practice these singularities will most assuredly cheat and defraud their neighbors during the rest of the week. Such," it is said, " are the religious sentiments of a people void of superstition ; of a people prone to hospitality, urbanity of manners, and innocent recreation ; and who present their daily orisons at the throne of grace with as much confidence of success as the most devout Puritans in existence."

Of course they were all Catholics ; but whilst great sticklers for their own form of worship, they were not disposed to interfere with the religious rights of others. In this they were far more liberal than were their laws. Thus, when the Holy Office endeavored to gain a footing in New Orleans, Governor Miro arrested the would-be inquisitor and shipped him back to Spain ; and when, a few years later, in upper Louisana, that sturdy Baptist, Abraham Music, asked leave to " hold meeting " at his house, Governor Trudeau is said to have answered : " It cannot be granted, as it is a violation of law. What I mean," he added, " is that you must not put a bell on your house and call it a church, nor suffer any one to christen your children but the parish priest ; but if any of your friends choose to meet at your house, sing, pray, and talk about religion, you will not be molested, provided you continue, as I suppose you are, good Catholics." The worthy governor knew that, as Baptists, they did not believe in infant baptism, and that they did not need the sound of a bell to show them the way to " meeting."

In a community so constituted, and under the rule of officers who were instructed to " maintain tranquillity and contentment among the inhabitants," and to cultivate friendly relations with their neighbors, red as well as white, there was but little to disturb the tranquil flow of what may, by courtesy, be termed public affairs. In fact, the records of the province contain but little save grants of land in the village and common fields, notices of the sales of the property of deceased persons, transcripts of deeds and wills, and occasionally an account of a suit for debt or slander. Even the coming and going of the lieutenant-governors is not unfrequently a matter of inference, to be determined by the date of the documents to which their signatures are attached. In spite, however, of the simple character of these records, tradition has preserved a few events that were regarded as being of sufficient importance to be perpetuated, and it may be well enough to glance briefly at some of them, more by way of showing the character of the occurrences that were thought worthy of commemoration, than for any influence which they had in shaping the destiny of the province.

Thus we find that, in 1770, St. Ange gave place as lieutenant-governor to Piernas. He, in turn, was followed in 1775 by Cruzat, and in 1778 by De Leyba, who remained in office until his death in 1780, when Cruzat was sent to the province for the second time, and held the command until 1787.

During these different administrations, which cover rather more than half the period of Spanish domination, the revolt of the English colonies, or, as it is called, the American Revolution, took place; and although it was indirectly fraught with important consequences to lower Louisiana and the Spanish crown, yet its influence seems hardly to have been felt in the portion of the colony with which we have to deal. Indeed, it only interests us so far as the capture, in 1778, of Kaskaskia and Cahokia by the Virginians, under General George Rogers Clark, and the presence of these troops on the east side of the river in the spring of 1780 can be said to have contributed to the defeat of the invasion which tradition has magnified into an attack upon St. Louis, and which has caused the year 1780 to pass into local history as *l'année du coup*, the year of the attack.

According to the account handed down by Stoddard, the British governor at Michilimackinac anxious to prevent the invasion of Florida by Governor Galvez of Louisiana, sought to create a diversion by sending a force of 150 white men and 1,500 Indians down the Mississippi for the purpose of attacking St. Louis. No direct assault was made upon the village, but during the short time that the hostile troops were in the neighborhood a number — some accounts say as many as sixty — of the inhabitants were killed and thirty taken prisoners. This is the story as it is usually told, and in the main it is correct, except in the number of killed and prisoners, which is greatly exaggerated. Another version of the affair represents " the attack " as having been brought about by a Canadian Frenchman named Ducharme, in revenge for the loss of his goods, which had been confiscated by the Spanish authorities because he was caught trading with the Indians of the Missouri. In this account, also, there is an element of truth, for Ducharme's goods had been seized, and he was engaged in the invasion. It is even intimated that it was owing, in part, to his treachery that the expedition proved a failure.

Recent investigations have thrown additional light upon this subject ; and it now appears that whilst it was expected that the posts which had been taken by Clark would be recaptured, yet the expedition, as planned in London, was a part of a comprehensive movement which had for its object the expulsion of the Spaniards from the Mississippi valley. Having captured St. Louis and the other villages in that neighborhood, these troops were to proceed down the river and coöperate with an English force from below in an attack upon New Orleans and the Spanish settlements on the lower Mississippi. It was a magnificent scheme, but, unfortunately for its success, the Spaniards and Americans in the valley learned of it almost as soon as the English, and they at once took measures to defeat it. In lower Louisiana, Governor Galvez, without waiting to be attacked, raised a force and took Natchez, Baton Rouge, and other English posts on the Mississippi; whilst in Illinois, the invaders found the Virginians under Clark so well prepared that they did not dare to attack them. For this reason, and owing also, it is said, to the treachery of Calvé and Ducharme, the expedition was broken up and returned homewards, though not until " twenty Canadians and a very few traders and servants had made an attack upon Pencour " — *Pain court* — St. Louis, in the course of which, according to the report of Lieutenant-Governor Sinclair, " 68 were killed, and 18 blacks and white people taken prisoners."

This is probably the truth of the affair, except as to the number of killed and prisoners, and we have dwelt upon it at some length for the reason that it exemplifies the difficulties that attend an investigation into the history, or rather the traditions, of the province, and because it is the only instance in which these settlements were ever seriously threatened by a hostile force. Undoubtedly there are numerous statements in the early records as to the depredations committed by the Indians, and it cannot be denied that, on more than one occasion, they murdered a settler and were guilty of other acts of hostility; but, as a rule, these outrages are believed to have been the work of individual savages on horse-stealing expeditions, and not the result of any concerted tribal action. The fact that the French always lived in compact villages and not on separate farms, in exposed positions, as was often the case with the English-American pioneers, insured them a certain amount of protection from Indian attacks ; and when, a few years later, bands of Shawnees, Delawares, and other tribes were brought westward and established on reservations, where they served as a barrier between the whites and their troublesome neighbors the Osages, this comparative immunity was converted into an absolute guarantee against all danger from that quarter. Indeed, it is questionable whether, even without these precautions, there would have been any very serious risk, for the reason that the Spanish government, in all its dealings with the Indians of the Mississippi valley, seems to have been actuated by a sense of humanity that was in advance of the times ; and because the officials of upper Louisiana, in their treatment of these people, were ordered to pursue a policy that was at once just and conciliatory in its character. Instead of enslaving them, O'Reilly, in 1770, notified the inhabitants of Louisiana that they would have to prepare for the emancipation of those who were already in bondage ; and so far from trying to dispossess them of their lands and drive them off, the French, and after them the Spaniards, endeavored to make use of them as hunters and small farmers, and to this end they did not hesitate to establish them, so far as they were able, in permanent settlements close to their own villages, as was the case at Kaskaskia, Ste. Genevieve, and other places. That such a course of conduct bore good fruit is well known to every student of border history; and it is not therefore improbable that the contrast between this method of treatment and that pursued by the English-American colonists may have given rise to the indignant remonstrance which a Shawnee chief is said to have addressed to General Harrison : "You call us your children," said he ; "why do you not make us happy, as our fathers the French did ? They never took from us our lands ; indeed, they were in common between us. They planted where they pleased, and they cut wood where they pleased, and so did we. But now, if a poor Indian attempts to take a little bark from a tree to cover him from the rain, up comes a white man and threatens to shoot him, claiming the tree as his own." Only on one occasion does there appear to have been a prospect of a war between these colonists and the Indians, and that was settled in such a curious manner that the story would not be credible, were it not vouched for by as trustworthy an authority as Major Stoddard. According to him, during a sort of predatory war which, in 1794, raged between the whites and a tribe of Missouri Indians, a chief, with a party of his warriors, boldly entered St. Louis and demanded an interview with Governor Trudeau, to whom he said : "We have come to offer you peace ; we have been at war with you many moons, and what have we done? Nothing. Our warriors have tried every means to meet yours in battle ; but you will not, you dare not fight us ; you are a parcel of old women. What can be done with such a people but make peace, since you will not fight ? I come therefore to offer you peace, and to bury the hatchet, to brighten the chain and again to open the way between us." The Spanish governor, it is added, was obliged to bear the insult, but there was no war.

The Indians, however, were not the only people against whom it was necessary to be on the watch. The recent incursion, though a failure, showed the possibility of an invasion by the English from Canada, and, accordingly, Cruzat, with the view of guarding against an attack from that direction, caused St. Louis to be fortified on the land side by a stockade, to which in after years was added sundry stone towers, a demi-lune, and a bastion. As against any force which the Indians could bring, these defenses were sufficient, though fortunately, perhaps, for the villagers their strength was never tested by the use of cannon.

During the remainder of Cruzat's term there was but little to note. A census taken in 1785 gives the total population of the province at about fifteen hundred ; and in this same year there was a freshet in the Mississippi which obliged the inhabitants of Ste. Genevieve to abandon the site of the " old " village, and to remove to the situation which the town now occupies, on higher ground. It was a memorable event in the annals of the colony, and gave to the year the significant title of *l'année des grands eaux*, the year of the high water.

In 1787, called *l'année des dix batteaux*, from the arrival at one time of ten boats from New Orleans, Perez came into office ; and it was during his administration that bands of the Shawnees, Delawares, etc., driven back by the advance of the whites across the Alleghany Mountains, were induced to forsake their homes in the region north of the Ohio, and to establish themselves upon the lands which had been granted them in the neighborhood of Cape Girardeau, Ste. Genevieve, and the other villages on the Spanish side of the Mississippi. Here they were permitted to remain for some thirty-five years ; and it is a sad commentary upon our treatment of these people that when, in 1825, they were called on to remove still farther westward, the improvements which they left behind them are said to have compared not unfavorably with those of the average of their white neighbors. On the expiration of Perez's term of office in 1793, Trudeau was appointed, and in 1799 he was succeeded by Delassus, a Frenchman by descent, if not by birth, who was the last lieutenant-governor of upper Louisiana under the Spanish régime, as St. Ange, another Frenchman, had been the first.

Under these two administrations, which embrace the last decade of Spanish rule in the Mississippi valley, there were a few events, as for instance the "hard winter" of 1798–99, the prevalence of "the small-pox" in 1801, and some others, which have been commemorated in the peculiar fashion of these villagers, but to which it is unnecessary to do more than refer, as, however important they may have appeared at the time, they were without any influence in shaping the future of the colony, and are, therefore, of but little moment when compared with the increase of population which took place during this period, and with the total change in its character.

To appreciate the full significance of these facts, it is necessary to bear in mind that the first settlers in this province were emigrants from Fort Chartres, Kaskaskia, and the other villages on the Illinois side of the river; that they were almost exclusively French or of French descent, and that for twenty years or more, in spite of the gradual increase in population, this distinct national character was maintained. Even as late as 1788, if we may judge from the village records, the registers of

deaths and marriages, there were but few of the two
thousand inhabitants that were then credited to the province who had not sprung from this stock.   About this
time, however, two events occurred, which, by turning in
this direction a fair share of the emigration from "the
States," increased the population of the province so rapidly, and wrought such a change in its character, that, in
1799, it amounted to six thousand, and in 1803 to about
ten thousand, of which number three fifths, or six thousand, were English-Americans.

The first in time, and perhaps the more important of
the causes which contributed to this result, was the adoption by Congress of the Ordinance of 1787, prohibiting
slavery in the region north of the Ohio and south of
the Lakes.   This ordinance, it will be remembered, was
passed by a vote of five slave and three free States, and
although it was intended to be prospective in its action,
yet its immediate practical effect was to deter those who
owned slaves from settling in the region to which it applied.   It also led some of those who had already established themselves in that region, and who were desirous
of retaining that kind of property in their families, to
take up their residence on the other side of the Mississippi, where the conditions were such as to enable them
to carry out this wish.   Powerful as this motive must
have been in turning the attention of slaveholding emigrants in this direction, its influence was vastly increased,
and its effect hastened, by the necessity which, in 1796,
the Spanish authorities conceived themselves to be under
of strengthening the people of upper Louisiana, so that
they might be able to defend themselves against a threatened invasion of the English from Canada.   To enable
them to do this successfully, it was thought necessary to

increase their numbers; and hence the great inducements which were held out to emigrants, especially to
those from the United States, as it was thought that
their hostility to the English would prove a guarantee
of their fidelity to Spain. Accordingly, lands were
freely granted to all settlers, attended with no other expenses than those of surveys and office fees. A farm
of 800 acres could be obtained for forty-one dollars,
exclusive of the amounts paid to the chainmen and for
the confirmation of the title at New Orleans. Even these
payments were not necessary to give possession. This
was certainly little enough; and when we add that every
such concession might be made to cover a lead mine, and
that there was practically no such thing in the province
as taxation, it will be seen that the temptation to emigrate was of a character that the average pioneer from
Kentucky and Tennessee would find it difficult to resist.
A less attractive prize had lured Boone and men of his
stamp across the Alleghanies, and it was therefore but
natural that, being unable to find their places in the
new order of things which they saw growing up around
them, they should yield to the tempting offers of the
Spanish authorities, and cross the Mississippi in search
of the homes which they had failed to find in regions
farther to the east.

In this connection, it is worthy of note, and the fact
certainly redounds to the credit of the Spanish government, that when making these grants, they practically
showed no discrimination in favor of Catholics as against
Protestants. In 1790 the king had given orders that
the settlers were not to be disturbed in the exercise
of their religion; in 1797, the land laws of Gayoso,
narrow and bigoted as they were in some respects, al-

lowed liberty of conscience for the first generation of emigrants to lower Louisiana ; and in the upper part of the colony, as we have seen, the officials conveniently ignored the regulations that interfered with emigration, including those that bore heavily upon all who did not belong to the established church. In fact, there is reason to believe that as early as 1788, Gardoqui, the Spanish minister at Philadelphia, in the concession which he made to Colonel Morgan of some millions of acres in the New Madrid district, not only granted the prospective colonists the right of self-government, but also freedom of religious worship. This concession, it is true, was not sanctioned by Governor Miro, and it was therefore inoperative ; but the fact that it was granted is proof of the growing liberality of the Spanish authorities, and of the free and easy manner in which the laws of the colony were interpreted. In refusing to confirm this grant, Governor Miro refers to the fact that it would have created an independent republic within Louisiana, and says : " The circumstance of their governing themselves whilst the king should pay the magistrates would attract here a prodigious multitude of people . . . who would, on the slightest provocation, declare themselves independent, and, what is worse, having the free use of their respective religions, they would never become Catholics." With grim humor, the worthy governor adds, that " on such conditions he would undertake to depopulate the greater part of the United States, and draw all their citizens to Louisiana, including the whole Congress itself."

With the incoming tide of emigration, there was a marked change in the values of certain kinds of property. Land which had heretofore been held in little esteem was now eagerly sought after; and all who were entitled to concessions solicited and obtained them. Among those who were thus fortunate were " most of the French inhabitants," and also those officials who were entitled to compensation, and whose services, in accordance with Spanish custom, were rewarded by grants of lands instead of by gifts of money. A few of these concessions were on a large scale, embracing a league square or more of land, but the great majority of them were far from extravagant; and yet so numerous were they that, according to Major Stoddard, " the quantity of land claimed in upper Louisiana under French and Spanish titles, amounted to one million seven hundred and twenty-one thousand four hundred and ninety-three (1,721,493) arpents, a quantity " which, we are told, " was not exorbitant when compared with the population of the province."

Of these grants, some were general and others special; and the titles which they conveyed were either complete or incomplete. The concessions were general when they could be located upon any portion of the public domain that was not taken up, and they were special when they were designated by certain metes and bounds. When the grant was derived directly from the crown, or when it was sanctioned by the regularly constituted authority at New Orleans, the title which it conveyed was said to be complete; but when the concession was based upon a " naked grant " of the lieutenant-governor or of a commandant, and had not received the approval of the proper officers at New Orleans, it was incomplete. Nineteen twentieths of the titles belonged to the latter or incomplete class, and this gave rise to much trouble and litigation before the evil was finally remedied. Congress, however, set to work to accomplish it, and though it took a good many years and several acts, yet, thanks to the liberal policy which was adopted, it is probable that there were but few *bonâ fide* grants made by the French and Spanish authorities that were not ultimately confirmed.

Such, in brief, is the history of upper Louisiana under Spanish domination, and the picture which it presents of the condition of the inhabitants at the close of the eighteenth century. This picture, it will be observed, is not sketched from materials furnished by the colonists themselves, but is made up from accounts given by those who, however favorably disposed towards them, were, with but few exceptions, either ignorant of what was really meritorious in the Spanish form of government, or were so hostile to it as to be able to see but little that was good in any of its measures. In either event, they were but poorly qualified for the work which they had in hand ; and yet, in spite of the prejudice which occasionally crops out even in trustworthy writers like Stoddard and Brackenridge, it is evident to any one who will take the trouble to read between the lines, that these people had attained to a degree of mental, material, and political progress which compared not unfavorably with the early stages of existence in the communities on the other side of the Mississippi. All things considered, it is safe to say that, so far as the acts of the constituted authorities could or did affect the lives of the colonists, they had nothing to learn from their English-American neighbors. They did not, it is true, have to pay as much for their homes and farms, contribute out of their scanty earnings to the maintenance of the priests, or of the magistrates for whom they had but little use; neither were they called on to tax themselves to any great extent for the support of the government. They had even managed to get along quite comfortably without the introduction of the trial by jury; and, what some of the early writers find it difficult to understand, they regarded these exemptions as positive advantages.

Whether, alone and unaided, they could have educated themselves to a contrary way of thinking, is a question which we are not called upon to consider. Such a thing is possible; and it is even possible that the English-American settlers who had crossed the Mississippi to escape taxation and in pursuit of cheap lands might have been foolish enough to revolutionize the province, as they were abundantly able to do, for the purpose of reincurring the obligations which such a course would have imposed; but there is no reason for thinking they would have done so, though the contrary has been often asserted and is generally believed. All that we are permitted to know about the matter is that the settlers were so well satisfied with their form of government, and with their mode of life, that the transfer of the colony, in 1804, to the United States was a source of undisguised regret to a great majority of the creoles, and that the English-American portion of the population was neither unanimous nor enthusiastic in its favor.[1]

[1] "Indeed, few of the French and part of the English-Americans only were at first reconciled to the change, though they never manifested any discontent." — Stoddard, *Sketches of Louisiana,* p. 311. Philadelphia, 1812.

CHAPTER IV.

In seeking for the causes that led to the treaties of
1800 and 1803, by which Louisiana was " retroceded "
to France and subsequently sold by that power to the
United States, it will be necessary to glance briefly at
the political condition of Western Europe as it then was,
and to note the steps by which the English colonies
along the Atlantic coast had become welded into the
United States of America, and had extended their western boundary to the Mississippi River.

By the first of these treaties, known to history as the
treaty of St. Ildefonso, and concluded on the 1st of October, 1800, France came into possession of Louisiana
with "the same limits that it now has in the hands
of Spain, that it had when France possessed it, and such
as it ought to have after the treaties subsequently entered into between Spain and other powers." Ostensibly this retrocession was made in return for the province
of Tuscany, which was to be erected into a kingdom
under the name of Etruria and handed over to the Duke
of Parma, one of the Spanish princes ; but in reality,
it was the result of a complication of affairs in which
Spain can hardly be said to have been a willing actor.
Under any circumstances, such a cession involved a
sacrifice of pride and prestige which must have been
exceedingly distasteful to a proud and haughty people,

and in the present instance, it was made more objectionable by the fact that, in many quarters, it was regarded as a military and political blunder. By some inexplicable process, the Spanish authorities had persuaded themselves that Louisiana might be made a sort of bulwark to their Mexican possessions, and hence the tenacity with which they clung to it although it had already brought them to the brink of a war with the United States, and although it must, if the policy of closing the Mississippi to the people of the Ohio valley were persisted in, inevitably hasten the very result which they were anxious to avoid. For these reasons, then, among others, it is permitted us to believe that the court of Madrid was not anxious to part with Louisiana, and that it would not have agreed to do so, but for the pressure which Bonaparte knew so well how to bring to bear upon all who were in positions to help or hinder his designs.

At this time, he was in the full flush of his Italian triumphs. He had just been made First Consul for ten years, and he was intent upon schemes for advancing France to a position in naval and commercial affairs which would be commensurate with the military supremacy he had reasserted for her on land. To do this, colonies were regarded as absolutely essential, and these France did not have. The ill-advised emancipation of the slaves in Hayti had handed over that flourishing island to Toussaint L'Ouverture and the party of the blacks, as distinguished from that of the whites or the mulattoes; and of all her other possessions in Asia and America, the English had left her but little that was worth having. The outlook was not favorable, but the First Consul, in nowise daunted by the prospect, made up his mind to reconquer Hayti on the first opportunity, and by way of furnishing that colony with a depot from which to draw supplies of " provisions, cattle, and wood," he determined to reclaim Louisiana.

In the condition in which France then was, such a course would, to-day, be looked upon as suicidal, but at that time it was regarded as sound policy by not a few of those who controlled the destinies of Europe. Even the First Consul himself, far-sighted as he was, seems only to have caught a glimpse of the truth, recognized everywhere twenty five years later, that a distant colony was " an element of weakness to a people who could be shut out from the sea on the outbreak of every maritime war." There were other considerations of a personal character, that had their weight in leading him to adopt this course. He knew very well that the family compact of 1762, by which Louisiana had been ceded to Spain, was considered a great mistake by the merchants of France, and he was satisfied that he could count upon their support in any efforts he might make to recover it. He seems also to have had a vague notion that the possession of the mouth of the Mississippi would enable him to exert a pressure upon the people of the Ohio valley which would, with a little judicious management, bend them to his will and thus give him a potential voice in North American affairs. But even if it did not come up to his expectations in each and every one of these particulars, he fancied that in some possible contingency it might furnish him with a base of operations from which he could threaten the English colonies in Canada or the West Indies ; and if the occasion should ever arise, it would afford him a position from which he could seize Mexico and the Spanish possessions in Central

America. Besides these advantages, which were rather prospective than real, he hoped to find here the means of rewarding the officers and soldiers whom the peace had thrown out of employment, and he also saw in it a safe and convenient outlet for certain turbulent spirits whom he might wish to keep at a distance from France.

Influenced by these considerations, he took occasion to open negotiations with the Spanish cabinet upon this subject; and skillfully availing himself of the critical condition of the relations which then existed between Spain and the United States, he found no difficulty in convincing the Spanish minister that it was to the interest of his country to retrocede Louisiana to France. France, it was urged, was the friend and ally of Spain, and in her hands Louisiana would be a protection to Mexico, and not a source of danger, as it now was. Powerful as this motive must have been, it was supplemented by the fact that the prevailing opinion at Madrid, at that time, seems to have been that she would prove a less dangerous neighbor than the United States, as she was not a colonizing power, the experience of a hundred and fifty years having demonstrated her inability to maintain a successful continental possession. Unquestionably these considerations had their weight, and backed, as they were, by the imperious will and victorious legions of Bonaparte, they were too powerful to be resisted. Accordingly, on the 1st of October, 1800, the treaty of St. Ildefonso was concluded, and Louisiana became once more a French colony.

Thus far, everything had gone on smoothly. Spain had given her consent to the retrocession, somewhat unwillingly, perhaps, but still she had given it; and thus by the mere stroke of a pen, the First Consul had acquired a clear title to a domain far more extensive than France itself. To take possession of it, however, was quite a different matter, and this was the lesson which he was now to learn. England was the mistress of the seas, and not only was it impossible for a French fleet to move without her permission, but it was quite within her power, in case the cession of Louisiana became known, to land a force at New Orleans and seize the colony before it had been formally transferred to its new owners. Under these circumstances, the high contracting parties found it necessary to move very cautiously; and hence the attempt to keep the terms of the treaty and even its existence a secret, until the peace of Amiens once more gave the French the free run of the ocean, and made it possible for the First Consul to proceed openly in the execution of his plans for colonial aggrandizement. When, therefore, in the autumn of 1801, the preliminaries of that peace were agreed upon in London, he at once took advantage of the opportunity and began secretly to make arrangements for the occupation of Hayti and Louisiana. With the expedition sent to Hayti, we are not concerned. It sailed in the winter of 1801–2, before the conclusion of the definitive treaty of peace in the March following, and except in so far as the difficulties and disasters which it encountered may have influenced the First Consul in his determination to part with Louisiana, it does not come within the scope of our investigation.

The second of these expeditions — the one intended to take possession of Louisiana — was organized during the ensuing summer and with the same secrecy, but its departure was delayed by a misunderstanding as to the interpretation of the treaty of St. Ildefonso, France contending that the Floridas were included in the act of cession, whilst Spain maintained that they were not. When, at length, after some months of contention, this point was settled, another year had rolled around, and the relations between France and England had become so strained that the order for the expedition to sail was countermanded, and the troops that had been intended to occupy Louisiana and garrison New Orleans were assigned to other duties.

In the mean time, notwithstanding the secrecy with which the terms of this treaty had been guarded, its purport was generally suspected in diplomatic circles. In March, 1801, Mr. Rufus King, the American minister to England, informed Mr. Secretary Madison of the rumors that were afloat on the subject, and Mr. R. R. Livingston was at once sent to Paris, with instructions to protest against a measure which was justly regarded as being hostile to the interests of the United States, inasmuch as it placed a strong military power at the mouth of the Mississippi, instead of a weak one as Spain then was. This vigorous action brought the United States prominently forward, and there can be no doubt that it was their hostility to the measure, joined to the warlike attitude assumed by England some months later, that determined the First Consul to make a virtue of necessity and sell a colony which he could not hope to retain, even if he were permitted to take possession of it.

To understand the part which the United States were henceforth to play in this transaction and the reasons for it, we shall have to take a retrospective glance, and note briefly the steps which had brought them to the Mississippi River, and to the very doors of New Orleans. In doing this it will not be necessary to go back of the treaty of 1763, by which, as we have already seen, France divided the possessions which she held upon the mainland of North America, between Great Britain and Spain, — all on the east side of the Mississippi, except the city of New Orleans and the island on which it is situated, being ceded to the former power, whilst the latter gained New Orleans and all of Louisiana that was situated west of that river. At the same time, Spain surrendered Florida in return for Havana which had been recently taken from her, so that, by virtue of these treaties, Great Britain was now the sole owner of all of North America east of the Mississippi, except the small triangle at the mouth of the river, which is bounded by the Mississippi on one side, the Gulf on another, and by the Iberville and Lakes Maurepas and Pontchartrain on the third or north.

In the same year in which she came into possession of all this broad domain, Great Britain divided Florida into two provinces, which were called, respectively, East and West Florida. At first the northern limit of West Florida was fixed at a line extending from the Mississippi to the Appalachicola along the 31st degree of north latitude ; but shortly after, in order to expedite the administration of justice in the Natchez district, a strip, a hundred miles and more in width, along its entire northern boundary, was added to West Florida, thus extending its limits in that direction to a line drawn due east from the mouth of the Yazoo River to the Chattahoochee, one of the main branches of the Appalachicola.

Such was the condition of affairs when the revolt of the thirteen American colonies made another revision of the map necessary. By the treaty of 1783 between Great

Britain on the one part and the United States and her allies, France and Spain, on the other, Great Britain acknowledged the independence of the colonies, and recognized as a part of their southern boundary a line drawn due east from a point in the Mississippi River, in latitude 31° north, to the middle of the Appalachicola ; and at the same time she ceded to Spain by a separate agreement the two Floridas, but without defining their northern boundaries. This omission gave rise to a dispute between Spain and the United States as to their respective limits. On the part of Spain it was contended that by the act of Great Britain, of 1764, the northern boundary of West Florida had been fixed at the line running due east from the mouth of the Yazoo to the Chattahoochee, and that all south of that line had been ceded to her ; whilst on the other hand, the United States as strenuously maintained that the act fixing and enlarging the limits of West Florida was superseded by the recent treaty, which extended their southern boundary to the 31st degree of north latitude, a hundred and ten miles further south than the line claimed by Spain.

Spain, however, had possession of the disputed territory by right of conquest, and evidently had no intention of giving it up. She strengthened her garrisons at Baton Rouge and Natchez, and built a fort at Vicksburg, and subsequently one at New Madrid, on the Missouri side of the Mississippi, just below the mouth of the Ohio ; and of the latter she made a port of entry where vessels from the Ohio were obliged to land and declare their cargoes. She even denied the right of the United States to the region between the Mississippi and the Alleghany Mountains, which had been ceded to them by Great Britain on the ground that the conquests made by Governor Galvez, of West Florida, and by Don Eugenio Pierre,[1]

The following is the account of this expedition : —

From the *Madrid Gazette* of the 12th March, 1786.

Translation. — By a letter from the commandant general of the army of operations at the Havana and governour of Louisiana, his majesty has advices, that a detachment of sixty-five militia men, and sixty Indians of the nations Otaguos, Sotu, and Putuatami, under the command of Don Eugenio Pierre, a captain of militia, accompanied by Don Carlos Tayon, a sub-lieutenant of militia, by Don Luis Chevalier, a man well versed in the language of the Indians, and by their great chiefs Eleturno and Naquigen, which marched the 2d January, 1781, from the town of St. Luis of the Illinois, had possessed themselves of the post of St. Joseph, which the English occupied at two hundred and twenty leagues distance from that of the above-mentioned St. Luis ; having suffered in so extensive a march, and so rigorous a season, the greatest inconveniences from cold and hunger, exposed to continued risks from the country being possessed by savage nations, and having to pass over parts covered with snow, and each one being obliged to carry provision for his own subsistence, and various merchandises which were necessary to content, in case of need, the barbarous nations through whom they were obliged to cross. The commander, by seasonable negotiations and precautions, prevented a considerable body of Indians, who were at the devotion of the English, from opposing this expedition ; for it would otherwise have been difficult to have accomplished the taking of the said post. They made prisoners of the few English they found in it, the others having perhaps retired in consequence of some prior notice. Don Eugenio Pierre took possession, in the name of the king, of that place and its dependencies, and of the river of the Illinois ; in consequence whereof the standard of his majesty was there displayed during the whole time. He took the English one, and delivered it on his arrival at St. Luis to Don Francisco Cruzat, the commandant of that post.

The destruction of the magazine of provisions and goods which the English had there (the greater part of it which was divided among our Indians and those who lived at St. Joseph as had been

of Fort St. Joseph, "near the sources of the Illinois,"
had vested the title to all this country in her; and she
insisted that what she did not own was possessed by the
Indians, and could not therefore belong to the United
States.   Even as late as 1795, she claimed to have
bought from the Chickasaws the bluffs which bear their
name, and which are situated on the east bank of the
Mississippi some distance north of the most northerly
boundary ever assigned by Great Britain to West
Florida.

Here, then, was cause for " a very pretty quarrel," and
to add to the ill feeling which grew out of it, Spain denied the right of the people of the United States to the
"free navigation of the Mississippi," — a right which
had been conceded to them by Great Britain with all the
formalities with which she had received it from France.
Whether it was competent for her, thus, to hand over to
a third party the right which she undoubtedly had of
passing, at will, through this portion of the dominions of
Spain is a point about which opinions may differ.   One
thing, however, is certain, that no self-respecting people,
powerful enough to prevent the exercise of such a right,

offered them in case they did not oppose our troops) was not the
only advantage resulting from the success of this expedition, for
thereby it became impossible for the English to execute their plan
of attacking the fort of St. Luis of the Illinois, and it also served
to intimidate these savage nations, and oblige them to promise to
remain neuter, which they do at present.

When you consider the ostensible object of this expedition, the
distance of it, the formalities with which the place, the country,
and the river were taken possession of in the name of his Catho-
lick majesty, I am persuaded it will not be necessary for me to
swell this letter with remarks that would occur to a reader of far
less penetration than yourself. — *Secret Journal*, vol. iv. (U. S.
Doc. 205.)

would ever suffer it to pass unchallenged. To this extent, then, it must be conceded that Spain occupied solid ground, and in the present instance her position was strengthened by the fact that, strictly speaking, the free navigation of the Mississippi was not the point in dispute. Of itself, this phrase meant nothing tangible, for a sea-going vessel, as then constructed, could not reach the Ohio; neither could a flatboat, such as the people of Kentucky generally used for sending their surplus produce down the river, navigate the ocean. What was needed to make the right of any value to the people of the Ohio valley was the additional right to take their produce into a Spanish port, New Orleans, and either sell it then and there, or else store it, subject to certain conditions, until such time as it suited them to transfer it to sea-going vessels. This right Spain would not concede; and as the people of the Ohio valley were determined to have it, cost what it might, it brought on a series of intrigues between the Spanish governors of Louisiana and certain influential citizens west of the Alleghanies which threatened the stability of the American Union almost before it was formed, and ultimately led to the purchase of Louisiana, and to the sectional struggle for political power which, aligning itself on different issues, finally culminated in the election of Lincoln and the war of secession.[1]

At length in 1795, after ten years of procrastination, the prospect of a European war, in which Spain and England were to be ranged on different sides, and the

---

[1] " We agreed and lamented the one inevitable consequence of the annexation of Louisiana to the Union would be to diminish the relative weight and influence of the Northern section." John Quincy Adams in *New England Federalism*, p. 148. Boston, 1877.

necessity which this imposed on the former power of guarding her American possessions by the interposition of a neutral and friendly state between upper Louisiana and Canada, brought about an agreement between Spain and the United States which resulted in the treaty of Madrid. By the terms of this treaty, Spain recognized the 31st degree of north latitude as the boundary between the United States and West Florida; and she agreed to permit the people of the United States to use the port of New Orleans as a place of deposit for their merchandise and effects, and to export the same free of all duty or charge except a reasonable consideration to be paid for storage and other incidental expenses. This agreement was to be in force for three years, at the end of which time, his Catholic majesty "promised either to continue this permission, if he found during that time that it was not prejudicial to the interests of Spain, or if he should not agree to continue it there, he agreed to assign, on another part of the banks of the Mississippi, an equivalent establishment." At the expiration of the three years, the agreement was continued by tacit consent, and it remained in force until October, 1802, when the intendant, Morales, in opposition to the advice of the governor, canceled it, and refused to name any other place of deposit, as the Americans contended he was bound to do under the treaty. This ill-judged act worked an injury to both parties. It caused a scarcity of provisions at New Orleans, and it effectually shut out the people of the Western States from a market for their surplus produce, thus provoking throughout all that region a storm of indignation not only against Spain, but also against France; for by this time the fact of the retrocession was known, and it was generally believed that the right of deposit would not have been revoked except at her request.

At this time the population of the Ohio valley amounted to about six hundred thousand souls, and they were in no mood to submit to a proceeding which they regarded as being inimical to their interests, as indeed it was, and also as a violation of treaty obligations, which was a matter of some doubt, "the law of nature" to the contrary notwithstanding. "The Mississippi," they said, "is ours by the law of nature. . . . Its mouth is the only issue . . . to our waters, and we wish to use it for our vessels. No power in the world shall deprive us of this right. . . . If our liberty in this matter is disputed, nothing shall prevent our taking possession of the capital, and when we are once masters of it, we shall know how to maintain ourselves there. If Congress refuses us effectual protection, if it forsakes us, we will adopt the measures which our safety requires, even if they endanger the peace of the Union and our connection with the other States. No protection, no allegiance."

In November, Mr. Madison wrote to the American minister at Madrid to the effect that the proclamation of Morales, prohibiting the right of deposit at New Orleans, was a direct and palpable violation of the treaty of 1795, and expressed the hope that the Spanish government would neither lose a moment in countermanding it, nor hesitate to repair every damage which might result from it. You are aware, he said, of the sensibility of our Western citizens to such an occurrence; and this sensibility, he added, is justified by the interests they have at stake. "*The Mississippi to them is everything. It is the Hudson, the Delaware, the Potomac,*

*and all the navigable rivers of the Atlantic States,
formed into one stream. . . .* It is to be hoped that the
intendant will be led to see the error which he has
committed, and to correct it before a very great share
of its mischief will have happened. Should he prove
as obstinate as he has been ignorant or wicked, nothing
can temper the irritation and indignation of the Western country but a persuasion that the energy of their
government will obtain from that of Spain the most ample redress." Mr. Livingston held much the same language in Paris, and made good use of the hostile outburst by way of enforcing the proposition which he had
previously submitted to the French cabinet for the purchase of New Orleans and the Floridas. Congress, too,
took up the matter, and in February, 1803, after a
lengthy debate, resolutions of a decidedly belligerent
character were adopted.

Before the news of this action could reach Europe,
the Spanish king " had disapproved of the order of Morales, prohibiting the introduction of goods, wares, and
merchandise from the United States into the port of
New Orleans, and had ordered that the United States
should continue to enjoy the right of deposit there, but
without prejudice to his right of substituting some
other spot on the banks of the Mississippi," as provided
in the treaty of Madrid. Unquestionably this was a
politic move, and a few years earlier it would have
been hailed as a harbinger of peace by the people of
the Ohio valley ; but of late, events had moved rapidly
both in Europe and America, and the time had gone by
when the destiny of Louisiana could be affected by anything that Spain might or might not do. The fact of
the retrocession, hitherto jealously guarded, was now

openly proclaimed, and England, armed for the struggle with France which had now become inevitable, stood ready to seize the mouth of the Mississippi on the firing of the first gun. This was well known to the First Consul, and, no doubt, it decided him ; for whilst as a matter of fact he could afford to ignore the protest of as weak a power as the United States then was, and probably would have done so, yet with the sword and purse of England in the scale against him, the conditions were changed, and he saw, at once, that the coveted prize had gone from him forever. Resolved, however, that what was France's loss should not be England's gain, and being in sore need of money, he determined to sell not only New Orleans, but the entire colony, and Talleyrand was instructed to sound the American minister on the subject. Accordingly on the 11th of April, 1803, he astonished Mr. Livingston, whose modest desires had scarcely reached beyond New Orleans, by asking him how much he would give for the whole of Louisiana ? Not being prepared to name a definite sum or even to negotiate for the entire colony, he answered twenty millions, "provided our citizens were paid for the losses inflicted on their commerce by French privateers." This was pronounced too little, and Mr. Livingston then proposed to defer the further consideration of the matter until after the arrival of Mr. Monroe, who was daily expected in Paris, and who was specially charged by President Jefferson to assist in this negotiation. Fortunately Mr. Monroe arrived at this time, and he and Mr. Livingston at once took up the negotiation. After a little finessing as to the price between them and M. Barbé-Marbois, the French representative, the terms were agreed on, and the treaty was concluded on the 30th of April, 1803.

By it the United States obtained " Louisiana, with all its rights and appurtenances as fully and in the same manner as they had been acquired by the French Republic from Spain, on condition that the Americans should pay to France eighty millions of francs, twenty millions of which were to be used in payment of what was due by France to the citizens of the United States." Certain commercial advantages were also conceded to France; and in Article III., written by Bonaparte himself, it was stipulated that " the inhabitants of the ceded territory shall be incorporated in the Union of the United States, and admitted as soon as possible, according to the principles of the Federal Constitution, to the enjoyment of all the rights, advantages, and immunities of citizens of the United States; and in the mean time they shall be maintained and protected in the free enjoyment of their liberty, property, and the religion which they profess."

As soon as the terms of this treaty became known, Spain protested against it, on the ground that France had no right to make the sale, because, first, she had agreed never to alienate the colony; and, secondly, because her own title was not yet complete, owing to the failure on her part to secure the recognition of the king of Etruria by the cabinets of London and St. Petersburg. In reply, Mr. Madison contended that the promise " never to alienate " formed no part of the original treaty between France and Spain, and that if it had done so it would not affect the purchase by the United States, which had been made in good faith, and in ignorance of any such understanding. He also called attention to the fact that, under date of May 4th, Spain had, herself, referred the United States to France as being the only power that could convey this territory, and he added somewhat sarcastically that if any further evidence were needed as to the validity of the French title, it might be found in the orders of the king of Spain, transferring that colony to France.

To this statement on the part of the United States, there could be no satisfactory reply ; and on the 10th of February, 1804, the Spanish minister, in a letter to Mr. Pinckney, denied that he had given any order to oppose the transfer of Louisiana, and declared that " his majesty thought proper to renounce his protest against the alienation of Louisiana by France." What the French government thought of the objections brought forward by the Spanish court may be inferred from the letter of the French *chargé* at Washington, dated October 14, 1803, in which he announced that as soon as the ratifications were exchanged, " he would proceed without delay . . . to the delivery of the colony to the persons whom the President of the United States shall appoint to take possession of it." In spite, however, of the harmony which prevailed between the two powers that were most directly concerned, the protest of Spain was taken advantage of by the opponents of Mr. Jefferson's administration, and made one of the grounds upon which they urged the rejection of the treaty. It proved of no avail, for, as John Quincy Adams subsequently truly said, " Notwithstanding the objections and apprehensions of many individuals, of many wise, able, and excellent men in various parts of the Union, yet such is the public favor attending the transaction which commenced by the negotiation of this treaty, and which, I hope, will terminate in our full, undisturbed, and undisputed possession of the ceded territory, that I firmly believe if an amendment to the Constitution, amply sufficient for the accomplishment of everything for which we have contracted, shall be proposed, as I think it ought, it will be adopted by the legislature of every State in the Union." This course, however, was not thought necessary by the friends of the measure. The constitutional objections to which Mr. Adams referred, and which were shared, to some extent, by both Jefferson and Madison, were brushed aside with characteristic disregard; and on the 26th of October, 1803, a few days after the ratification of the treaty, an act to enable the President to take possession of the ceded territory was passed in the Senate by a vote of 26 to 6; and on the 28th it was carried in the House by a vote of 89 to 23. On the 29th of the same month, the House passed a bill authorizing the creation of a stock to the amount of eleven million two hundred and fifty thousand dollars, for the purpose of carrying this treaty into effect, and when, on the 3d of November, 1803, it came before the Senate, Mr. Adams, rising superior to sectional considerations, was found side by side with Breckenridge, of Kentucky, among its stoutest supporters.

With the adoption of this measure, congressional action upon the subject was at an end, and it now only remained for the United States to take possession of the territory which they had purchased. This was done without difficulty. On the 30th of November the Spanish authorities at New Orleans handed over the colony to Laussat, the French representative, and on the 20th of December following, he formally transferred it to General Wilkinson and Governor Claiborne, of Mississippi, who were authorized to receive it on the part of the

United States. When the French flag that was floating in the square was hauled down and the American flag was run up, " a group of American citizens, who stood at the corner of the square, waved their hats in token of respect for their country's flag, and a few of them greeted it with their voices." No emotion, it is said, was manifested by any other portion of the assemblage, unless the tears which, according to another account, were shed on the occasion should be taken as an index of the feelings of those who witnessed the ceremony.

With but little change, save in the actors, this scene was repeated on the 9th of March, 1804, in the then village of St. Louis. On that day, the American troops crossed the river from Cahokia, and Don Carlos Dehault Delassus delivered upper Louisiana to Captain Amos Stoddard, of the United States Army, who was commissioned to receive it on behalf of France. The next day he transferred it to the United States, and thus put an end to the rule of Spain in the valley of the Mississippi, which, counting from the landing of Ulloa at New Orleans, had lasted thirty-eight years.

CHAPTER V.

ON the 26th of March, 1804, only about two weeks after Captain, or, to give him the title by which he is better known, Major Stoddard took command at St. Louis, and in evident anticipation of that event, President Jefferson approved of the act of Congress by which Louisiana was divided into two parts, and all north of the 33d parallel of north latitude was formed into a district, and styled the District of Louisiana. For judicial and administrative purposes this district, or upper Louisiana as we shall continue to call it, was attached to the territory of Indiana, and in October of that year the governor and judges of that territory prepared a series of ordinances, and inaugurated the new government within the district, thereby relieving Major Stoddard from the anomalous position which he had hitherto held of first civil commandant of upper Louisiana, under the appointment of Governor Claiborne, of Mississippi, with all the powers and prerogatives of a Spanish lieutenant-governor.

To that portion of the act which attached the district to Indiana, as well as to those clauses which declared all grants of lands made subsequent to the treaty of St. Ildefonso to be void and of no effect, and which related to the prospective removal of the Indians from the east side of the Mississippi to the west, the people of upper Louisiana were violently opposed ; and in a remonstrance signed on the 29th of September, 1804, by " Representatives elected by the Freemen of their respective districts in the District of Louisiana," they prayed for the repeal of the act, and petitioned for the erection of the district into a territory of the second grade, the rank to which their numbers entitled them. They also claimed the right, under the treaty, of importing slaves into the district, which was prohibited in the territory of Orleans, as lower Louisiana was now called, but which had not been denied to them ; and they asked that " funds should be appropriated for the support, and lands set apart or bought for the building and maintaining of a French and English school in each county, and for the building of a seminary of learning, where not only the French and English languages, but likewise the dead languages, mathematics, mechanics, natural and moral philosophy, and the principles of the Constitution of the United States should be taught."

Of the fifteen signers of this " Remonstrance and Petition," as it was termed, eight were unquestionably of French extraction — a proof, if any were needed, of the ease with which they adopted the methods of their neighbors from the other side of the river. On the 4th of January, 1805, this petition was presented in the lower house of Congress, and was referred to a committee which reported, on the 25th of the same month, a resolution declaring that " provision ought to be made, by law, for extending to the inhabitants of Louisiana the right of self-government," though with singular inconsistency they accompanied the resolution by a number of so-called " wise and salutary restrictions " as to the subjects upon which freedom of action was to be allowed.

This report was adopted, and a committee, of which John Randolph was chairman, was appointed to draw up an act in accordance with its provisions; but before they could report, a bill was received from the Senate which erected the district into a territory of the first or lowest grade, and changed its title from the District to the Territory of Louisiana. This bill was at once passed, and on the 3d of March, 1805, it received the signature of President Jefferson and became a law, though it was not to go into effect until the 4th of the July following. By it, the President was empowered to appoint a governor and three judges, who were to act together in a legislative capacity, and who were authorized to adopt such regulations as they might deem proper for the government of the territory, subject of course to the approval of Congress. No mention is made in the act of the land grants of the French and Spanish commandants, nor is there any reference to the removal of the Indians to the west side of the Mississippi, the two measures in which the people of the territory were most interested.

So far as the Indians were concerned, it was not perhaps necessary that there should have been any action, at this time, as the intentions of the general government in this respect had been made sufficiently manifest, during the preceding autumn, by a treaty in which the Sacs and Foxes had relinquished some three million acres of land situated immediately north of the Missouri and in the angle formed by the junction of that stream with the Mississippi. In regard to the land grants, however, there were no such assurances; and it was not until April, 1814, that an act was passed confirming all claims made " by virtue of incomplete French or Spanish grants or concessions, or any warrant, or order of survey which was granted prior to the 10th of March, 1804," the day on which the United States took formal possession of upper Louisiana.

Exactly why this just and politic measure was so long delayed is a question which it is useless now to discuss. Possibly, it may have been due to an unwillingness on the part of the United States to admit the right of Spain to dispose of any portion of the soil of Louisiana during the time that she continued to hold it, after the cession to France and before the final transfer to themselves, that is, from October 1, 1800, to March 10, 1804 ; or it may have been the result of certain well-grounded suspicions as to the fraudulent character of some of the grants made by the last two Spanish lieutenant-governors of upper Louisiana. In either event, it was a mistake, for as matters turned out it would have been productive of less harm if the government had, in the first place, submitted to the small loss with which it was threatened, instead of trying to save a few thousand acres of land by delaying the confirmation of these grants and thereby prolonging the period of " alarm and apprehension " which, we are told, prevailed very generally throughout the district in regard to these claims.

That this delay, or rather the uncertainty of which it was, in some measure, the cause, may have led a number of the holders of these concessions, and of the entries made under them, to dispose of their claims at prices that were merely nominal is very probable ; but that it induced " many families to abandon the country," as was asserted on the floor of Congress, is believed to be a bit of exaggeration, excusable, perhaps, in view of the end sought to be obtained, but hardly to be taken as the literal statement of a truth. Indeed, the evidence all seems to point the other way; for upon examination it will be found that in a majority of the thirteen hundred and forty-two confirmations made prior to January, 1813, the claims were still in the hands of the original holders of the concessions or of their immediate representatives; and the fact that in 1810 the population amounted to over twenty thousand, about double the number it was estimated to have been when Major Stoddard took possession of the district, indicates beyond all cavil that the number of families that had come into the territory during this interval was largely in excess of those that had quitted it.

In spite, however, of the silence of this act in regard to these titles, and although it stopped short of what the people of the district thought they had a right to expect in the way of territorial advancement, it was a step in the right direction. It did not, it is true, allow the citizens of the newly formed territory to choose their own officers, frame their own laws, or do much else that a self-governing community is usually supposed to do; but it gave them officers whose field of duty was limited to the territory; and, theoretically, it made of that territory a sort of preparatory school, in which the inhabitants were to take their first lessons in the science of self-government, though, practically, except in the introduction of the trial by jury, it made but few changes either in the laws or in the manner in which they were administered.

Under the circumstances this was no doubt the best thing that could have been done. The experiences of a large minority of the citizens of the territory, accustomed as they had been to the summary methods of the Spanish commandants, was hardly of a character to fit them for some of the duties that were now to devolve upon them, and though they adapted themselves to the new order of things with marvelous ease and rapidity, yet our fathers, wiser, perhaps, in their generation than we have been in ours, appear to have been of the opinion that a certain amount of training was not a bad preparation for the responsibilities of citizenship. Accordingly they assigned Louisiana to a position in the first or lowest grade of territories, and not in the second, as was expected and desired.

Under this new régime the first governor was General James Wilkinson, and with him were associated, the one as chief justice and the other as secretary, J. B. C. Lucas, a Frenchman by birth and a former member of Congress from Pennsylvania, and Dr. Joseph Browne, of New York, who is said to have been appointed upon "the special and single recommendation of Aaron Burr," whose brother-in-law he was.

Wilkinson at this time stood high in the favor of the authorities at Washington, and though the suspicious character of the dealings which he had formerly carried on with the Spanish officials in lower Louisiana must have been well known, yet he seems to have retained the confidence of Mr. Jefferson and his cabinet to the very end. He was, if we may credit Postmaster General Granger, " one of the most agreeable, best informed, most genteel, moderate, and sensible Republicans in the nation ; " and if to this be added his high military rank and his familiarity with border life and Indian affairs, it would seem as if he must have been almost an ideal man for the place. And yet, notwithstanding these qualifications, real and supposed, his career as governor was a failure ; not that he did anything in his official capacity that was positively harmful to the people of the territory, or left undone anything, within his power, that might have contributed to their welfare, but for the reason that, during the year or more that he was in authority, that is, from July, 1805, to August, 1806, he succeeded in so embroiling himself with the territorial officials with whom it was his duty to act, as to interfere very seriously with his chances of usefulness. In less than four months after his arrival in the territory, his relations with Rufus Easton, one of the most honorable men in all that region, and the first postmaster St. Louis ever had, were of such a character that he refused to send his mail through that office ; and before the end of the year, according to his own statement, Judge Lucas, Colonel Hammond, who had been commandant of the district of St. Louis under Governor Harrison, of Indiana, and other leading citizens of the territory were engaged in " a cabal " to bring about his removal.

Of the causes that led to this opposition it is impossible to speak with certainty. The little that we know about the matter has to be picked out, item by item, from his own letters and from the evidence of his friends and enemies, submitted in a case in which his conduct as governor was not a point at issue, and hence the difficulty of reducing the charges against him to anything like a definite form, and the many grains of allowance with which they are to be taken. Without attempting, therefore, anything like a detailed statement of the causes of complaint against him, it will be sufficient to say that in one of his letters we find a reference to the charge " of improper interference in the conduct of the commissioners ; " and that Major Bruff, who seems to have been a personal as well as political enemy, asserts that he was in favor of keeping the territory under military rule, and complains that he was not only " averse to the first American settlers and Democrats," of both of which classes he is said to have entertained an unfavorable opinion, but that he was " prepossessed in favor . . . of the rich French landholders under antedated and other large grants, royalists, federalists, and Burrites, *alias* the new honest Republicans, who came out with him expecting appointments." Reduced to plain English, this simply means either that he had been engaged in land speculations on his private account, or had interfered with those of some of his neighbors; and that in the distribution of the few offices that were within his gift, he had not met the expectations of one wing, at least, of the political party to which he owed his appointment.

In regard to the first of these charges there is not much to be said. Wilkinson was a speculator, and no matter how high the position he happened to hold, there was never a time when he was not ready to engage in schemes for improving his pecuniary condition. This course was not necessarily criminal, neither was it always improper, though there were times when it was undignified, and when it led him into the performance of acts that were open to suspicion. Such, indeed, seems to have been the case in the present instance; for although in purchasing a large tract of land adjoining the spot he had selected as a cantonment for the troops, he laid himself open to the accusation of using his official position for the purpose of advancing his private interest, yet he afterwards sold it to the government for the same price he had paid for it, and this fact is sufficient to induce those who are charitably disposed to acquit him of the charge.

But whilst cheerfully absolving him from blame in this particular transaction, it is not so easy to relieve him of the political offenses that are laid at his door. Upon this count of the indictment he is clearly guilty, though it may perhaps lighten our verdict to know that, in pursuing the independent course which he seems to have marked out for himself, and which received the approval of the authorities at Washington, he claimed to have been actuated by a desire to unite the honest and moderate men of both parties, Federal as well as Republican, in an effort " to save the Constitution and prevent a division of property which the Democrats," led by that arch aristocrat Randolph, of Roanoke, are said to have " aimed at." Absurd as this explanation now seems, it was the reason, according to Major Bruff, that Wilkinson assigned for the course which he had thought proper to pursue in administering the affairs of the territory ; and we therefore give it, not that his conduct stood in need of any justification even in that era of intense political feeling, but for the reason that it furnishes us with what may be considered either as a statement of the dangers that were then thought to threaten the existence of the infant republic, or as a specimen of the claptrap in which our fathers, under the pressure of party necessity, were wont to indulge. Be this as it may, there can be no question as to the extent of the opposition which Wilkinson managed to excite, and of the high character of some of those who took side against him ; neither, on the other hand, can there be any doubt as to the honesty and integrity of those who defended him, among the stanchest of whom we must continue to reckon President Jefferson.

Aside from the character of this opposition, which is of

interest as showing the rapid growth of what are sometimes termed American political ideas, but which is too
often but another name for the vulgar greed for money
or office, the only event of importance that occurred during Wilkinson's term was the short visit which, in September, 1805, Aaron Burr made to his brother-in-law
Dr. Browne, of St. Louis. Of the secret purposes of this
visit, or rather of what are supposed to have been such,
it is not my province to speak; neither does it come
within the limits marked out for my guidance to investigate the connection which may or may not have existed
between Burr and Wilkinson. All that we are permitted to know on the subject is that both of these
gentlemen were afterwards placed upon trial, the former
in 1807 for conspiring to break up the federal Union,
and the latter, several years later, for being an acces-
sory to this and other crimes; and that the government
not only failed to prove that Burr was engaged in any
such conspiracy, but that Wilkinson, who was the chief
witness against him, was able to show that, in October,
1804, he had written to Robert Smith, Mr. Jefferson's
Secretary of the Navy, that "Burr was about something," whether internal or external he could not say,
but that "an eye ought to be kept on him." This letter, it will be observed, was written and received a year
and more before the final collapse of Burr's plans,
whatever they may have been; and of course in the
face of such evidence and of Wilkinson's subsequent
conduct, it was impossible to convict him of any complicity with them. Accordingly, after one of the most
searching investigations of which we have any record,
he was, in December, 1811, acquitted by the court of
inquiry which had been summoned to investigate the
charges made against him.

Of the substantial justice of this verdict there is, to-day, but little doubt, though Burr, in after years, whilst ridiculing the idea that he had been engaged in any conspiracy against the federal Union, did not hesitate to say that his object had been to revolutionize Mexico, and that Wilkinson had been a party to the scheme, but that at the critical moment he had betrayed and defeated it. That he did expose and defeat the movement is most true; but whether he was ever a party to it is a point about which opinions may well differ. Burr's unsupported assertion is not sufficient to establish the fact; and whilst there are circumstances in Wilkinson's career at this time which, taken by themselves, are calculated to make us doubt his integrity, yet inasmuch as they can, when considered with reference to the hostile attitude which the United States and Spain then held towards each other, be explained without in any way impeaching his honor, it is but fair to allow him the benefit of the doubt, and of the acquittal which necessarily goes with it.

In September of the year following this visit, a few weeks only after Wilkinson had left for the scene of the boundary dispute between Spain and the United States on the banks of the Sabine, Lewis and Clark returned from their overland journey to the Pacific, bringing with them as one of the results of the expedition a better knowledge of the extent and course of the Missouri and the Columbia rivers, and of the valleys through which they flow. It was the first expedition of the kind ever undertaken by our government, and the return of the party, safe and successful, after an absence of over two years, was hailed with delight throughout the entire West. Congress, too, sharing in the general acclaim, voted a grant of land to each person engaged in the expedition ; and in the spring of 1807, in further recognition of his services, Captain Lewis was appointed governor of the territory which he had done so much to make known.

When, after a delay of some months, he arrived in St. Louis, he found the affairs of his government in a very disorderly condition. The officials are said to have been distracted by " feuds and contentions," and the people themselves, who seem to have caught the infection, " were divided into factions and parties." Unsatisfactory as is this picture, for which we are indebted to Mr. Jefferson, it is not as discouraging as is the one which Major Bruff has left us of the condition of affairs that then prevailed. According to him " the territory was convulsed ; society and confidence destroyed ; American citizens obliged to arm with dirks and pistols, and the old inhabitants lamenting the change of masters." To a certain extent this account is true, but taken as a whole, the impression it conveys is decidedly erroneous. Thus, for instance, whilst it is true that the " old inhabitants," meaning thereby the creoles, were opposed to the transfer of the colony to the United States, as were a large number of the English-American residents as well, and whilst it is also true that there was more or less uneasiness throughout the territory, growing out of the delay of Congress in confirming certain classes of land grants, yet it is not true that society and confidence were destroyed ; neither were the American citizens obliged to arm themselves, though the custom of carrying weapons was at that time, and for some years afterwards, so general that " the judges on the benches had their pistols and ataghans by their sides." Indeed, so far is the picture from being true to life that courts were held regularly in the different districts into which the territory had been divided, and, what is more to the purpose, they appear to have found no difficulty in enforcing their decrees, even in cases where the supreme penalty of the law was adjudged. Real estate, too, had increased enormously in value, in some quarters as much as five hundred per cent.; and the eager demand for it that prevailed everywhere, a demand which seems to have been shared by the witness himself, was scarcely compatible with the state of lawlessness that is said to have existed.

Whilst, therefore, so much of this testimony as refers to the overthrow of social order may be rejected safely, it cannot be denied that there were causes at work which, among a people so combative naturally as the American emigrants were, occasionally brought on one of those bloody personal encounters which gave the territory the reputation of being an uncomfortable abiding place for persons of weak nerves. Among these causes may be mentioned the prominence of the military element at certain social centres, and the tone which it gave to society; the personal character which the heated political discussions of that day were wont to assume; and the lawsuits and disputes which sprang from conflicting land claims, mining rights, and other similar sources, and which were not unfrequently submitted to the arbitrament of the pistol. "'Mr. P.,' said the well-known Colonel S. to a neighbor with whom he had a dispute about a mining claim, 'we have been friends for a long time, and I feel great regret that any misunderstanding should have arisen between us; here we are entirely alone, and there is no one to interrupt us — let us settle the matter in an amicable way. You know my aversion to law and lawyers, and their quibbles ; I have here a couple of friends that have no mistake in them. Take your choice, they are both loaded and equally true.' Mr. P., without losing his presence of mind, thanked him and declined the proffered civility on account of important business which could not be transacted by a ghost, whereupon Colonel S. resumed the conversation, which he had interrupted for the purpose of making what he considered a friendly offer."

Fortunately, the circles within which these influences were active were necessarily small, being confined almost entirely to the two extremes of the social scale. At the one end were to be found "the persons of note," as Brackenridge calls them, or "the small class that denominate themselves the gentlemen," as they are styled by Flint, among whom the duel was still recognized as the proper mode of settling personal quarrels, as it still was in some of the more favored localities of the east. At the other were the miners, consisting of "some of the rudest and most savage of the uncivilized portion of civilized society," who were exceedingly jealous of their "natural rights," as taking lead from public lands seems to have been termed, but who, even when engaged in this illegal pursuit, were so far from being lawless that they had found it necessary to frame a set of regulations which, with but little change, may have served as models for those that, long afterwards, brought order into the mining camps of California.

Among these two classes, comprising at best but a small part of the total population of the territory, fatal duels and bloody "rencontres" were relatively frequent, though they were not so common as they are sometimes represented to have been, nor were they so general. Upon this point Timothy Flint, a New England clergyman, who lived in upper Louisiana from 1816 to about 1820, and who traveled extensively not only in that territory, but also in what are now the States of Arkansas and Louisiana, is certainly good authority. Protesting against the injustice of ascribing to a whole community the crimes of a few fierce and ungovernable natures he tells us that " it is true there are worthless people here, and the most so, it must be confessed, are from New England. It is true there are gamblers, and gougers, and outlaws; but there are fewer of them than, from the nature of things and the character of the age and the world, we ought to expect. . . . I have," he adds, " traveled in these regions thousands of miles under all circumstances of exposure and danger . . . and this, too, in many instances where I was not known as a minister, or where such knowledge would have had no influence in protecting me. I have never carried the slightest weapon of defense. I scarcely remember to have experienced anything that resembled insult, or to have felt myself in danger from the people. I have often seen men that had lost an eye. Instances of murder, numerous and horrible in their circumstances, have occurred in my vicinity. But they were such lawless rencontres as terminate in murder everywhere, and in which the drunkenness, brutality, and violence were mutual. They were catastrophes, in which quiet and sober men would be in no danger of being involved."

Of the backwoodsman of the West, that representative in fact as well as in name of the great majority of the emigrants, the same writer says : " He is generally an amiable and virtuous man. . . . He has vices and bar-

barisms peculiar to his situation. His manners are rough. He wears, it may be, a long beard. He has a great quantity of bear or deer skins wrought into his household establishment, his furniture and dress. He carries a knife, or a dirk in his bosom, and when in the woods has a rifle on his back and a pack of dogs at his heels. An Atlantic stranger, transferred directly from one of our cities to his door, would recoil from a rencounter with him. But remember, that his rifle and his dogs are among his chief means of support and profit. Remember, that all his first days here were passed in dread of the savages. Remember, that he still encounters them, still meets bears and panthers. Enter his door and tell him you are benighted, and wish the shelter of his cabin for the night. The welcome is indeed seemingly ungracious : ' I reckon you can stay,' or ' I suppose we must let you stay.' But this apparent ungraciousness is the harbinger of every kindness that he can bestow, and every comfort that his cabin can afford. Good coffee, corn bread and butter, venison, pork, wild and tame fowls, are set before you. His wife, timid, silent, reserved, but constantly attentive to your comfort, does not sit at the table with you, but like the wives of the patriarchs stands and attends on you. You are shown the best bed which the house can offer. When the kind hospitality has been afforded you as long as you choose to stay, and when you depart, and speak about your bill, you are most commonly told with some slight mark of resentment that they do not keep tavern. Even the flaxen-haired children will turn away from your money. . . . If we were to try them by the standard of New England customs and opinions, that is to say, the customs of a people under entirely different circumstances, there would be many things in the picture that would strike us offensively. They care little about ministers, and think less about paying them. They are averse to all, even the most necessary, restraints. They are destitute of the forms and observances of society and religion; but they are sincere and kind without professions, and have a coarse but substantial morality." In a word, they were " a hardy, adventurous, hospitable, rough, but sincere and upright race."

These were the people who were now coming into the territory, and who were to shape its destiny. As a rule they were sturdy, self-reliant scions of British stock, emigrants chiefly from the States that were afterwards known as Southern, though Pennsylvania had already sent a colony of hard-working Germans, and among those who came from New York and New England we recognize such honored names as Easton and Hempstead. Especially liberal were Kentucky and Virginia in the contributions which they made to the life of the new territory, just as in after-years Missouri sent her sons and daughters to people the regions still further to the west and south.

Unlike the early French settlers, who preferred to live in villages and were content with an allotment in the common fields, these new-comers were farmers after the English-American fashion, and their objects in coming to the territory were to acquire land in as large tracts as possible, and to avail themselves of the vast extent of free pasturage or " range " which the unoccupied government land afforded. To secure these advantages, they passed by the villages and settled neighborhoods near the river, and penetrating into the wilderness they established themselves on detached farms, usually at some distance from each other; for the average emigrant from the States "never wished to live near enough to hear the bark of his neighbor's dog," unless the prospect of danger from the Indians obliged him to build his cabin within easy reach of some central fort or station, to which, in case of necessity, he might repair.

With the incoming tide of emigration and its steady flow westward, the frontier, which at the time of the purchase in 1803 may be said to have been limited to the villages and settlements along the west bank of the river, was gradually pushed forward, until at the close of the first decade of the century the inhabited portion of the territory comprised an area some fifteen or twenty miles in width, extending from the Arkansas to a point a short distance above the mouth of the Missouri, and embracing the districts of New Madrid, Cape Girardeau, Ste. Genevieve, St. Louis, and St. Charles. At this rate of progress, it was a question of only a few years before the advance guard of pioneers would be upon Indian territory, if it was not already there; and as such contact had always led to hostilities, it became an object with the authorities at Washington, as it was their policy, to lessen the chances of collision by buying the land next adjoining the settlements of the whites, and removing the Indians further westward. In pursuance of this plan, Pierre Chouteau, acting under the instructions of Governor Lewis, concluded a treaty with the Osages in 1808, by which it was agreed that the boundary between them and the whites should begin at Fort Clark, a post on the Missouri thirty-five miles below the mouth of the Kansas, and "extend due south to the Arkansas, and down the same to the Mississippi." All east of this line, comprising, as it was then estimated, about forty-eight millions of acres, was ceded to the United States. By the same treaty, though this seems to have been rather a formality, all the lands north of the Missouri to which the Osages had any claims were also relinquished. Of the territory so ceded, something over one half is said to have been within the limits of Missouri, and this amount, somewhat exaggerated, it is true, added to the three millions of acres purchased in the autumn of 1804 from the Sacs and Foxes, gives an estimated total of about twenty-seven millions of acres, — almost two thirds of the present area of the State, — to which the Indian title was extinguished.

With the terms of this treaty, or the circumstances under which it was concluded, we are not now concerned, except in so far as the knowledge of the manner in which these purchases were sometimes made may cause us to look with less austerity upon the free-and-easy way in which the French and Spaniards were accustomed to deal with questions of this sort. According to their theory, the land belonged to them, and not to the Indians, and hence they were never troubled by any conscientious scruples as to the title by which they held it. When they wanted a tract, be it large or small, they did not think it necessary to go through the farce of a treaty in order to get it, but they simply took what they wanted and indemnified the Indians, or, if the exact terms be preferred, "kept them quiet" by a system of presents, a mode of procedure which the savages could understand, and which was " more acceptable to them than the same articles would have been if given in payment of a debt." Such a course, no doubt, savored of the strong hand, but it was open and above board ; and if, as was usually the case, the Indians were the sufferers in the transaction, so also were they in their dealings with the United States. Indeed, on the score of justice and morality, it may be questioned whether the high-handed measures of the French and Spaniards were not less objectionable than were the devious methods to which our government sometimes resorted when seeking to consummate a so-called purchase. Thus, for example, when Brackenridge, speaking of such transactions in general, but with evident reference to this particular case, tells us that " our agents may have gone too far in procuring the consent of the chiefs," or that " the chiefs may have been created for the express purpose" of giving their consent, it is but another and a gentler way of saying that the sale may have been brought about by bribery, or in some other indefensible way. Happily, the evidence is not sufficient to justify us in asserting that either of the methods referred to was adopted in this instance ; but there were others, not less efficacious, which were equally available, and the fact that the great body of the Osages were dissatisfied with the terms of the treaty is proof that there were some features about it that did not commend themselves to the Indians' sense of fairness. This, however, was a matter of but little moment to the other contracting party. For reasons that were perfectly satisfactory, it was deemed necessary to insist upon the purchase, though the authorities at Washington suffered two years to elapse before they took any steps towards complying with their part of the bargain. At the end of this period, the Osages were informed that the first payment for their land was ready, and, accordingly, some thirty or forty of their chiefs and head men repaired to St. Louis, apparently not so much for the purpose of receiving the amount due them as to protest against the enforcement of the treaty, which, they contended, had been unfairly made. In a council held for the purpose, Le Sonneur, who was the orator for the occasion, and who is said to have " spoken with great art and some eloquence," addressed the governor as follows: " He was much surprised to hear of this purchase, which had been forgotten by his nation, and he supposed had also been forgotten by his great father. The sale was made by those who had no authority; and his great father not having complied with his part of the bargain, by delaying two years the stipulated payment, and not performing the other parts of the treaty, his nation ought not to be held to their part of it, even if fairly entered into. But," said he, " the Osage nation has no right to sell its country, much less have a few chiefs, who have taken it upon themselves to do so; our country belongs to our posterity as well as to ourselves; it is not absolutely ours; we receive it only for our lifetime, and then to transmit it to our descendants. . . . No, my father, keep your goods, and let us keep our lands." To this statement, admitting its truth, there can be no answer, whether we regard it from an Indian's point of view, or whether we look upon it, as in fact we are bound to do, as the protest of a weak but independent people against the unjust pretensions of a powerful neighbor. Such, at all events, seems to have been the opinion of Governor Howard, who was appointed to office on the death of Captain Lewis in 1809, and in whose hands the negotiation now rested. Instead of attempting to defend the course of the whites either in making the treaty or in carrying out its provisions, he contented himself with telling the chiefs that their great father did not compel the Indians to sell their lands, but that when they did they must adhere to the bargain ; "that the annuities for two years were ready for them : if they chose they might accept, if not it was of no consequence ; the land would still be considered as purchased, and their obstinacy would have no other effect than that of displeasing their great father."

With this decision the Indians were obliged to be content, and it speaks well for the influence of the chiefs who took part in this council and for their pacific disposition that, notwithstanding the injustice with which they felt they had been treated, they were able and willing to hold the fighting men of the nation to the terms of the treaty, except, perhaps, so far as it related to horse-stealing. Upon this point the Osages were incorrigible ; and whilst it was their boast that they had never shed the blood of a white man, the reclamations made upon them for stolen property were so numerous that they exceeded the amount of their annuities, and at a treaty made in September, 1818, the United States agreed to assume some four thousand dollars of their indebtedness in return for another liberal slice of territory, which the Indians duly relinquished.

But whilst the Osages may be said to have submitted quietly to this wholesale appropriation of their land, there were portions of the tribes who claimed the region north of the Missouri who were by no means disposed to bear with what they considered as a similar injustice. To understand the condition of affairs that prevailed along this portion of the frontier, it is necessary to bear in mind that, in 1803, when Louisiana was purchased, all of this part of what is now known as the State of Missouri, as well as the northwest quarter of Illinois and a part of southern Wisconsin, were claimed by the Sacs and Foxes and their allies the Iowas. Having driven out the Missouris and practically destroyed the tribes that formed the Illinois confederacy, they held the most of this region by right of conquest; and so far as our acknowledgment of this fact could give them a valid title, they were its undoubted owners, and they so continued until November, 1804, when they ceded to the whites all of their possessions east of the Mississippi, including the Rock River valley of Illinois and other favorite localities. In the same treaty they agreed that, west of the Mississippi, the boundary between them and the whites should be a line drawn in a direct course from the Missouri River, opposite the mouth of the Gasconade, to a point on the Jeffreon River (Salt?) thirty miles above its mouth, and down the said Jeffreon to its junction with the Mississippi. West and north of this line, they reserved all the rest of this portion of Missouri; and there can be no doubt that, as against us, they held it by an indisputable title until they sold it in August, 1824, — three years after Missouri was admitted into the federal Union, though long before that time the whites had crossed the boundary, and were establishing themselves upon forbidden ground.

To this treaty, especially to that portion of it which related to the cession of their lands in Illinois and Wisconsin, the Sacs and Foxes who lived east of the Mississippi were bitterly opposed. They complained that the sale had been concluded by chiefs who were sent to St. Louis on other business, but who, while there, had been made drunk, and when in that condition had been induced to agree to it. For this reason they held, and justly, too, from their point of view, that it was not binding; and there is every reason to believe that the part

which they took against us then, and in the war of 1812
with England, was due not so much to the intrigues of
British emissaries and traders, as it was to the determination of the Indians not to give up their homes without a struggle. Their opposition, however, was of no
avail. They were divided among themselves as to their
true policy; and though for several years, from the beginning of the war of 1812 until its conclusion in 1815,
those of the Indians who took up the hatchet were able
to keep the northern frontiers of Missouri and Illinois
in a state of constant alarm, yet in the end they were
obliged to succumb. The whites had become too numerous, and were too well organized, to be successfully
resisted. Their leaders were men like Governor Howard and his successor Clark, of Missouri, and Governor
Edwards, of Illinois, who were familiar with every phase
of border life, and who were as prompt in action as they
were skilled in the arts of Indian warfare and diplo-
macy. Under their direction, important points on the
Illinois and Mississippi were garrisoned, forts, or " sta-
tions " as they were called, were established at suitable
intervals along the frontier, and troops were raised for
service in the field, and for patrol duty on the rivers and
in the more exposed districts. The Indians of the Missouri, too, especially the Sioux, were instigated to take
up arms against the hostile tribes on the upper Mississippi; and if we may credit the statement of Manuel
Lisa, the agent employed in the matter, they did good
service.

By the adoption of these vigorous measures, the hostile Indians were held in check; and the fighting, so
far as there was any, may be said to have been confined
to the efforts of the Americans to capture and hold

Prairie du Chien. With the exception of the expeditions undertaken for this purpose, and the defensive and retaliatory measures which were improvised in the different neighborhoods, the people of upper Louisiana were not called upon to take any active part in the war, or to bear, except in a general way, any of its burdens. Owing to the early successes of the Americans, the English troops that might have been spared for service on the Mississippi were needed for the defense of the Canadian frontier ; and the defeat of the Indians at Tippecanoe in 1811 had so shattered the strength of the confederated tribes that when, in 1812, on the outbreak of the war with England, Tecumseh called on them to take up arms against the United States, it was found that they were hopelessly divided among themselves, and that but a moiety of their warriors were ready to follow him into the British camp. Large and influential bands of the most hostile of the tribes, as for instance, the Shawnees and the Sacs and Foxes, refused to take any part in the war, preferring, as did those of their friends and congeners that lived west of the Mississippi, to trust to the friendship of the Americans, fatal as it sometimes proved, rather than to risk the chances of a collision. In such a contest, with the advantages all on one side, the result could not long be doubtful. A few desultory inroads were made into the territory by small parties, usually from the east side of the river, and occasionally an isolated cabin was destroyed and its inmates slaughtered ; but beyond this the Indians effected nothing. The time had gone by when they could reënact, here, the scenes which had marked the early struggle for Kentucky and the region between the Ohio and the Lakes. In the changed condition of affairs,

the invasions in force, the determined attacks upon fortified positions, and the bloody battles that characterized
that era were no longer possible.

Under these circumstances, the struggle on the part of
the Indians was soon seen to be hopeless even by themselves. Accordingly, when the Treaty of Ghent made
it incumbent on the United States to put an end to the
hostilities against the tribes with whom they were then
at war, they found the Indians ready to meet them half
way. In response to the invitations that were sent out,
representative chiefs from nearly all the hostiles tribes
repaired, in the summer of 1815, to Portage des Sioux,
a small village on the west side of the Mississippi a few
miles above the mouth of the Missouri, where they were
met by the American commissioners; and as both parties were anxious for peace there was no difficulty in
agreeing upon the terms. Among the tribes represented
in this council were the Sacs and Foxes, or rather
those of them who had adhered to the United States
during the late war, and who on that account had been
obliged to separate themselves from the rest of their
nation and remove to the Missouri. The Rock River
band, though, as it was called, still held out, and it
was not until the next year that they finally gave in,
and agreed to a settlement upon the basis of the treaty
of 1804.

With the conclusion of these treaties, Indian wars in
the territory of Louisiana, and we may also add in the
State of Missouri, came to an end; for although the
mad attempt, in 1832, of Blackhawk and his band to
repossess themselves of the Rock River valley caused
great alarm in the northeastern portion of the State, and
volunteers were sent out to protect the settlers in that

quarter, yet the struggle, if that term can be applied to what seems to have been the last frantic effort of a small party of desperate men, was confined to the region east of the Mississippi, and was soon settled by the capture of Blackhawk and most of his warriors. Considered as a part of the history of Missouri, and with reference to the share taken by the State in suppressing it, this outbreak is too insignificant to merit more than a passing notice. It has, however, a certain dramatic interest from the fact that President Lincoln and his whilom opponent Jefferson Davis — the former as a captain of Illinois volunteers, and the latter as lieutenant in the regular army — were both engaged in the pursuit and capture of this marauding band of savages.

Returning from this digression, which has led us to anticipate by some years the current of events, and resuming the thread of our narrative, it will be found that the concluding year of Governor Howard's administration, memorable as it was in the history of the United States for the declaration of war with England, was notable in the local annals of the territory for certain events which have been more or less far-reaching in their consequences. Prominent among these was the earthquake of 1811, by which the village of New Madrid and the settlements at Big and Little Prairie were, for the time being, practically broken up, and the surface of all that portion of the State was essentially changed. The first and one of the severest of these shocks, or series of shocks, was felt on the night of December 16, 1811 ; another of equal violence was experienced some months later ; and after that they were repeated at intervals, but with lessening intensity, until finally, after the lapse of some years, they ceased altogether. Eye-witnesses have told us that these concussions were divisible into two classes, in one of which the motion was perpendicular, whilst in the other it was horizontal. Of these, the latter were the more destructive; " when they were felt, the houses crumbled, the trees waved together, and the ground sunk." The undulations at such times are described as resembling waves, which " increased in elevation as they advanced, and when they had attained a certain fearful height, the earth would burst, and vast volumes of water and sand and pit-coal were discharged, as high as the tops of the trees, leaving large crevices or chasms where the ground had burst." Lakes of twenty miles in extent and more were made in an hour, whilst others were drained, and whole districts were covered with white sand, so that they became uninhabitable. " Large tracts, including the graveyard at New Madrid with all its sleeping tenants, were thrown into the river ; " and " the whole country extending to the mouth of the Ohio in one direction, and to the St. Francis in the other, including a front of three hundred miles, was convulsed to such a degree as to create lakes and islands, the number of which is not yet known."

Fortunately, the country was thinly settled, and as the cabins were low and built of logs it was not easy to overthrow them ; so that although many of them were shaken down, the loss of life resulting from this cause was small. In fact, if we except those who are said to have been drowned by the sinking of the boats in the river, of which there is no record, there were but two persons whose deaths can be attributed to the earthquake, and one of them " died from fright." The settlers, as soon as they saw that " the chasms in the earth were in direction from southwest to northeast, and that they were of an extent to swallow up not only men, but houses," immediately felled the tallest trees at right angles to these chasms, and upon these trees they took refuge when warned of an approaching shock. By this simple device "all were saved." As the people did not dare to dwell in houses, they passed this and the ensuing winter in booths and camps, such as were in use among the neighboring Indians. Meanwhile their crops were neglected and nearly all their cattle died. This was a serious loss, and would inevitably have resulted in a general scarcity, but, that so many heavily laden flatboats were wrecked, "and their contents driven by the eddy into the bayou near the village of New Madrid," that provisions of all sorts were in great abundance. Flour, beef, pork, bacon, butter, cheese, apples, in a word all the articles that usually found their way at this season of the year to the New Orleans market, were in such quantities "as scarcely to be matters of sale."

After the violence of the earthquake had somewhat subsided, the country is said to have exhibited "a melancholy aspect of chasms, of sand covering the earth, of trees thrown down or lying at an angle of forty-five degrees, or split in the middle." The settlement at Little Prairie was broken up, but two families remaining out of a hundred, whilst that at Big Prairie, one of the most flourishing on the west bank of the Mississippi, was greatly reduced, and New Madrid itself had sunk into insignificance, the people trembling in their miserable hovels at the distant rumbling of an approaching shock. Even as late as 1819, this district, "once so level, rich, and beautiful, still presented the appearance of decay. Large and beautiful orchards, left uninclosed, houses uninhabited, deep chasms in the earth, obvious at frequent intervals, — such was the face of the country, although the people had for years become so accustomed to frequent and small shocks, which did no essential injury, that the lands were gradually rising again in value, and New Madrid was slowly rebuilding with frail buildings, adapted to the apprehensions of the people." [1]

In the mean time Congress had been appealed to, and had responded with an act allowing those whose lands had been damaged or destroyed by the earthquake to locate the same quantity of land in any other portion of the territory that was open to entry. It was a generous provision, but it proved to be of but little benefit to the actual sufferers, for the reason that almost all of them sold out their claims at a price which is said to have averaged less than ten cents per acre. " Out of five hundred and sixteen certificates issued, only twenty were located by the original claimants or sufferers. Three hundred and eighty-four were held by persons who resided in St. Louis, one of whom had thirty-three, another forty, another twenty-six, another sixteen, and others from one to five each."

Unfortunate as was the failure of this act to effect the end desired, it was not the worst of the evils to which it is said to have given rise. Perjury and forgery followed in its train, and were so common that there came a time when a New Madrid claim was considered as a synonym for fraud.[2] According to Mr. H. W. Wil-

[1] Flint's *Recollections*, Letter XX. Boston, 1826.

[2] As a sample of the frauds perpetrated under this act we have the following, taken from *American State Papers*, title Public Lands, vol. iv. p. 609 : —

"A claim was made by one George Tenelle (who had eighteen other New Madrid claims) for two hundred and forty acres,

liams, whose familiarity with the land laws of Missouri entitles him to speak with authority, no less than one hundred and forty-two claims, set up by persons who falsely represented themselves to be the legal representatives of New Madrid sufferers, were confirmed; and the holders were permitted to surrender lands which they never owned, receiving, in lieu thereof, certificates for location elsewhere. These certificates, as well as those that were genuine, were located throughout the State, wherever a desirable piece of land could be found, often without regard to prior claims, and this of course caused a vast amount of litigation, some of which has continued to our day.

Of a totally different character, but not less influential in its consequences, was the act of Congress of June 13, 1812, which confirmed the titles of the inhabitants of the different villages of the territory to the lots which they had occupied prior to the 20th of December, 1803; and which provided "that all town or village lots, out-lots, common-field lots, and commons in and adjoining and belonging to the towns or villages of the territory, which are not rightfully owned or claimed by

which he claimed as assignee of Elisha Jackson, producing documents to that effect, and also proof, under oath, that the land had been materially injured by earthquakes. He obtained his certificate, and relinquished the injured land to the United States. It was then entered on the books of the land office as public land subject to entry. In 1825 it was entered by one Evans or Ogden, who proceeded to take possession. It then transpired that Jackson had sold the land in 1796, that the purchaser had constantly lived on it until he died in 1819, that one of his heirs had lived on it until it was claimed under the entry at the land office, and, further, that it was a valuable farm, which had never been injured by the earthquakes." — Scharf's *History of St. Louis,* p. 328. Philadelphia, 1883.

any private individual, or held as commons belonging
to such towns or villages, or that the President of the
United States may not think proper to reserve for military purposes, shall and the same are hereby reserved
for the support of schools in the respective towns or
villages aforesaid; *Provided*, that the whole quantity
of land contained in the lots reserved for the support of
schools in any town or village shall not exceed one
twentieth part of the whole lands included in the general survey of such town or village."

With the first of these provisions we do not propose
to concern ourselves further than to say that it was one
of the amendments made to the law of 1804, to which
we have already referred, and that whilst it brought relief to a number of deserving persons, whose cases had
hitherto been ruled out under the stringent regulations
of Congress, it also opened wide the door to fraud and
perjury, by making a number of these claims depend
for their validity upon the recollection by witnesses of
events which, in some cases, had happened years before.
Under these circumstances, and in view of the mania
for speculating in land which at this time prevailed in
the territory, the inducement to recollect circumstances
that were, to say the least, of doubtful occurrence, was
often very great, and it need not surprise us, therefore,
to be told that weak human nature not infrequently
yielded to the temptation. Out of some twenty-five
hundred claims that were presented for confirmation between the passage of this act and February, 1816, when
the commissioners made their report, eight hundred
were rejected; and of this number, it is probably safe
to say that a large majority were either notoriously
fraudulent, or were based upon evidence that failed to
establish either their character or amount.

For the second of these provisions, that by virtue of which certain lots were reserved for school purposes, we have only words of commendation. Its effect has been uniformly beneficial; and it is a pleasure to be able to say that the grant has never been perverted from its original purpose, but that its sphere of usefulness has gone on steadily widening, and that it bids fair to be productive of even more good in the future than it has been in the past. It is no doubt true that, owing to subsequent legislation, the gift was somewhat shorn of its fair proportion before it was finally handed over to the State in 1831; but in spite of this fact, such was the number of these unclaimed lots, and so great has been their increase in value in certain favored localities, that in St. Louis alone they constitute the bulk of the real estate held by the schools for purposes of revenue, and furnish to-day an income which may be roughly estimated at from fifty to sixty thousand dollars per annum.

For this magnificent gift the people of St. Louis, and of the other villages which shared in the bounty of Congress, are indebted to the exertions of Thomas F. Riddick, a Virginian by birth, and one of the earliest immigrants to the territory. He was secretary to the first board of land commissioners, and by virtue of his office became cognizant to the fact that there were in each of the villages in the territory a number of lots for which no legal owners could be found. With rare foresight, he conceived the idea of securing them as the beginning of a fund for the support of common schools, and in accordance with his suggestion the section quoted above, reserving them for this purpose, was inserted in the act, the primary object of which was to quiet land titles. When the proposition came before Congress, such was his interest in its success that he made the trip from St. Louis to Washington on horseback, and at his own expense, to urge its passage ; and it was owing to his exertions and those of Edward Hempstead, who then represented the territory, that it finally became a law.

The last of the measures to which we find it necessary to refer at this time was the act of Congress of June 4, 1812, by which, on the 12th of the December following, Louisiana was to be advanced from the first to the second grade of territories, and its name changed to Missouri. It was time that this change should come, for the territory had a population of over twenty thousand, exclusive of Indians. This was four times as many as were necessary, under the law for the government of the Northwest Territory, to entitle them to the promotion, and they had begun to grow restive under a mode of treatment which discriminated unfavorably between them and their neighbors on the other side of the Mississippi. By the terms of this act, the territorial affairs were to be administered by a governor appointed by the President, and a general assembly consisting of a house of representatives elected by the people, and a legislative council of nine members, chosen by the President from a list of eighteen returned to him by the territorial house of representatives. In accordance with this law, Governor Howard issued a proclamation dividing the territory into five counties instead of districts, as they had hitherto been called, and ordering an election to be held in the November following for a delegate to Congress, and for members of the territorial legislature. It was one of the last of his official acts, for soon after he was appointed a brigadier-general in the army, which position he held with honor to himself and advantage to the territory until his death in 1814.

After an interregnum of some months, during which the duties of the office were satisfactorily performed by Frederick Bates, the secretary of the territory, Captain William Clark, the worthy companion of Merriwether Lewis in the expedition to the mouth of the Columbia, was appointed governor. It was a fortunate selection in view of the hostile relations that then existed between the whites and the tribes of the Northwest, and it was no doubt his skill in dealing with these people and the influence he had acquired over them that led to his appointment. His administration proved successful, and he was continued in office until 1820, when Missouri became a State, though it was a year and more before she was formally admitted into the Union. At the election which then took place, Alexander McNair was chosen governor, but General Clark, as he was usually called, was still kept at the head of Indian affairs, and it was in this capacity that he negotiated the treaties of 1824–25, by which the Osages, Kickapoos, and Sacs and Foxes, relinquished the lands which they still held within the limits of the State. It was a position for which he was preëminently fitted, for with perhaps the exception of Sir William Johnston, there has never been a white man whose influence among these wild and wayward children of the forest was comparable with that which he wielded. Up to the day of his death in 1838, he was their tried and trusted friend and counselor ; and but few of them ever came to St. Louis (and in those days such an occurrence was by no means rare) whose first visit was not made to the " Red-head," the name by which he was known among them.

CHAPTER VI.

DURING the eight years that Governor Clark was at the head of affairs, the territory, in spite of certain drawbacks, made rapid progress in wealth and population. For a year or two at the outset of his administration, during the continuance of the war with England, the tide of immigration was somewhat interrupted ; but on the return of peace in 1815, it set in afresh and with increased force. In fact, so great was the rush from Kentucky, Tennessee, Virginia, and the Carolinas that the "Missouri Gazette" of October 26, 1816, was moved to exclaim that " a stranger witnessing the scene would imagine that those States had made an agreement to introduce the territory as soon as possible into the bosom of the American family." As many as one hundred persons are said to have passed through St. Charles in one day " on their way to Boone's lick, Salt River, or some other region which for the time being was the centre of attraction ; " and this rate was kept up for many days together." Many of these " movers " brought with them a hundred head of cattle, besides horses, hogs, and sheep, and from three to twenty slaves. The few rude ferries that were then in existence on the Mississippi were kept busy crossing them.

As one of these long trains moved slowly through the woods or over the prairie, the huge wagons drawn by four or six horses and loaded down with the household goods or "plunder," as it was called, of the family; the cattle with their hundred bells; the negroes, who, we are told "seem fond of their masters," and are quite as much delighted and interested in the migration; and, finally, the mistress and her children strolling leisurely by the side of the heavily laden teams, "often stretch for three quarters of a mile or more along the road, and present a scene which is at once pleasing and patriarchal." As night comes on, the band halts near some creek or spring where there is a supply of wood and water. "The pack of dogs sets up a cheerful barking. The cattle lie down and ruminate. The huge wagons are covered so that the roof completely excludes the rain. The cooking utensils are brought out. The blacks prepare a supper which the toils of the day render delicious; and they talk over the adventures of the past day, and the prospects of the next." Meantime they are going where the land is inexhaustibly fertile, and "where there is nothing but buffaloes and deer to limit the range even to the western sea." Well might the worthy preacher, in view of such a picture, exclaim that "it carried him back to the days of other years and to the pastoral pursuits of those ancient races, whose home was in a tent wherever their flocks found range."[1]

When the immigrant arrived at his journey's end, his first business was to look out a suitable spot where he might open a farm and once more set up his household gods. This was not always an easy matter, especially if he were going to an unknown region or among strangers, for speculators beset his path at every turn and

[1] Flint's *Recollections*, p. 202.

confused him with glowing accounts of their own lands, whilst, at the same time, they decried the possessions of their rivals by all the arts known to the profession. Amid such a conflict of opinions, and in view of the diversity of claims founded, some upon settlement and improvement rights, others upon Spanish or New Madrid grants, some of which had been confirmed, whilst others had not, it was often a difficult matter to decide ; but when, at last, a choice was made, the necessary log-cabins were soon raised, the neighbors all joining in and helping on the work. A field of suitable size was cleared and fenced after the Virginia fashion, and at the proper season a crop was " pitched." In due time it was harvested, and ever after the Missouri farmer, with a moderate force, if gifted with health and possessed of a fair share of industry, was sure of food, shelter, and clothing, and was thus " as independent as it was fit that a man should ever get to be."

It is true that, owing to their abundance, farm products were often in but little demand, and that hence money was scarce and but little of it ever found its way into his possession ; but, on the other hand, it may be urged that except for the purchase of the necessary farming implements or in the payment of his taxes, he had but little use for it, as the necessaries of life and many of its luxuries were within his reach without the expenditure of a dollar in cash. Thus, for example, the materials for his clothing were grown in his own fields or sheared from his flocks, and their preparation and manufacture were among the duties that devolved upon the women of the family; his cabin of logs, rude at first and soon replaced by the more ambitious frame house, gave him shelter ; while the woods and streams, his fields, flocks, and well-filled " truck patch " or vegetable garden, all contributed to furnish forth a table that was as abundant as it was varied.

Of foreign wines and brandies he, of course, had none ; but in a few years, when his orchard came into bearing, he had an abundance of cider, and if with increasing years he felt the need of a more potent stimulant, he was at liberty to convert the nutritious corn or the fragrant peach into the most seductive of liquors, without the fear of a visit from the tax-gatherer.   Tea and coffee, too, were at times a recollection rather than a reality, and here, it must be confessed that the ingenuity of the housewife was at fault, as sassafras and rye furnished but poor substitutes for these well-nigh indispensable articles. However, he had an abundance of milk, or if he did not, it was generally his own fault ; and with a plentiful supply of maple syrup and honey, known as " long sweetening," he had no reason to complain of the absence of foreign sugar.

Being thus relieved from the dread of poverty, the economic restrictions upon marriage that prevail in old communities had no existence among them, and a prudent father might reasonably expect to see his children comfortably settled about him, in homes of their own, long before his own days of usefulness were over.   Land was cheap, and in two years an active, energetic young man might, by his own exertions, open a farm and be in a condition to support a wife and children.   After this, the necessity for persistent, exhaustive labor would not be so great, as it was " calculated " that two days' work in Missouri would contribute as much to the support of a family as the labor of a week would do in the North. In good time the miller, the blacksmith, and the country storekeeper would be attracted to the settlement, and soon the school, the church, and the post-office would follow. At this stage of progress the community would contain within itself the nucleus of the coming village and be virtually self-supporting. Soon there would arise the need of something more regular and authoritative than neighborhood law or custom, powerful as that was in newly-settled districts; and steps would be taken for the establishment of courts and the enforcement of their decrees. At first the little community would be attached to the nearest county or judicial circuit, with the seat of justice perhaps a hundred miles away, but this was a mere temporary expedient; and when, sooner or later, the requisite population was attained, a suitable extent of territory would be cut off and erected into a county, with judges, representatives, and all the other officers necessary to a separate political life.

Such, in brief, was the process by which neighborhoods grew, and ultimately became welded into counties; and some idea of the rate at which this was going on within the territory may be formed from the fact that, between 1812 and 1820, the counties had increased from five to fifteen, and the population, exclusive of Arkansas, which in 1810 amounted to twenty thousand souls, now numbered over sixty-six thousand, of whom about ten thousand were slaves.

Of this increase, amounting in the ten years to over two hundred per cent., a large majority were farmers, and the gain in population, therefore, was chiefly in the agricultural regions, though the villages also felt the impulse and shared in the general prosperity. Especially was this true of St. Louis, which, owing to its advantageous situation, and to the fact that it was the political capital of the territory as well as the depot for the purchase and distribution of supplies for the different military and trading-posts on the upper rivers, soon acquired a lead which it has ever since retained.   In 1804, at the time of the purchase, there were in the village one hundred and eighty houses, consisting ordinarily of but one room, and built after the French fashion, which differed from the American in the fact that the logs, instead of being laid horizontally, were set upright in the ground, or upon plates, and were then connected by cross-pieces, the interstices in each case being filled in with stones and mud.   A few of these houses, as for instance those of the Chouteaus and the government buildings, were of stones laid rough cast and coated with mortar ; and as they were " inclosed with massive stone walls like a demi-fortress," they may well have been regarded as palaces when compared with the more humble dwellings by which they were surrounded.   All, however, were alike in having porches on one or more sides ; and as they were all whitewashed and usually stood in gardens, surrounded by fruit-trees, they appeared beautiful when seen from a distance, though most of them " were mean and comfortless when contemplated near at hand."

As soon as the United States came into possession of all this region, " the influence of the guardian spirit of liberty," whatever that may mean, is said to have made itself felt, and the place rapidly lost the distinctive features of a French village.   In 1809 it was incorporated as a town, and before the close of the second decade of the century there arose " lines of brick houses that would not have disgraced Philadelphia."   By actual count it was found that in the spring of 1821 there were two hundred and thirty-two dwelling-houses of brick and stone in the village as against four hundred and nineteen of wood, to say nothing of warehouses, stables, shops, and outbuildings. Land, too, had increased enormously in value, and a few of the old French settlers, hostile as they were at first to the new régime, by prudently investing their savings in this form of property, had reaped the benefit of the advance, and were comparatively rich.

To facilitate intercourse between different parts of the territory, roads were cut out ; post-offices, too, were established, and routes opened between the different villages and the east, though it was many years before the arrival and departure of the mails became either frequent or regular. In July, 1808, a newspaper was established, which under different names has continued down to the present time, and is now known as the " Missouri Republican." It was the first paper published west of the Mississippi River, but not the first in Louisiana, as one had been issued in New Orleans as early as 1794, while the Spaniards were yet in possession of that portion of the valley.

A few good private libraries seem to have existed in the territory from the earliest times, notably that of Colonel Auguste Chouteau, which is said to have been strong in works relating to the early history of America, and was probably made up of books sent from France for the Jesuit College at Kaskaskia. It was not much used, if we may credit contemporary evidence ; and for some years after the purchase, but few new books were brought into the territory. To this rule, though, there must have been some honorable exceptions, as the library of Mr. Secretary, Frederick Bates is spoken of with commendation, and in 1820 Bishop Dubourg is credited with having gathered together some eight thousand volumes. Besides this library, he had secured for the new cathedral, which was then in course of erection, a " collection of sacred vases, ornaments, embroideries, and paintings " that is said to have been without a rival in the United States. Among the paintings there were, so we are told, " originals by Raphael, Rubens, Guido, Paul Veronese, as well as by the modern masters of the Italian, French, and Flemish schools." It was also during this period that Governor Clark made a collection illustrative of the arts and industries of the Indians, which was open to the public, and which, to-day, would be of incalculable value to the ethnologist.

Limited as was the supply of reading matter, it was fully equal to the demand, for among the old French settlers there was a large proportion who could not read, and the new-comers were so busy making farms, speculating in lands, and otherwise providing for their temporal wants, that they had no time to indulge in the luxury of reading. But while they were thus careless of their own literary improvement, they were by no means neglectful of the education of their children. Upon this point they displayed a commendable anxiety, and there were but few settlements in the territory so insignificant that they did not have, during some part of the year, a school, in which reading, writing, and a little arithmetic were taught. A lady who had resided two years at Fort Osage, some two hundred miles up the Missouri River, told Brackenridge " that descending the river on her return from that place, she had observed on the very spot, where on ascending she had seen a herd of deer, several children with books in their hands, returning from school." The settlement, it is added, had been formed, and the school opened, during the two years that she had lived at the fort.

According to the same writer there were in 1811 two schools in St. Louis, one English and one French; and from other sources we learn that the former was "kept" by George Tompkins, who afterwards became chief justice of the State, and the latter by Jean Baptiste Trudeau, whose career as a teacher, extending from 1774 to about 1825, covers a period of fifty years. Although only two are mentioned, yet there must have been others, as it was about this time that the "Missouri Gazette" contained the advertisement of the erratic C. F. Schewe, a graduate of the College of Berlin and of the Saxony School of Mines, who seems to have divided his time between teaching French and German and "moulding candles out of deer's tallow." There were also Lancastrian schools, Pestalozzi establishments, and institutions for "*instruction mutuelle.*" Hebrew was taught in twelve lessons, and Latin and Greek with equal dispatch, by professors whose knowledge of even their own mother tongue was exceedingly limited. Dancing, especially the waltz, — then just introduced, — fencing and music (the piano and clarinet) were also taught; and in a young ladies' academy, in addition to French and English grammar, geography, and arithmetic, the pupils were instructed in sewing and embroidery, and "their minds were enlightened and their hearts formed by a course of select reading either in ancient or modern history or morality."

Of course these were all private institutions, as was the college founded by Bishop Dubourg, from which the St. Louis University may be said to have sprung. As yet there was no such thing in the territory as a public school. Not until 1838, and after much tribulation, was one opened in St. Louis, though in 1817 the first step was taken towards organizing the system which has since grown into such magnificent proportions, by incorporating a board of trustees, whose duty it was to superintend the schools of that town.

In 1811, at the time of Brackenridge's visit, the population of St. Louis amounted to about fourteen hundred, and was composed of Canadian French, a few Spaniards and other Europeans, with a somewhat larger proportion of Americans, to which may be added a slight sprinkling of Indians, half-breeds, and negro slaves. It was a motley crowd, and they differed among themselves as much in appearance, character, and occupation, as they did in nationality. Here might be seen the French *paysan* and the American farmer who was destined so soon to supersede him; the boisterous, bragging, fighting boatman of the lower Mississippi and the gay, good-humored *voyageur* from Canada and the upper rivers. "Vagrant Indians still loitered along the streets, and now and then a stark Kentucky hunter," — the veritable gamecock of the wilderness, — "with rifle on shoulder and knife in belt, strode along. Here and there were new houses and shops just set up by bustling, driving, and eager men of traffic from the Atlantic States; while, on the other hand, the old French mansions with open casements still retained the easy, indolent air of the original colonists; and now and then the scraping of a fiddle, or strain of an ancient French song, or sound of billiard balls showed that the happy Gallic turn for gayety and amusement still lingered about the place." In appearance the town is said to have been less like a rural village than Ste. Genevieve or any of the other

French settlements, as the inhabitants depended upon trade for their support rather than upon agriculture. Indeed, it was owing to this fact, and to the scarcity which, in early times, it had sometimes occasioned, that St. Louis was derisively styled by its more fortunate neighbors *Pain court*, or "short loaf," as it may be roughly translated. We are also told that the town contained " twelve mercantile stores," and that the value of its imports amounted to two hundred and fifty thousand dollars per annum, which amount probably represents rather more than half the cost of all the goods annually brought into the territory. Except the sixty thousand dollars which the troops stationed at Belle Fontaine, near St. Louis, yearly put in circulation, almost all the rest of the domestic trade of this region was still carried on by barter. Lead and its product in the shape of shot, and peltry were most in demand, for the reason that, practically they were monopolies, and besides furnishing a recognized currency for the country, they were the two articles most eagerly sought after for shipment, as, no matter what the condition of the market in New Orleans or the Atlantic cities in regard to the other products of the territory, they always commanded a ready sale at fair prices.

Of the former of these articles, it was estimated that the Maramec mines alone produced, annually, one million five hundred thousand pounds, and " gave employment to three hundred and fifty hands, exclusive of smelters, blacksmiths, and others." The Dubuque mines were not worked at this time, but those on the opposite side of the river, near Prairie du Chien, were; and it may, perhaps, interest those of us who are concerned about the future of the Indians to know that, in 1811, the Sacs and Foxes, who still held the region where these "diggings" were situated, "having no other instrument but the hoe," made five hundred thousand pounds of lead, which they sold to the traders, and which ultimately found its way down the river. A fair share of the lead produced in the territory was cast into shot, a tower for that purpose having been erected on a river bluff between Ste. Genevieve and St. Louis, as early as 1809, by J. Maklot, who seems to have been the pioneer in this business. His shot is said to have equaled the best English patent ; and in the newspaper of that day the opinion is expressed that he would " be able to supply the Atlantic States on such terms as would defeat competition."

The fur-trade, too, which, as we have seen, amounted in 1804 to two hundred thousand dollars per annum, was prosecuted with much vigor, though there is reason to believe that it was hardly as profitable as it had once been, and that its increase had not been commensurate with the growth of the commerce of the territory in other respects. In 1807–8, one year after the return of Lewis and Clark from their journey to the mouth of the Columbia River, Manuel Lisa, an experienced Indian trader, and one " who had few equals in perseverance and industry," wintered on the Yellowstone at the mouth of the Big Horn. The next year, a company with a capital of forty thousand dollars was formed for the purpose of " monopolizing," as it was said, " the trade of the tribes of the lower Missouri, who understand the art of trapping, and of sending a party to the head waters of that stream, strong enough to defend itself in case of necessity, and which should engage, practically, in the work of taking beaver and other skins." This was a decided innovation, or rather an improvement, for hitherto this branch of the business had been left almost altogether to the Indians, the trader being obliged to take the furs as they were brought to him, or to go without. Of course, so long as this was the case, there was always an element of risk growing out of the competition of the traders, and the irregular and uncertain habits of the Indians; and it was to remedy this evil that the company proposed to employ white men, regularly, in the work of hunting and trapping, thereby giving to these pursuits a degree of stability which, thus far, they had not possessed. Accordingly, in 1809, Mr. Henry, one of the partners, started up the Missouri River at the head of two hundred and fifty men, and after establishing small trading-posts among the Sioux, the Arickaras, Mandans, and other tribes, he proceded to the three forks of the river, where he built a fort, and began at once the business of hunting and trapping as well as trading. It was a magnificent scheme, and one which promised a large measure of success, but unfortunately for the company, all their plans miscarried; and after a series of unforeseen misfortunes, the partnership was dissolved at the end of the time for which it had been formed. In spite of this apparent failure, the company, thanks to the energy of Lisa, saved its original investment, and began life afresh with a slightly increased capital. It met with no better success, however, and after a precarious existence of a few years, it gave way, in 1819, to still another, the third company, which is said to have bought it out for ten thousand dollars. At this time, if we may credit the report of Major Biddle, the whole amount of capital embarked in the fur-trade of the Missouri amounted to barely fifty-three thousand dollars, seventeen thousand of which, including the plant, belonged to the company, whilst the rest was owned by a number of individuals, among whom the Chouteaus were prominent. From these figures it is evident that the trade had not made any great increase, for even if a possible profit of five hundred per cent. be allowed, it would only carry the total to about three hundred thousand dollars; and it is probable that this amount would cover, not only the receipts from the Missouri, but those from all other sources.

To carry on this commerce, and transport the farm products, live stock, etc., that were annually sent down the river, various kinds of craft, as for instance the keel-boat, the barge, and the flatboat or " broad horn," were called into requisition. Of these, the two first mentioned were the most important, though not, perhaps, the most numerous, as they could be used for a return trip, whilst the flatboat could not, and was, therefore, broken up and sold at the end of the voyage.

Some of these boats were of good size, carried as much as forty or fifty tons, and were owned and run by men who acted as " patrons " or captains, and who made the transportation of freight and passengers a regular business. In manning them it was the custom to proportion the number of the crew to the size of the cargo, one hand being allowed for every three thousand pounds. A trip from St. Louis to New Orleans and back usually occupied from four to six months, the upward voyage being especially long, laborious, and by no means free from danger. Even with the aid of sails and oars, it could not be made in less than an average of ninety days. Besides these means of propulsion, the crew were often obliged to resort to " warping, cordelling, poling," and, when the occasion offered, to a process known as " bushwhacking," or pulling the boat forward by means of the bushes and willows that grew along the shore. It was a hard life, full of toil and danger, and developed a class of men each one of whom, in the vernacular of the river, claimed to be " half a horse and half an alligator."

In truth, they were a wild and reckless set, ever ready for a fight or a frolic ; but to their credit be it spoken they were honest and true and patient after their fashion under labors and privations that would have daunted less resolute spirits. The best man in every crew was entitled to wear a feather or some other emblem as a challenge, which he was bound to make good against all comers ; and the worthy Mr. Flint, on the occasion of his first visit to St. Louis, was surprised to learn that the term " best " had no reference to the moral qualities of the possessor, but that it meant " he who had beaten, or, in the Kentucky phrase, had whipped all the rest."

Such were the men and the methods employed in carrying on the commerce of the valley when, in December, 1811, the New Orleans, the first steamboat built west of the Alleghany Mountains, made the trip from Pittsburgh to New Orleans, and thus settled at once and forever the question of the use of steam as a motive power upon the Western waters. Although the career of this vessel was very short, yet so satisfied were the people of the Ohio valley with the result of the experiment, that they went into the business of boat-building with an energy that must have savored of recklessness to any one not acquainted with the volume of trade that annually floated down the Mississippi. In the eight years that intervened between 1811 and 1819, sixty-three steamers, varying in capacity from twenty to some hundreds of tons, were constructed and running upon the Western rivers, and of these fifty-six were built on the Ohio, four at New Orleans, and one each at Philadelphia, New York, and Providence, R. I.

Rapid as was the increase in the number, size, and speed of these vessels, at first and for several years they found employment only on the Ohio and the lower Mississippi, and it was not until the 2d of August, 1817, that the General Pike, Jacob Read master, the first steamboat that ever ascended the Mississippi above the mouth of the Ohio, arrived at St. Louis.

From the description that has come down to us, she must have been an ungainly sort of craft, with a hold constructed on the model of a barge, and a cabin situated on the lower deck inside of the "running boards." She had no wheel-houses and but one smoke-stack. The motive power was furnished by a low-pressure engine, reinforced occasionally by the exertions of the crew, who pushed the boat along with poles much as they had been accustomed to do with barges. She did not run at night, and this may partially account for the length of time she was on the way. In the course of the next few months she made other trips to and from Louisville, and in much better time. In October of the same year, another steamer, the Constitution, also reached St. Louis. During the ensuing season of 1818, these arrivals and departures were more numerous, some of them from New Orleans, and the sight of a steamboat soon became so common as no longer to excite the curiosity of the dwellers on the banks of the Mississippi. As yet no attempt had been made to ascend the Missouri, and such was the swiftness of that stream that the result of an effort to stem its mighty current

was awaited with some anxiety, not to say doubt. At
length the feat was accomplished; and the return in
June, 1819, of the Independence, Captain Nelson, from
Old Franklin, a town situated about one hundred and
fifty miles up the river and long since washed away, led
to an outburst in the " Missouri Gazette," in which it was
said : " The Missouri has hitherto resisted almost effectually all attempts at navigation ; she has opposed every
obstacle she could to the tide of emigration which was
rolling up her banks and dispossessing her dear red children, but her white children, although children by adoption, have become so numerous, and are increasing so
rapidly, that she is at last obliged to yield them her
favor. The first attempt to ascend her by steamboat
has succeeded, and we anticipate the day as speedy,
when the Missouri will be as familiar to steamboats as
the Mississippi or Ohio."

With the gradual increase in population and the consequent growth in the agriculture, commerce, and other
material interests of the territory, the necessity for a
better system of currency became daily more apparent.
Lead, peltry, and tobacco, which had furnished the principal mediums of exchange during the days of the Spanish régime, and useful as they still were in the way of
barter, were no longer adequate to the demands made
upon them, though as late as the winter of 1807 transactions were made upon the basis of a payment in furs.
Even the supply of small change was totally insufficient,
and Spanish dollars cut up into halves, quarters, and
eighths or "bits" were made to do duty in this respect.
For any less amount, pins, needles, sheets of writing-
paper, and other articles of small value were used.

To remedy this evil, the territorial legislature chartered the Bank of St. Louis, which went into operation in the summer of 1816, and in the following year the Bank of Missouri, with a capital of two hundred and fifty thousand dollars, was also organized. A partial list of the stockholders of this latter concern is preserved, and it is of interest as showing the part which the French element of the population still played in the monetary affairs of the territory. Out of seven hundred and eighty shares held in the city of St. Louis, two hundred and seventy-six belonged to persons who were unmistakably French, or of French descent ; and among them we recognize the name of Charles Dehault Delassus as a subscriber for five shares.

For a time the community felt the benefit of these institutions, and the volume of business was increased by the flood of money which they poured into the channels of trade. The merchants not only imported more largely of goods and wares, but the spirit of speculation in land, which was already rife, received additional momentum. The people of the territory, one and all, appeared to be possessed with a mania for it. No claim was so indefinite, no title so uncertain, and no piece of property so shadowy, as not to find a purchaser. A tract of land, the only description of which was that it was situated thirty miles north of St. Louis, was put up at auction and actually bid off. Sometimes the same tract was offered by two or three claimants, and on one occasion the whole county of St. Charles, containing several thousand inhabitants, was sold for thirteen hundred dollars under a grant that had never been confirmed. The immigrants, who were pouring into the territory in such a continuous stream, were possessed by the usual Anglo-Saxon land-hunger, and bought, or " took up," more than they needed or could pay cash for, trusting to the future to be able to sell out at a profit and in time to meet their engagements. At this period, government lands were sold at two dollars per acre, one fourth cash and the balance in two, three, and four years, so that to enter a quarter section of one hundred and sixty acres required only a cash payment of eighty dollars. This was a temptation too strong to be resisted by the average immigrant, and consequently we are told that, for every eighty dollars brought into the territory, a quarter section was taken up, upon which two hundred and forty dollars, three fourths of the purchase money, was unpaid. The dealings with the stores, too, were largely increased, and were also upon credit, for with money in abundance, the merchant could afford to be liberal, and customers bought recklessly, as " every one expected to get rich out of the future emigrant. The speculator was to sell him houses and lands, and the farmer was to sell him everything he wanted to begin with and to live upon until he could supply himself. Towns were laid out all over the country, and lots were purchased by every one on credit; the town-maker received no money for his lots, but he received notes of hand which he considered to be as good as cash; and he lived and embarked in other ventures as if they had been cash in truth."

In this way the year 1818 found almost everybody in debt, but this made no difference as long as immigrants continued to arrive, and bank-notes, good, bad, and indifferent, circulated freely and without question. But when about 1819 settling day rolled around, and the stringency in the Eastern money market prevented the people who were desirous of immigrating from sell-

ing their lands, the flow of Eastern capital westward
was checked, and as a consequence the local institutions
were unable to respond to the demands made upon them
by the United States Bank for specie, and were forced
into suspension or hopeless bankruptcy.

The merchants, feeling the pressure, called for a settlement of their outstanding claims, but in vain.   Bank-
notes had driven out the specie, and as they were now
worthless, there was no longer any money in the country with which to make payment.   Farm products, it
is true, were abundant, but they were unsalable.   So,
also, was real estate ; and then was presented the singular spectacle of a people living in the midst of a
rude plenty, who were practically without a circulating
medium.   They did not even have the means to pay
their taxes ; and those of them who were so unfortunate
as to owe a balance on their farms, be it ever so small,
saw no way of saving them from forfeiture.   At this
stage of the crisis the general government came to the
rescue, and devised " a system of relief which, by extending the time of payment, and authorizing purchasers to
secure a portion of their lands by relinquishing the remainder to the government, in the course of eight years
extinguished a large portion of those debts, and eventually . . . absorbed the whole without injury to the citizen, and with little loss to the government."   The legislature, too, that had been called into existence by the
enabling act of 1820, not to be behindhand in the work
of relief, passed stay laws, and endeavored to accomplish
the impossible feat of paying something with nothing.
Among the other measures to which they resorted was
the issue, in sums varying from fifty cents to ten dollars,
of some two hundred thousand dollars' worth of certifi-

cates, which were predicated upon the credit of the State, and were to be loaned by commissioners, appointed for the purpose, to the citizens of the several " loan districts," upon certain conditions. These certificates were made receivable " not only for taxes and debts of whatever kind due the State, but for the salaries and fees of all officers, civil and military, and in payment of salt sold by the lessees of Salt Springs."

Owing to losses sustained by reason of insufficient security, and to the adverse decision of the courts as to the constitutionality of the act under which they were issued, these certificates were discredited almost as soon as they were put in circulation ; and when they ceased to pass current, the holders of them were in a worse condition than they were before. Probably in no part of the West was the scarcity of money and the consequent derangement of business more keenly felt than in Missouri. Her people had been so generally engaged in speculative enterprises, and had so uniformly conducted their affairs upon a basis of credit, that the process of liquidation was severe, and that of recuperation slow.

But whilst the closing years of this second decade of the century were a season of trial, the people of the territory, engrossed though they must have been with their private troubles, yet found time to devote to political affairs, and to securing for Missouri the position to which her population entitled her. By an act approved in April, 1816, she had been advanced to the third or highest grade of territorial government, and during the session of the legislature which met in November, 1818, and whilst the first mutterings of the financial storm which soon spread over the whole country were but faintly heard in the distance, application was made to

Congress for authority to frame a constitution and establish a state government.

A bill to effect this purpose was at once introduced
into the House, and in February, 1819, it came up for
consideration.   Mr. Tallmadge, of New York, then offered an amendment, making it a condition precedent to
admission "that the further introduction of slavery or
involuntary servitude shall be prohibited, except for the
punishment of crimes, whereof the party shall have been
fully convicted ; and that all children born within the
State after the admission thereof shall be free at the age
of twenty-five years."   This amendment, in so far as it
"restricted" their freedom of action, was exceedingly
objectionable to the people of Missouri, and it also gave
rise to a long and acrimonious debate in Congress, which
convulsed the whole country and threatened the stability
of the Union itself.   Ostensibly, it was a protest in the
interest of morality against the evil of slavery, and an
effort to legislate it out of territory where it lawfully
existed ; but in reality it was, as Rufus King frankly
admitted, a struggle for political power, and it did not
differ from that which had taken place in 1803, when the
treaty for the purchase of Louisiana was under consideration, except in being aligned upon a different issue.   The
admission of Alabama in 1819 and the organization of
the territory of Arkansas in the year following, without
any restriction as to slavery and whilst the Missouri
question was still pending, to say nothing of the addition
to Missouri in 1836 of the Platte Purchase, — a territory
larger than some of the States, — indicate very clearly
that hostility to slavery was not at all times the controlling motive of all of those who sought to prevent the
increase of slave States.

CHAPTER VII.

THE MISSOURI COMPROMISE.

To understand the condition of affairs that prevailed at Washington at this time, it is necessary to bear in mind that when the fifteenth Congress assembled, in December, 1817, the free States, as we shall call them, had acquired a large and constantly increasing preponderance in the House of Representatives, whilst in the Senate, with its representation based on States, not on population, the inequality was not so great; and when Congress met in this year there were in the Union ten free and nine slave States, counting Delaware among the latter. Early in the session Mississippi was admitted, and in December, 1818, a year later, Illinois, a free State, was brought in, thus preserving the proportion between the two sections as it had existed at the time of the adoption of the Constitution, and as it had hitherto been maintained. So far all had gone well, notwithstanding the delay that attended the admission of Kentucky, and it is possible that if the same rate of increase could have been kept up on both sides, the angry controversy which took place at this time and the ill-feeling which it engendered might have been indefinitely postponed. Such, however, was not the case. For reasons that seem to be inherent in the system of slavery the South spread territorially more rapidly than the North, and in the session of 1818–19, — the second of this Congress, — Alabama and Missouri, two slave territories, applied for authority to frame constitutions, preparatory to their admission into the Union. This of course precipitated the issue as to the balance of power ; for, obviously, if these two applicants were to be brought into the Union with slavery, as in all probability they would elect to be, the proportion hitherto existing between the free and slave States would be destroyed, and the preponderance of power in the Senate would be handed over to the South. This the representatives from the North were determined to prevent, and to this end it was necessary either to defeat the admission of one of these territories, or to bring it in as a free State.

So far as Alabama was concerned, Georgia, when ceding the territory out of which that State was subsequently carved, had made certain stipulations in regard to slavery which were regarded as deciding, in the affirmative, the question of the existence of this form of labor in all that region. At all events, for this or some other equally good reason, there was no attempt made at Washington to dictate a constitution to the people of Alabama, and they were left free to come into the Union with or without slavery, as to them might seem best. To an unprejudiced mind, this appears to have been a just and fair method of settling the matter, or rather of letting it settle itself ; and as it had worked well in the case of Louisiana, it is difficult to understand why the same rule should not have been applied to Missouri, save on the theory that the balance of power required that if she were to come into the Union at this time, it must be as a free State. On no other ground can the action of Congress be explained and justified. The article in the Louisiana treaty which guaranteed to the people of that territory the possession of their property including slaves, was certainly as sacred as was the clause in the Georgia deed of cession which is assumed to have legalized slavery in Alabama. So far, too, as the action of Congress could give them validity these two instruments stood upon an equal footing; for both had been reaffirmed, the one by the admission of Louisiana, and the other by that of Mississippi. In fact, the two cases are believed to be strictly analogous and were therefore equally binding. If, then, Congress had the power to forbid slavery in Missouri, it had the power to prohibit it in Alabama; and it was clearly the duty of those who favored the Missouri "restriction," if they believed slavery to be the great evil which they said they did, to have insisted upon doing so, even though it involved them in as utter disregard for the Georgia deed of cession as they subsequently showed for the Louisiana treaty. Such, however, does not appear to have been their opinion, for in December, 1819, Alabama was received into the Union with slavery, and without any serious opposition on their part, at the very time that they were insisting most strenuously upon forcing the people of Missouri to adopt a clause in their constitution which should put an end to slavery, under penalty of being refused admission into the sisterhood of States.

Out of this measure, as formulated in the amendment of Mr. Tallmadge, of New York, sprung up a debate, in which, for the first time, parties were divided by a geographical line, and in which hot words and threats were bandied to and fro with a frequency and freedom that showed how deep and determined was the feeling that underlaid the struggle. On the part of those who opposed the imposition of this "restriction," as it was called, upon the people of Missouri, it was contended that the measure was contrary to the precedents established by Congress in the cases of Kentucky, Tennessee, Louisiana, Mississippi, and Alabama, all of which had been admitted into the Union with slavery; that it infringed upon that article in the treaty of purchase which guaranteed to the people of Louisiana the possession of their property; and that Congress had no power to prescribe to a State any particular form of government, other than that it should be republican; and that even if they had the abstract power, it would be folly to use it, since the people of the State would have a perfect right to change or amend their constitution whenever, and in whatever way, they might think proper.

In answer to these arguments, it was objected that Congress had imposed restrictions upon other States, as, for instance, in the case of Louisiana; that in the bill now under consideration, there was a clause which forbade Missouri to tax, for five years, the lands that had been granted to soldiers; and that even if this were not so, the power to admit, or to refuse to admit, a State, which Congress unquestionably possessed, necessarily carried with it the power to impose the conditions upon which such State should be admitted. In regard to the argument based upon the treaty of purchase and the infringement which this amendment, if adopted, would work in the rights of property, it was held that slavery existed only in virtue of local law; that it was not only unrepublican in its nature, but it was also a moral wrong as well as a political and economical evil; and hence, no matter if the treaty and the subsequent enactments of Congress did sanction it, self-interest and a higher law demanded that it should be abolished. These objec-

tions were urged with great warmth and persistency,
and there can be no question as to the influence they
exerted upon the people of the North, though a moment's reflection will convince any fair-minded person
that they were more specious than solid. If the effort
to extinguish slavery in Missouri had been in conformity
with the will of the people of that State, and in undoubted
accord with the treaty of purchase and the Constitution
of the United States, the position of those who favored
the " restriction " would have been absolutely impreg-
nable. But this was not the case, and hence the anal-
ogy which, it was claimed, existed between this restriction and those which had been imposed on other States
fell to the ground. So, also, in regard to the wrong and
the evil of slavery, both of which, we may remark in
passing, were admitted. Indeed, on this point the representatives from the South went quite as far as did
their neighbors from the North ; and it is probably safe
to say that, as an original proposition, any measure that
looked to the introduction of slavery into territory then
free would have found but few defenders. But this
was not the point at issue, and its discussion was therefore irrelevant. The question to be decided was whether
Congress had the right to abolish slavery in a region
where it legally existed, regardless of treaty stipulations
and of the wishes of the people most directly interested. It was, it will be seen, a matter of law, not
of morality ; and in justice to themselves and to their
friends and kindred who had immigrated to Missouri,
the South could not afford to surrender the point.
Accordingly, they planted themselves upon their constitutional rights and the faith of treaties, and though
this position was hotly contested at the time, yet, to-day,

there are probably few who will venture to question
its legality, whatever may be thought of its morality.
As a matter of law, there can be no doubt that Missouri was entitled to admission in 1820, and with slavery, if her people so willed it, just as Louisiana had
been in 1812, and as Arkansas was in 1836 ; and
the attempt on the part of one branch of Congress to
force her people to do away with slavery as a *sine qua
non* of admission into the Union was, as was afterwards
affirmed by the supreme court, a stretch of power not
warranted by the Constitution, and therefore illegal.
Upon this point the argument of John Quincy Adams is
unanswerable. Speaking, some years later, on the motion to admit Arkansas, he said : "She is entitled to
admission as a slave State . . . by virtue of that article
in the treaty for the acquisition of Louisiana which secures to the inhabitants of the ceded territories all the
rights, privileges, and immunities of the original citizens
of the United States ; and stipulates for their admission,
conformably to that principle, into the Union. Louisiana was purchased as a country wherein slavery was
the established law of the land. As Congress have not
power in time of peace to abolish slavery in the original
States of the Union, they are equally destitute in those
parts of the territory ceded by France to the United
States under the name of Louisiana, where slavery
existed at the time of the acquisition. . . . Arkansas,"
or Missouri, for the argument applied equally to her,
"therefore, comes, and has the right to come, into the
Union with her slaves and her slave laws. It is written in the bond, and however I may lament that it was
so written, I must faithfully perform its obligations." [1]

Benton's *Abridgment of the Debates,* vol. xiii. p. 33.

In spite of the strength of this position and the doubts that must have prevailed as to the validity of a contrary course, the opponents of the " restriction " were outvoted, and the amendment of Mr. Tallmadge, abolishing slavery in Missouri (for that was what it amounted to), was carried. When the measure came before the Senate, this feature was stricken out by a decided vote, and the bill was returned to the House in the shape in which it had been originally introduced. This body refused to concur in the change, and as the Senate adhered to its position, the fifteenth Congress adjourned without coming to any agreement, and the bill was lost.

With the opening of the new Congress, in December, 1819, the question again came up, but under somewhat different auspices. The House, it is true, showed very plainly that it was not prepared to abandon the position it had taken in favor of abolishing slavery in Missouri ; but the application of Maine for admission into the Union, which was made about this time, enabled the Senate to exercise a little gentle pressure upon their neighbors of the lower house by a resort to the well-known device of coupling the two measures into one and the same bill. This was done, and with a candor that was worthy of a better cause, the opponents of the Missouri restriction in both houses of Congress declared that the two measures must stand or fall together ; that unless Missouri was admitted into the Union and without conditions as to slavery, Maine should be kept out. This brought on a debate, which ran through several weeks, and finally culminated in a dead-lock, the appointment of a committee of conference, and the adoption of a measure, or rather a series of measures, known as the

Missouri Compromise. By the terms of this agreement, which, it may be well to observe, was understood and not expressed, the clause prohibiting slavery was stricken from the bill authorizing the people of Missouri to form a constitution. This left them nominally free to organize the State with or without slavery, as they might prefer, but without any express guarantee as to its admission into the Union, though it seems to have been clearly understood that this was to be the effect of the measure. In return for this concession, which, in the light of a subsequent decision of the supreme court, yielded nothing, Maine was brought into the Union, and a provision was inserted into the Missouri bill, by which it was stipulated that slavery should be excluded from all " the territory ceded by France to the United States, under the name of Louisiana, north of thirty-six degrees and thirty minutes north latitude."

In securing the adoption of this compromise, if that term can be truly applied to a transaction in which one party gained everything and conceded nothing, the representatives of the free and relatively populous North achieved a decided success. For the first time in the history of the country, they had openly attempted to limit the power of the South by preventing the admission of a slave State, and they certainly had no cause to be dissatisfied with the result of the experiment. By the admission of Maine, they had regained the supremacy in the Senate which was temporarily lost when Alabama came into the Union; and if they had not succeeded in carrying a measure for the abolition of slavery in Missouri, they had secured the passage of a law by which all that vast domain situated north of the line of thirty-six degrees and thirty minutes north latitude, and lying between the Rocky Mountains and the Mississippi River, was transformed, as far as an act of Congress could effect that purpose, from possible slave to actual free territory.

Like all arrangements that are based upon expediency alone, this agreement was not lasting. Subsequent Congresses did not hesitate to violate it whenever it suited their purposes to do so ; and individual States, even those that had most to gain by insisting upon its observance, indicated clearly what they thought of its character when they declared, as Massachusetts did in 1845, that they did not intend to abide by it. In fact, neither of the great political parties ever regarded it as being peculiarly sacred save when there was something to be gained by so doing. As early as 1836 it was violated, and that without a protest on the part of the North, by the addition to the State of Missouri of the triangle known as the Platte purchase ; in 1854 it was formally abrogated ; and in 1857 it was pronounced unconstitutional in an *obiter dictum* of the highest tribunal in the land.

This was certainly a most lame and impotent conclusion, but for this verdict the Southern men who had sanctioned the compromise were not responsible. In good faith, and in the interest of peace and the Union, they had sacrificed what they believed to be, and what have since been decided to have been, their constitutional rights ; and, so far as they could, they had dedicated to freedom a much larger extent of country than that which their fathers had given, when in 1787, by a vote of five slave and three free States, they had passed the famous ordinance that made free all the region north of the Ohio and south of the Lakes. In so doing they certainly had not been guilty of any act of aggression, whatever else it may have been; and the fact that a majority of them in each house, small though it was, were willing to make the concession is proof not only of their devotion to the Union, but it indicates very clearly what are believed to have been their sentiments, at this time, in regard to the extension of slavery.

Were other evidence on this point necessary, it may be found in the ratification by the Senate, at this very session of Congress, of the treaty with Spain, in virtue of which all of Louisiana territory south of the line of thirty-six degrees and thirty minutes, except Arkansas and a strip reserved for certain Indian tribes, was exchanged for the Floridas. Of the merits of this treaty, or of the hidden motives that may have led the Southern members to vote for its ratification, it is not my province to speak. All that it concerns us to know is the fact that, in relinquishing their claims to all this region, the United States sold the only territory they owned west of the Mississippi, except Arkansas, into which slavery could be legally carried. Indeed, if we also except Florida, which was acquired by the treaty, there was not then a foot of land on either side of the Mississippi, belonging to the United States, in which slavery had not been extinguished, and that with the approval and by the votes of Southern slaveholders.

CHAPTER VIII.

ALTHOUGH the adoption of this compromise put an end to the attempt on the part of the North to abolish slavery in Missouri, it did not secure her admission into the Union, neither was it the work of Henry Clay. The honor of having suggested it as a means of escape from a dead-lock which threatened the integrity of the Union belongs to Jesse B. Thomas, a senator from Illinois, and a Southern man by birth, though it is proper to add that Mr. Clay lent to the measure the weight of his great name and abilities, and that it probably could not have been carried without his assistance. What he really brought about, and what earned for him the title of the peace-maker, was the adoption of a second compromise, by virtue of which Missouri was admitted into the Union, not in the usual way, but through a sort of side door, opened to her in return for a certain concession which she was assumed to have made.

As a compromise, using this term in its usual acceptation, this second measure was as one-sided as the first, but differed from that in being altogether in the interest of the South. By it, a few Northern men (fourteen in the House, and eight in the Senate), joined to an almost solid Southern vote, were able to secure the admission of Missouri, on the condition that her legislature should adopt a " solemn public act," which was ostensibly a modification, or rather a repeal, of an article in the constitution she had just adopted, and which, therefore, from its nature, was of no binding force, moral or legal, upon any human being whatsoever.

To understand this curious page of legislative history, it is necessary to transfer the field of investigation from Washington to Missouri, and note briefly the change which the adoption of the first, or Missouri Compromise proper, had wrought in the political condition of the people of the territory.

For a few years previous to this time, ever since 1816, they had been living under the third or highest form of territorial government, but when the news of the passage of this "act" reached them, they at once took steps to organize the State. An election was held for members of a convention which met in June, 1820, and proceeded to frame a constitution. It was a fairly representative body, and numbered among its members some who were afterwards called upon to play conspicuous parts upon a more extended theatre. As might have been expected, it was composed altogether of men who were in favor of making Missouri a slave State, though they were not necessarily in favor of a still further extension of the slave area; and it is a curious commentary upon the changes that subsequently took place in men and measures that Edward Bates, who was attorney-general under President Lincoln, and one of the best and purest men this country has produced, was one of its members, having been returned from St. Louis in the pro-slavery interest. The fact is that the attempt of the Northern representatives to regulate the domestic affairs of the territory had reacted upon themselves, and instead of strengthening the hands of their friends, it had alienated not a few, even of those who agreed with them upon the question of slavery. It was looked upon as a high-handed effort at usurpation, and such was the opposition it provoked within the State that, owing to this and to other causes that will readily suggest themselves, no one whose views upon the slavery question were in the least doubtful stood any chance of an election. Even among the free-state men the issue had become so complicated that the "Missouri Gazette," whose editor, Joseph Charless, was one of the leaders on that side, declared, on one occasion, when speaking of the effort in Congress to abolish slavery in the incoming State, that "the question was not whether slavery shall or shall not be prohibited, . . . but whether we shall meanly abandon our rights and suffer any earthly power to dictate the terms of our constitution."

After a session of a little over a month, and an expenditure for stationery, etc., of a total of twenty-six dollars and twenty-five cents, the convention adjourned, having completed the work for which it had been called together. The constitution, as adopted, was not submitted to a vote of the people for ratification, but took effect of its own motion. It did away with the territorial government, and provided for the election of officers, state as well as national. In August of that year this election was held, and the officers then chosen were duly inaugurated ; and although it was a year and more before Missouri was finally admitted into the Union, yet the wheels of her government were promptly set in motion, and she found herself occupying the somewhat anomalous position of a State outside of the Union.

Of course this constitution sanctioned slavery. That was a foregone conclusion : but as it was the very contingency against which the compromise that had been so recently adopted was intended to provide, it did not furnish any just and tenable ground for opposing the admission of the State. So far as the Southern representatives were concerned, they had complied with their part of the agreement. Maine had been received into the Union ; slavery had been excluded from all the rest of Louisiana, or Missouri territory as it was then called, north of thirty-six degrees and thirty minutes, so far as an act of Congress could effect that purpose ; and it now only remained formally to advance Missouri to the dignity of a State, in order to carry out in full the well-understood terms of the compromise. This a large majority of the Northern representatives were unwilling to permit, so long as her constitution sanctioned slavery. They had voted steadily and up to the very last to make Missouri a free State, regardless of the wishes of her people ; and for them now to wheel around and consent to receive her into the Union with slavery would have indicated a change of heart too sudden to be genuine, and one which, in the temper then prevailing at the North, they might have found it difficult to explain and defend. Besides, although they had been temporarily defeated upon the question of prohibiting slavery in the State, yet the contest had been close, and there were not a few among them who did not despair of ultimate success, though they seem to have recognized the propriety of shaping their course so as to avoid, if possible, the appearance of coming to an open conflict with the recently adopted compromise. Accordingly, when the constitution which the State of Missouri had adopted was presented for approval, they seized upon the clause rendering it obligatory upon the legislature to enact a law to "prevent free negroes and mulattoes from coming to and settling within the State," and made it the occasion for renewing the struggle. Free negroes, they contended, were recognized as citizens in some of the old States, and as emigration was a privilege possessed by all citizens, they insisted upon the rejection of Missouri's application, on the ground that this article was contrary to that provision of the federal Constitution which guaranteed to " the citizens of each State the privileges and immunities of citizens in the several States."

That this was a mere pretext, intended to cover up the real grounds of their opposition, hardly admits of a doubt. The fact that, at this time, there was, probably, not a single State, north or south, that did not in some shape discriminate against blacks and in favor of whites certainly indicates it ; and if further proof be required, it will be found in the chance utterances of different speakers during the course of the debate, in the proceedings of the legislature of at least one of the Northern States, and in the fact that if the objectionable article came in conflict with the federal Constitution, as it was said to do, it was, *ipso facto*, null and void, and would be so decided by the supreme court, whenever the matter came up for adjudication. However, be this as it may, it served the purpose for which it was intended ; and whether the objection to which it gave rise was feigned or real, it furnished the opponents to the admission of Missouri with what they most needed, — a plausible excuse for keeping her out of the Union without an open violation of their part of the compromise. To all outward appearance, they now opposed her admission, not because she had legalized slavery, but because she proposed to do as some of her neighbors had already done, and as one of them did as late as 1846, — prevent an undesirable class of persons from settling within her borders. In urging this objection they were apparently occupying high constitutional grounds, but in reality their opposition was simply a continuation of the struggle which had been begun some two years before ; and disguise the fact as we may under high-sounding phrases and nice verbal distinctions, it was, after all, but another attempt on the part of the North to prevent the increase and limit the power of the South. That it was a movement in the interest of morality and a higher civilization may be admitted, but that will not alter the fact. The path was different, though the end aimed at was the same.

In the debate which grew out of this question some of the ablest men in the nation took part. The evils of slavery, the value of the Union, the terms of the Louisiana treaty, the true intent and meaning of the Missouri Compromise, and the powers of Congress in the premises were all discussed at length, but to no purpose. The key to the debate lay in the interpretation that was to be put upon that clause in the federal Constitution, according to which "the citizens of each State shall be entitled to the privileges and immunities of citizens of the several States," and upon this point opinions were hopelessly divided. Even Charles Pinckney's declaration that when he drew up this clause " there was not such a thing in the Union as a black or colored citizen," and that consequently it could not have been intended to include that class of persons, important as it was to a proper understanding of the provision, seems to have had little or no weight in bringing about a decision. Under the circumstances, and from a political point of view, it was more important to interpret the Constitution so as to make it fit the changed condition of affairs than to find out what the framers of that instrument had intended to say. Accordingly, when it was urged that free blacks were not citizens in the sense of the Constitution, it was replied that now they were citizens in some of the States, and that the Constitution spoke of citizens of the " several States," and not of citizens of the United States. In answer to this, it was shown that if this interpretation prevailed, it would be possible for one State to impose citizens upon another ; and that it might be made to grant to a free colored citizen, say of Massachusetts, immigrating to Missouri, rights and privileges in the latter State which he did not possess in the former, both of which propositions were declared to be absurd. In this way the debate ran on from day to day and week to week, only to end at last in a disagreement, the Senate being in favor of the admission, whilst the House was opposed to it.

In this condition of affairs Mr. Clay found his opportunity ; and he introduced a resolution to appoint a joint committee, " to consider and report to the Senate and House respectively whether it be expedient or not to make provision for the admission of Missouri into the Union on the same footing as the original States, . . . and if not, whether any other, and what provision, adapted to her actual condition, ought to be made by law." This resolution was carried by an overwhelming vote in both branches of Congress ; and a committee, of which Mr. Clay was chairman, and which, so far as the House was concerned, he may be said to have named, was appointed. In due time it reported a resolution admitting the State, provided its legislature " by a solemn public act" shall declare that the fourth clause of section 26 of article 3 of the constitution submitted by the State shall never be construed to authorize the passage of any law, by which "any citizen of either of the States in this Union shall be excluded from the enjoyment of any of the privileges and immunities" to which he is entitled under the Constitution of the United States. It was also provided, and the reason for it is obvious, "that when this declaration shall have been made, and a copy of it furnished to the President, he shall, by proclamation, declare the State to be admitted." This resolution was passed without discussion, though its efficiency may well be doubted in view of the fact that the clause in the state constitution, here described, did not contain the provision to which Congress objected and consequently could not have been the one it was intended to limit.

With the adoption of this measure the Missouri question passed out of the hands of Congress, and it now only remained for the legislature of that State to go through with the farce of pretending to set aside a constitutional provision. This they did with commendable alacrity, though they evidently were well aware of the extent of their own powers, and had a keen sense of the absurdity of the part they were called upon to play. After reciting the act of Congress containing the condition under which Missouri was to be received into the Union, they went on to declare that, "forasmuch as the good people of this State have, by the most solemn and public act in their power, virtually assented to the said fundamental condition, when, by their representatives in full and free convention assembled, they adopted the constitution of this State, and consented to be incorporated into the federal Union, and governed by the Constitution of the United States, which among other things provides that the said Constitution and laws of the United States, made in pursuance thereof, and all treaties made or which shall be made under the authority of the United States, shall be the supreme law of the land ; and the judges in every State shall be bound thereby, anything in the constitution or law of any State to the contrary notwithstanding. And although this general assembly do most solemnly declare that the Congress of the United States have no constitutional power to annex any condition to the admission of this State into the federal Union, and that this general assembly have no power to change the operation of the constitution of this State, except in the mode prescribed in the Constitution itself, nevertheless, as the Congress of the United States has desired this general assembly to declare the assent of this State to said fundamental condition, and forasmuch as such declaration will neither restrain nor enlarge, limit nor extend, the operation of the Constitution of the United States or of this State ; but the said constitutions will remain in all respects as if the said resolution had never passed, and the desired declaration was never made ; and because such declaration will not divest any power or change the duties of any of the constitutional authorities of this State or of the United States, nor impair the rights of the people of this State, or impose any additional obligation upon them, but may promote an earlier enjoyment of their vested federal rights, and this State being, moreover, determined to give to her sister States and to the world the most unequivocal proof of her desire to promote the peace and harmony of the Union — therefore

" *Be it enacted and declared by the General Assembly of the State of Missouri, and it is hereby solemnly and publicly enacted and declared*, That this State has assented and does assent that the fourth clause of the twenty-sixth section of the third article of the constitution of this State shall never be construed to authorize the passage of any law, and that no law shall be passed in conformity thereto, by which any citizen, of either of the United States, shall be excluded from the enjoyment of any of the privileges and immunities to which such citizens are entitled under the Constitution of the United States."

Upon the receipt of a certified copy of this act, which, considered with reference to the preamble which accompanied it, can hardly be called solemn, President Monroe issued a proclamation announcing the fact of its passage, and declaring that the admission of Missouri was complete. This proclamation bears date the 10th of August, 1821, and consequently that is the day upon which Missouri took her place in the sisterhood of States, and upon which the long and bitter controversy of which she had been the innocent occasion was brought to an end.

In looking back over this exciting period and noting the results that were obtained, we cannot but be struck with the absurdity, inconsistency, and illegality that characterized almost every phase of the proceedings of Congress upon this question. Thus, for instance, we find that before admitting Missouri into the Union " upon an equal footing with the other States," an effort was made to deprive her of the privilege which her sister States had exercised, and which they still possessed, of deciding for herself whether she would or would not legalize slavery,

unmindful apparently of the fact that if the measure had
been carried and could have been enforced, it would have
established her inequality at the very outset of her career.
This was, to say the least, somewhat inconsistent; and
what added to the absurdity of the situation was the fact
that, although the attempt on the part of a majority of
the representatives from the North to prohibit slavery
in Missouri was, as was afterwards decided, unconstitutional, yet by way of inducing them to abandon their
opposition upon this point and consent to the admission
of the State with or without slavery, as her people might
decide, the South agreed to a condition, which was also
subsequently decided to be unconstitutional, by virtue of
which slavery was excluded from all the territory north
of thirty-six degrees and thirty minutes north latitude.
Thus we have the singular spectacle of a great political
party agreeing to refrain from an act which would have
been a violation of the organic law of the land, and which
they therefore could not legally perform; in return for
which their opponents agree to a measure, and actually
embody it into a law, which was also null and void, because it, too, was in opposition to this same Constitution.   This, it will be observed, was compromise number
one, the far-famed Missouri Compromise of March 6,
1820; or rather it is all that was left of it after passing
through the hands of the supreme court in 1857.   In
view of this decision it seems like waste of time to repeat
that Missouri was not admitted into the Union under
this agreement, but that she was brought in under another and a totally different one, entered into March 2,
1821; and hence that, in the opinion of not a few, even
of those who had aided in passing it, the first, or Missouri Compromise, was violated within the year by the

very Congress that adopted it, and the agreement as to the exclusion of slavery north of the line of thirty-six degrees and thirty minutes thus became void and of no effect, the consideration for it having failed. Unsatisfactory as this attempt at compromise proved to be, it did not by any means complete the chapter of errors and inconsistencies that marked the proceedings of Congress in all their dealings with this question. Indeed, so curious was the next step taken that it is impossible to understand it, save on the theory suggested by Benton, that the Democrats, or Republicans as they were then called, of the North had become sensible of the error into which, when judged from a party point of view, they had been led by keeping Missouri out of the Union, and were now anxious to regain their lost ground and bring her in, provided it could be done without jeopardizing their individual positions at home. Certainly nothing but a supposed dire political necessity could account for such action as that which resulted in the adoption of what, for the want of a better term, may be styled compromise number two. By it Missouri was, as we have seen, admitted into the Union, but on condition that her legislature adopted a "solemn public act," which not only came in conflict with a provision of her organic law, and was therefore null and void, but which, if it meant anything and had been legal and could have been carried out, would have resulted in bringing her in, not on an equality with the other States, but shorn of the privilege which they had enjoyed, and which Illinois exercised as late as 1846, of deciding for herself as to the qualifications of those who were to live within her borders, thus relegating her at once to a position of marked inferiority.

In other words, to protect a handful of so-called citizens in one or two of the older States, not one of whom would ever have thought of immigrating to Missouri, her legislature was required, as a condition precedent to her admission, to assent to a measure that was illegal in itself, and could not, therefore, in any possible way affect the class of persons which it was ostensibly intended to benefit.

When this assent was given, although the legislature that gave it took especial pains to declare that their action was of no legal force, yet the demands of Congress were satisfied; and President Monroe, at the head of whose cabinet was that sterling patriot and statesman, John Quincy Adams, issued a proclamation announcing the fact, and declaring that the admission of Missouri was complete.

Amid all this confusion and conflict of ends and means, laws and constitutions, and we have by no means exhausted the list, the resolution admitting Maine and the proclamation by which Missouri was brought into the Union are about the only measures that stand out distinctly and without challenge. They were final; and it is probable that they would both have been passed without serious opposition, if Maine had been ready to take her place in the Union when Missouri made application for permission to frame her constitution. Unfortunately, this was not the case; and it was this fact, which, threatening as it did to disturb the proportion that had hitherto existed between the free and slave States, gave the Federalists of the North the opportunity of bringing the slavery question to the front as a political issue. Intended, no doubt, at first, for effect in the local elections, it proved to be so popular, and made such inroads into the ranks of the opposite party, that it speedily outgrew the narrow proportions designed for it and became of national importance. Instead of being a struggle between the Federalists, and Republicans for supremacy in their respective States, it brought about a new division of parties, by which Congress and the country at large was divided geographically upon the line of slavery, with political power as the prize of the contest.

CHAPTER IX.

CALLED upon to prepare a constitution in the midst of great political excitement, and at a time when the monetary affairs of the country were in a state of disorganization, the people of Missouri, acting through their chosen delegates, set about the work with coolness and deliberation, and, all things considered, they framed an instrument that was a marvel of moderation and political sagacity. Among its provisions were a few, as for instance the one that declared ministers of the gospel ineligible to certain offices, that might have been improved, or better still, perhaps, left out altogether; but, take it all in all, it was a very creditable piece of work; and if we may judge of its character from the length of time that it remained in force without any material alteration, it compared not unfavorably with the best similar instruments, no matter when or by whom they may have been " ordained and established."

Especially was this true of the way in which it dealt with the financial question. The lesson the people of the State had just been taught by the failure of their local banks and by the evils of which this was in some measure the cause, severe as it was, seems to have been thoroughly learned, and it now brought forth good fruit. As a result of the experience of those years, a healthy distrust of banks and corporations of every kind pervaded all classes of the community ; and although the establishment in St. Louis, in 1829, of a branch of the United States Bank gave to the people of the State a currency that was safer and more convenient than any to which they had hitherto been accustomed, this fact was not sufficient to eradicate the feelings of hostility with which they regarded all such institutions, and which they imbedded in their organic law in the shape of an article limiting the power of the legislature to " the incorporation of one bank and no more, to be in operation at the same time." Theoretically, and so far as legislative action was concerned, they were a hard-money people, and it was not until 1837, five years after President Jackson's veto of the bill rechartering the United States Bank, that the legislature, in answer to the demands of the business interests of the State, availed themselves of the liberty allowed them, and agreed to the establishment of a bank. Meanwhile the notes of institutions organized and doing business in other States formed the bulk of the circulating medium ; and as many of these institutions were short-lived, their collapse entailed a loss that was only measured by the extent of their circulation, and that fell with peculiar force upon those who were least able to bear it. In spite, however, of the uncertainty as to the solvency of many of these banks, and the consequent fluctuation in the value of their notes, their issues, or " shin - plasters " as they were contemptuously called, continued to pass current until the refusal of the Bank of Missouri, in 1839, to receive or pay them out placed them at a discount so far as specie and her own bills were concerned.

At first this measure created not a little indignation,

and the merchants of St. Louis, the chief distributive point of the State, denounced it in unmeasured terms, but the bank officials remained firm, and the course of events soon justified their action. By drawing a broad line between currency and specie or bankable funds, they furnished a standard, safe and steady, for the adjustment of values ; and this brought about a much needed reform, though it was powerless to drive the discredited bills out of circulation. They continued to pass current in small daily transactions, but when tendered in payment of large amounts they were subjected to the rate of discount that ruled at the time ; and those of us who were familiar with the business methods that prevailed in those days can hardly have forgotten the numerous Counterfeit Detectors, Bank-Note Reporters, and other publications of a similar character, that were intended to keep the merchant and trader advised of the condition, from week to week, of the banks whose notes he was called upon to handle.

After some fifteen or twenty years of this experience, during which time private individuals and savings institutions supplied, as far as could be done, the place of banks, the constitution of the State was amended ; and, in 1857, it was so changed as to authorize the establishment of banks of issue, with branches in different parts of the State. With the conservatism that has ever been one of their marked characteristics, the people of Missouri did not plunge recklessly into the business of banking, but they very wisely limited the number of these parent institutions to ten, and provided that their aggregate capital should never exceed twenty millions of dollars, an outside limit that cannot be considered extravagant in view of the population of the State and of the amount of business annually transacted. An additional safeguard was also inserted in the constitution, in the shape of a clause requiring these banks to be " based upon a specie capital ; " and in the law of 1857, under which they came into existence, they were still farther hedged in by such provisions as experience had seemed to render necessary. So far, then, as it could be done by law, every care was taken to insure the stability of these institutions ; and it is but just to say that they were founded upon a solid basis, and that with but few exceptions they have been well managed.

Unfortunately, they were begun at a most inauspicious time. The panic of 1857, as sharp as it was short, found them unprepared for the demands that were made upon them, and a few years later, almost before they had recovered from its effects, they were called upon to share in the reverses that marked the opening years of the civil war. With but one exception, that of the Exchange Bank of St. Louis, they were obliged to bend before the storm ; and during the whole of that eventful period they had to suspend specie payments. The legislature, however, refused to forfeit their charters, so that with the return of peace they were able to resume their accustomed functions ; and to-day they are doing their legitimate work in facilitating the business of the communities in which they exist, though almost all of them, taking advantage of different acts of Congress, have ceased to be state institutions, and are now known as national banks.

But whilst the people of the State have in the main shown themselves to be decidedly conservative in the management of their monetary affairs, public as well as private, there have been times when they appear to have been unable to resist the tendency to speculation and overtrading which seems an inevitable attendant upon all new and rapidly developing communities. As a consequence, they have not been exempt from the penalty that attaches to such faulty methods of doing business, and makes itself felt in the storms which, from time to time, sweep over the financial world. Probably the severest of these storms, not so much on account of the amount destroyed as from the number of sufferers, was the one which visited the country in 1837, and which, following close upon the expiration of the charter of the United States Bank, is often ascribed to that event, though it would be going too far to assign it to that as the sole, or even a sufficient, cause. The truth is that so far from having been a prime factor in bringing on the " hard times " of 1837, the fate of the bank had little or nothing to do with it. This is, no doubt, contrary to the impression most sedulously cultivated by the Whigs of that day, but it can hardly be questioned in view of the fact that although the charter of the bank did not expire until 1836, yet the death-blow was really given to the institution in 1832, four years earlier ; and this measure, instead of causing a stringency in the money market and a depression in prices, as it would have done if there had been any necessary connection between the fate of the bank and the hard times of 1837, was followed, first, by a season of prosperity, and subsequently, as such seasons often are, by one of inflation, when for a time, say from 1834 to 1837, a fever of speculation ran riot throughout the land. Not only individuals, but States, caught the infection, and it is to the reaction following upon this condition of affairs that the student must look for an explanation of the crisis which has given Van Buren's administration such an undesirable prominence in the financial annals of the country.

To picture the saturnalia that prevailed during these years of inflation were an idle task. All classes seem to have engaged in it, and no portion of the country was exempt. During its prevalence schemes without number, some of which would have taxed the resources of the wealthiest communities, were launched upon the market; and there were few of them that did not find earnest advocates. Only a fraction of the number, it is true, ever came to anything, but to carry them on required more money than was then in circulation. To supply this deficiency the people in some of the States, forgetful of the lesson of 1819, resorted to an indefinite increase of local, or as they were sometimes called "pet," banks. They seem to have imagined that these institutions, instead of being mere instruments for facilitating commercial intercourse, were, in some mysterious way, to create wealth. Hence in some portions of the country they were chartered in great numbers, without any regard to the demands of the communities in which they were expected to do business, and in defiance of all laws of finance, and occasionally, we may add, of honesty. In one of the Western States, an agricultural one, and therefore relatively independent of such facilities, there was at one time a bank for every five thousand inhabitants. This number is said to have been subsequently increased, and a writer of that day, speaking of the condition of affairs which then prevailed, says, with pardonable exaggeration, " that every village plat with a house, or even without a house, if it had a hollow stump to serve as a vault, was the site of a bank; " and " that it was easy for any one to obtain their bills who could give reasonable assurance that he would circulate them at a distance and keep them afloat."

In this way, moving steadily on, but ever in a vicious circle, affairs went from bad to worse, and when finally the crash came, Missouri, in so far as she had held a conservative course and kept aloof from the ruinous systems of internal improvement in which certain of her sister States had indulged, was spared some of the calamities that they were called on to endure. Still she was not permitted to escape. With her growth in wealth and population, there had been a corresponding increase in commerce; and her business interests were so closely united with those of other and less conservative communities that they could not be separated. For good or evil they were inextricably bound together, and it was impossible that one should suffer without affecting the other injuriously.

Her people, too, in the management of their private affairs, appear to have been forgetful of the prudential considerations that governed their public action. For years they had witnessed the steady tide of immigration that had poured into the State, had noted the advance in different kinds of property, especially real estate, which was thus brought about; and it was but natural, as this stream of settlers still rolled in unchecked, to look forward to a continuance of the era of prosperity of which it was at once the cause and a visible sign. So long as they saw the State gaining in all the elements of wealth, they did not think it possible that a condition of affairs could arise in which individuals composing that State were to suffer. In this belief they acted, and, heedless of the impending storm, they made every preparation to share in the golden harvest which was so confidently anticipated. They bought and sold with a freedom that savored of recklessness ; engaged in enterprises that under other circumstances would have been regarded as too rash for consideration ; and when at last the day of reckoning came, it found them steeped in debt, and with lines of credit extended far beyond the limits of safety. Many of them sank under the weight ; but the great majority, after a few years of patient labor and enforced economy, were able to resume their positions in the world of commerce. It was a season of trial for all, relieved somewhat by local stay laws and such expedients, but none the less enduring and full of distress. The laws of finance had been set at naught, and the penalty had to be paid. Slowly and after much suffering the process of liquidation was accomplished, and an era of prosperity once more dawned upon the stricken people ; but the record of these years, written in the dockets of the courts and in the long list of bankruptcies, will ever remain as a warning.

Naturally enough, the " hard times," as this period of distress was called, entered largely into the political discussions of the day, and there can be no doubt as to the important part it was made to play in bringing about the defeat of Van Buren in the presidential election of 1840. It had come upon the country during his administration ; was associated in the minds of many with the veto of the bank bill, which had taken place some years previously and whilst his political friend and predecessor was in power ; and although, as has been said, it owed its origin to causes which neither he nor his party could control, yet the Whigs, as the opposition was then termed, taking advantage of the order in which these events had occurred, succeeded in making it appear that there was some necessary connection between them, and consequently that he and his political allies were responsible for the distress which then prevailed. It was an old fallacy, brought forward for the occasion, but it proved effective among a people whom financial troubles had made eager for a change ; and taken in connection with the military reputation which General Harrison, the opposing candidate, had acquired in the war of 1812, it led to the political revolution that resulted in his election and the success of the Whigs. It was the first time in the century that they or the party of which they were the legitimate descendants had won a popular verdict at the polls, and however desirable this may have been for other reasons, its merit is somewhat obscured by the fact that it was due, not so much to an intelligent dissent from the policy of the Democrats as it was to the adroit use made of a condition of affairs for which the people at large were responsible, and to a wild and senseless, but shrewdly manufactured, excitement over military events that were of secondary importance.

In this revolution, the people of Missouri had no part. They were essentially agricultural, and therefore comparatively independent of banks and banking facilities. They were earnest believers, too, in gold and silver as being not only the most desirable, but in fact the only, kind of money that Congress could legally authorize, and consequently they sympathized fully with the Democrats in their hostility to the national bank, which they had come to regard as an engine of political corruption. For these reasons among others, they had no faith in the explanation which the Whigs were wont to give of the origin of the financial distress that then prevailed ; and as they were correspondingly distrustful of the promised prosperity that was to follow upon a change in the administration at Washington, they could see no reason for surrendering their political convictions. Hence it was that in the election of 1840 they refused to " bend the knee to Baal," and voted with the Democrats, as they had done from the time that parties were organized upon the basis upon which they then stood, and as indeed they have continued to do, to this day, whenever they have been permitted to give a full and free expression to their wishes at the polls.

Of the causes, then, that led the people of the State thus early to identify themselves with the Democratic party, hostility to the bank may be said to have been the most influential. At all events, the bill to recharter that institution was the first distinctively national issue upon which they were called to act, and there can be no doubt that the position which they then assumed in favor of " hard money " was due in great part to the recollection of the bitter experience through which they had passed during the closing years of Missouri's career as a Territory and the beginning of her life as a State.

That this direction may have been given to the drift of opinion by the hostility which the Federalists had shown to the admission of the State into the Union is undoubtedly true ; and so far as opposition to slavery can be said to have been the cause of this hostility, it may properly be counted as a factor in the problem. But even if this be granted we shall have to admit that its influence was but short-lived; for, owing to the necessity which then existed of providing a remedy for the disorder into which the business affairs of the country had fallen, the feeling of irritation engendered by the course of the Federalists upon this occasion disappeared almost as rapidly as it had sprung up. Long before the close of President Monroe's administration in 1824, the slavery question had given way to more pressing considerations, and political parties, being left free to crystallize around new centres, gradually took on the forms under which they fought the battle that resulted in the destruction of the national bank.

But whilst it is true that, so far as the country at large was concerned, the slavery question had disappeared thus suddenly and entirely from the field of politics, it is a singular fact that there never was a time when, within the State, the sentiment of opposition to this institution was so active as it was during the twelve years covered by the administrations of the younger Adams and General Jackson, or when it made such headway. To a certain extent this was due to the movement in favor of gradual emancipation, of which Henry Clay was the great exponent, and of which the Whigs, considered as a party, are thought to have been the peculiar advocates. In Kentucky, no doubt they were so, and it may also have been true of other portions of the South and West; but in Missouri it was not the case. Here and upon this point both parties were in accord; and as early as 1828 a number of prominent men, "representing almost every district in the State, and consisting of about equal numbers of Whigs and Democrats," agreed upon a plan by which they hoped to secure the passage of a law that would provide for gradual emancipation, and thus in time get rid of slavery. At a private meeting which was then held, they determined to urge all candidates at the approaching election to approve of such a measure, and resolutions to this effect were drawn up and secretly dis-

tributed, " with the understanding that they were to be
placed before the people of the State in the shape of
memorials, and both parties were to urge the people to
sign them." Among those who took part in this meeting were United States Senators Benton and Barton,
the former of whom was at that time, and for many
years after, the recognized leader of the Democrats in the
State, whilst among the others there were those whose
influence within their respective spheres was not less
potent. Indeed, such was the strength of the " combina-
tion " that the Hon. John Wilson, to whom we are indebted for this curious bit of history, and who was a prominent Whig politician of that day, does not hesitate to
declare that they had the power to carry out that project. Unfortunately, however, before the day arrived
upon which the attempt was to be made, "it was published in the newspapers generally that Arthur Tappan,
of New York, had entertained at his private table some
negro men ; that, in fact, these negroes had rode in his
private carriage with his daughters." This may or may
not have been true, but it was generally believed in Missouri, and such was the furor it raised throughout the
State that those who had been instrumental in getting
up the meeting did not dare to let their memorials see
the light.[1]

[1] Mr. Wilson continues : " As well as I can call to mind, of the
individuals who composed this secret meeting, I am the only one
left to tell the tale ; but for that story of the conduct of the great
original fanatic on this subject we should have carried, under the
leadership of Barton and Benton, our project, and began in future
the emancipation of the colored race that would long since have
been followed by Kentucky, Maryland, Virginia, North Carolina,
Tennessee, etc. Our purpose further, after we got such a law
safely placed on the statute book, was to have followed it up by a

To those who are accustomed to look at the occurrences of those days through the medium of subsequent events, it is difficult to understand how so slight a matter as the entertainment of a negro by a somewhat noted abolitionist of New York could have influenced the action of earnest, sensible men who were engaged, with good promise of success, in what they must have felt to be a great social reform ; but among those of us who can remember the tremendous influence which such trivial incidents, when skillfully handled, excited throughout the South, there will be no hesitation in accepting the fact as here given, nor will it be necessary to go very far to find the explanation. Color, it will be remembered, was in all this region a badge of servitude, the one mark of inferiority that could neither be concealed nor gainsaid, whilst, on the other hand, every white man, whatsoever his condition, was in theory, at least, the equal socially of his neighbor. Starting from this point, the average Southerner, by a process of reasoning wholly illogical but not unnatural, had worked himself into the conviction that freedom to the blacks necessarily meant their social recognition ; and when called upon for the proof, he referred to the Tappan dinner and similar incidents. Of course it is easy at this late day to detect the fallacy in this mode of reasoning, but at that time, and situated as he was, it was not so. From his point of view the argument was sound, and it was owing to the belief in the experimental as well as logical truth of the conclusion to which he had come that the movement

provision requiring the masters of those who should be born to be free to teach them to read and write. This shows you how little a thing turns the destiny of nations.''—*Commonwealth of Missouri*, p. 223. St. Louis, 1877.

in favor of gradual emancipation, which, up to this time, had made such notable progress among the slaveholders of the State, was brought to an untimely end.

A few years after the events here narrated, Lovejoy took up the work and began his ill-advised agitation in favor of the same cause, but under very different conditions. Owing to the denunciations which the abolitionists of the North were now heaping upon slavery and slaveholders, the Southerners not only refused to take any measures for ridding themselves of what a large number of them regarded as an evil, but they would not listen to arguments in favor of a policy with which, only a few short years before, they had been in full sympathy. Accordingly, when in 1833, on his return from the theological school at Princeton, Lovejoy began, in St. Louis, the publication of his paper, his condemnation of slavery and pleas for gradual emancipation fell upon unwilling and even hostile ears, though there was nothing new or objectionable in the doctrines he advocated ; and the tone and temper of his utterances, when contrasted with the fierce philippics of later times, were as gentle as the cooings of a dove. In spite of this fact, they gave occasion to much ill feeling, and by way of allaying the excitement, and paving the way to the continuance of his Journal as a religious publication, pure and simple, a number of his friends and principal supporters, among whom was Hamilton R. Gamble, the Union Governor of Missouri during the war of secession, advised him " to distrust his own judgment so far as to pass over in silence everything connected with slavery." This he would not agree to do, having sworn, as he himself tells us, " eternal enmity to slavery, and being determined by the blessing of God never to go back." In consequence of his persistence in this objectionable course, he found, at the end of a year or two, that a longer residence in St. Louis was neither profitable nor safe; and in July, 1836, he so far deferred to public opinion that he announced his intention of removing to Alton, Illinois. Before he could do so, his office was sacked, his press and types were thrown into the street, but no personal injury was done him. When he arrived in Alton, he resumed his crusade against slavery, in defiance of pledges which his opponents assert he had made to the contrary, and this speedily involved him in fresh trouble. One press after another was destroyed, and it was while defending a third that he was shot, though not until he, or some of his friends, had fired upon and killed one of the mob.

With the circumstances of this sad tragedy, or with the subsequent attempt of certain admirers to apotheosize Lovejoy, we do not propose to concern ourselves. He did not meet his death in a slave State, or at the hands of slaveholders; and so far as the influence which he is said to have exerted in bringing about the final settlement of this question is discernible, it would have been better for the cause he had so much at heart, and for the people whom he sought to benefit, if he had never been born. That he had the abstract right to speak and write as he did, holding himself amenable to the laws of his country, is true, and so, also, it is true that a person may have the right to go into a powder mill with a lighted candle; but if any one should insist upon doing so, he would soon be taught that his neighbors had certain rights, not perhaps expressly guaranteed by law, but which it would not be prudent to ignore. Thus it was with Lovejoy. Whether rightly or wrongly

it matters not, the teachings which a few years before
had been received in Missouri with a fair share of favor
were now considered as being not only injurious, but
positively dangerous; and in putting a stop to them, the
people of St. Louis took the law into their own hands,
but in doing so, they exercised a right or a power — it
is immaterial by which name you call it — which is inherent in all communities, and which has been uniformly
exercised in our country whenever and wherever the
occasion demanded.

With the removal of Lovejoy from St. Louis, the
movement in favor of gradual emancipation in Missouri
came to an end. It was, certainly, a most dismal failure, and yet in some respects it is one of the most interesting and instructive episodes in American history.
Properly interpreted, it teaches us how prompt the
Anglo-American is to resent anything that looks like
outside dictation even from his own countrymen, and
how futile it is to attempt to improve the domestic institutions of our neighbors by a system of abuse, no matter
how much it may be deserved. It also shows us that
there was a time, and that not very long ago, when the
people of slaveholding St. Louis and free Alton were
equally intolerant of the anti-slavery agitation; and if
it does not throw any clear light upon the formation
of political parties as they existed at the time, it fore-
shadows, to some extent, the course of the border states
in the war of the rebellion, and it enables us to say with
certainty that, in the Missouri of that day, there was in
the Democratic party a strong contingent of emancipationists, just as there was some fifteen or twenty years
later, when Frank Blair and Gratz Brown raised the
banner of freedom and carried it to victory.

Another problem with which the Missourians of that day were called upon to grapple, and which, at one time, threatened the peace of the State, was the so-called Mormon war. As early as 1831, Joseph Smith, " the Seer, Revelator, Translator, and Prophet " of the new faith, visited Western Missouri, then but thinly populated, on a tour of inspection; and soon afterwards bands of Mormons, or, as they call themselves, Latter Day Saints, began to arrive and settle in the neighborhood of Independence, a town situated on the south bank of the Missouri River near the border of the State. This spot, we are told, is " the place selected by God for the centre stake of Zion ; " and although there is to-day but little of that fair land of which the Saints can claim full and undisturbed possession, yet they still look forward to a return to the homes which they once had there, and to the time when they shall build there " the most magnificent temple on the face of the earth to the name of Jehovah."

In the year succeeding the first settlements of the Mormons in this neighborhood, their numbers were largely increased by arrivals, chiefly from Ohio, where they appear to have been badly treated, Smith himself having been " daubed with tar and feathers " at a place called Hiram. They established a " mercantile house," as it was termed, in Independence ; opened some two hundred farms in the adjoining country ; planted orchards, and " commenced many extensive improvements." They also issued, in June of this year, the first number of a periodical which was devoted, among other things, to " publishing the revelations of God to the church." These revelations must have been of a somewhat partial character, for they are said to have promised most wonderful things to the faithful, whilst, at the same time, " they denounced equally wonderful things against the ungodly Gentiles." As a consequence, the Gentiles became much incensed, for in those days people were not as tolerant in such matters as they are to-day. It may be, too, that they were angered by the interference, real or supposed, of the Mormons with their slaves; and they certainly had very serious misgivings as to the safety of their persons and property whenever the Mormons should obtain the control of the county, as they were certain to do if the rate at which they were then increasing should be kept up for any length of time. For these and other reasons that seemed to them good and sufficient, they determined to drive the new-comers from the county, and accordingly they destroyed the house in which the objectionable paper was printed, and pitched the press and types into the street. They also tarred and feathered the presiding bishop and one or two of the leading members of the church, whipped others, and burned down a number of their houses. These outrages brought on an armed collision, which seems to have resulted in favor of the Mormons. Their success was but temporary, for in a few days they were completely overawed, and as a condition of safety they were required to give up their arms and leave the county within a specified time. This they did, some fifteen hundred of them, according to their own account, crossing the river and taking refuge in Clay and the neighboring counties. Here they suffered greatly, for, owing to the want of transportation, they had been obliged to leave most of their goods and chattels behind, and, consequently, they were but illy prepared to withstand the winter cold that was then upon them. In the spring, an effort was made to bring about some arrangement by which they were to be paid for the property which they had not been able to take with them, and a committee, composed of some of the leading citizens of Jackson County, was sent over to see if it were possible to agree upon the basis of a settlement. The effort came to naught, as the demands of the Mormons were thought to be excessive, and equally fruitless was their appeal to the Executive of the State and to the courts for protection and redress.

At the end of three or four years, during which time these misguided people had been driven from Clay and Carroll counties, the great bulk of them, reinforced by large accessions from the east, had gathered together in Caldwell county, where they had built up a town which they called Far West. Speaking from a material point of view they were, in the main, a hard working people, chiefly given to agriculture, though there was no lack among them of skilled mechanics and shrewd merchants. As an evidence of the prosperity which had thus far attended their efforts, they are said to have opened in this and the neighboring counties two thousand farms, and we are also told that from the time of their arrival in Missouri until their expulsion, they had paid to the United States government, for land alone, three hundred and eighteen thousand dollars. At the minimum price of one dollar and a quarter per acre this would give them over two hundred and fifty thousand acres, for the most of which they still hold the patents. [1] This is certainly a very favorable showing, but it is only one side of the

[1] *Discourse by President George A. Smith*, delivered in the New Tabernacle, Salt Lake City, July 25, 1869.

story. On the other hand, they are represented, and no doubt with some degree of truth, as having been ignorant, bigoted, and arrogant, easily led by the designing and unscrupulous men whom their very prosperity had attracted, and not overly observant of the rights of their neighbors. Preaching and believing, or affecting to believe, that " the Lord had given the earth and the fullness thereof to his people," and that they were his people, bands of the more lawless among them are said to have spent their time strolling about the country, helping themselves to whatsoever they pleased and otherwise spoiling the Egyptians, or in their more homely phrase, " milking the Gentiles." As they were largely in the majority, and the county officers were of their way of thinking on this point, they were not interfered with " until their lawless course excited the indignation of the Gentile settlers, who, not being able to obtain justice in a lawful manner, resorted to violence and retaliation in kind, until many a dark and unlawful deed was perpetrated on both sides." [1]

In this condition of thinly disguised hostility, matters remained until 1838, when the Mormons began to resist by force what they were pleased to term the attacks of the mob, but which, according to Gentile authority, were nothing more than the efforts of a sheriff's posse to execute the duly authorized processes of the courts. This of course placed the Mormons in the wrong, and gave Governor Boggs the opportunity, which he promptly seized, of calling out the militia for the purpose of putting down the insurrection and enforcing the laws. Under his proclamation a large body of troops entered

[1] Switzler, in the *Commonwealth of Missouri*, p. 244. St. Louis, 1877.

Caldwell county, and after a skirmish at Haughn's mill, which seems to have been rather a butchery, the Mormons were obliged to give up their arms and agree to leave the State, except their leaders, who were to be surrendered for trial. These conditions were certainly very hard, but they were the best that could be obtained; and if we may credit Mormon writers, it was owing to the determined stand of Alexander W. Doniphan that they were not more rigorous. As it was, the scenes that took place when the time came for carrying out these terms are said to have beggared description. The season was already far advanced, transportation was totally insufficient, and yet notwithstanding these silent appeals for delay some thousands [1] of these unfortunate creatures of all ages, sizes, conditions, and of both sexes were driven from their homes, and compelled to cross almost the entire northern part of the State before they could hope to find a resting place. As a rule, they were poor, had nothing but the small farms from which they were driven, but such was the pressure put upon them, or their anxiety to get away, that not infrequently "a valuable farm was traded for an old wagon, a horse, a yoke of oxen, or anything that would furnish them with the means of leaving." To take advantage of the necessities of a people so situated, even when their misfortunes were brought about by their own misdeeds, was certainly bad enough; but what adds immeasurably to the shame of the transaction is the fact that there are

---

[1] In the *Succinct History* the number of refugees is given at fifteen thousand; Switzler, on the other hand, p. 249, tells us that "at this time there were about 5,000 inhabitants in Caldwell county, nearly 4,000 being Mormons, most of whom went to Nauvoo, Illinois."

grounds for believing that not a little of the intolerance shown on this occasion may have been due to a desire on the part of the Gentiles to get possession of the Mormons' land. At least, this is the not unnatural inference from the statement made, not by one of themselves, but by a gentleman who has enjoyed exceptional advantages for acquainting himself with the facts of the case, and who tells us that "in many instances conveyances of land were demanded and enforced at the mouth of a pistol or rifle."[1]

With the leaders who were held for trial nothing was ever done, though they were indicted for treason, murder, robbery, arson, resisting legal process, and almost all the other crimes known to the calendar. In removing them to Boone, to which county they had obtained a change of venue, Joseph Smith escaped, by bribing the guards say the Gentiles, or, possibly, as the Mormons assert, by the connivance of the state authorities. One or two of the others were brought to trial, and after an impartial hearing, in which they were defended by General Doniphan, and James S. Rollins of Boone, they were acquitted. In view of this decision, the prosecuting attorney for that district wisely determined to dismiss the indictments against the others, and at the August term of the court, 1840, they were discharged from custody.

Immediately on their release they repaired to Hancock County, Illinois, where the other refugees from Missouri

[1] Switzler, in the *Commonwealth of Missouri*, p. 249. In the *Succinct History* we are told that "Several hundred persons were driven in a defenseless condition into a hollow square of armed fiends, and compelled to sign away their property to the republic of Missouri, to defray the expenses which had been incurred in committing these crimes."

had already established themselves. Here they were most hospitably received as their co-religionists had already been, for the Saints were looked upon as martyrs to their faith, and their sufferings had excited the sympathy of all, even of those who knew how incompatible were their social, political, and religious ideas and customs with the peace and welfare of the community in which they dwelt; but even here their stay was short. In June, 1844, less than four years after their expulsion from Missouri, Joseph Smith and Hyrum, his brother, prisoners in the hands of the law at Warsaw, Illinois, were shot down by a mob; and in 1846, the last of the Mormons were finally driven from Illinois, under circumstances that entailed heavier sacrifices and more suffering than had attended their enforced flight from Missouri.

Other measures there were of more or less importance which called for settlement during this most eventful period, and were, happily, free from the element of violence that characterized the treatment of Lovejoy and the Mormons. Prominent among them were the establishment of the State University, at Columbia, and the addition to the State of the triangle situated north of the Missouri, between that river and a continuation of the southern half of the western boundary line to the northern limits of the State. This region is popularly known as the Platte Purchase. It contains an area about equal in extent to that of Delaware, is of exceptional fertility, and has since been divided into six counties, one of which, Buchanan, is among the wealthiest and most populous in the State. In 1832, when the legislature first took definite action for the acquisition of this region, it belonged to the Sacs and Foxes, to

whom it had been granted in exchange for their possessions further to the eastward ; and hence before the proposed measure could be carried out, it became necessary
to abrogate the treaty with those tribes, — no very difficult matter so far as they were concerned and as such
affairs were usually managed. But besides this obstacle it involved a violation of the Missouri Compromise, as the whole of the coveted territory lay to the
north of the line of thirty-six degrees and thirty minutes ; and this, it would seem, ought to have been a more
serious consideration. Fortunately just at this time and
for a satisfactory reason, it was not as important for
the North to insist upon the sacredness of that compact as it afterwards became ; and consequently in 1836
a bill making this addition to the State was passed
through Congress without causing so much as a ripple
of excitement. Under its terms a treaty was made with
these Indians by which all this tract was relinquished to
the whites, and in 1837 it was formally annexed to the
State. In speaking of the legislation by which this was
brought about, Colonel Benton ignored his own services,
and in his large-hearted way was in the habit of giving
all the credit of the measure to his colleague, Senator
Lewis F. Linn. He also bore willing testimony to the
generosity and magnanimity of the Northern Congress-
men, without whose aid it could not have become a law.
To this award we do not object, though, possibly, our
admiration of the liberality of the Northern members
may be tempered by the reflection that, politically speaking, this concession to what is sometimes styled "the
slave power" cost them nothing. It did not and could
not add to the voting strength of the South in the Senate, the only place where the numerical superiority of

the North was in the least danger ; and it is probably safe to say that the representatives from that section, in permitting the bill to pass, were influenced by this consideration quite as much as they were by feelings of generosity, or by the personal popularity of Dr. Linn, great as that deservedly was. To have acted otherwise would have been, on their part, a useless and aggravating exhibition of strength on a point which, practically, could neither injure them nor benefit their opponents ; and as such a display was not called for, either as a matter of principle or policy, they wisely kept out of a contest in which they had nothing to gain. Had the circumstances been changed and the stake been worth fighting for, the result would perhaps have been different ; for whatever may have been the shortcomings of the Northern members of Congress in other respects, they were never in the habit of wasting their strength upon idle issues, nor did they fall into the error of mistaking the shadow for the substance when a question arose involving the possession of political power.

Turning now from individual business troubles and matters of purely local concern to subjects of national interest, the people of Missouri and of the country at large found abundant occupation during the next few years in dealing with questions that were connected, directly or indirectly, with the hard times of 1837. The presidential election of 1840, as we have seen, turned largely upon this issue ; and though the Whigs were successful in the contest, yet, owing to the death of their candidate in one short month after his inauguration, and to the treachery, as they termed it, of Vice-President Tyler, who succeeded him, they failed to reap the reward of their hard-earned victory. Indeed, if we except the protective tariff of 1842, of which he approved, Mr. Tyler, in his administration of affairs, may be said to have followed the policy outlined by his Democratic predecessor. Not only was this true of the financial legislation of this period, but it also held good in relation to the management of foreign affairs, and especially in regard to the annexation of Texas — the one measure that has given to this otherwise uneventful administration a right to the memorable place in American history which it unquestionably holds.

CHAPTER X.

THE ANNEXATION OF TEXAS AND THE CONQUEST OF NEW MEXICO.

In the question of the annexation of Texas, the people of Missouri were deeply interested; and as it was the immediate cause of the war with Mexico, in which they played a most important part, it may not be out of place to take a rapid glance at some of the causes that brought it about. And first of all it must be premised that it was not a new measure broached now for the first time and as the result of a deep laid conspiracy for the increase of slave territory, but on the contrary, it was the outcome of forces which were perfectly natural, which are constantly at work among all strong, colonizing nations, and which were shared to a very great extent by the people of the whole country, North as well as South. For twenty years, in fact ever since John Quincy Adams, acting under the instructions of President Monroe, but in opposition to his own better judgment, had concluded the treaty by which all the vast tract of country, now known as Texas, was handed over to Spain in exchange for the Floridas, the policy of the United States, it mattered not which political party happened to be in the ascendant, had been to recover it, whenever it could be done on satisfactory terms. To this end, Adams, on more than one occasion during the four years that he was at the head of affairs, endeavored to buy it back, either in whole or in part; and later, Jackson and Van Buren both made ineffectual efforts in the same direction. Nothing daunted by these repeated failures, Tyler took up the good work; and it was in 1844, during the closing year of his administration, that a treaty of annexation was made with Texas, the rejection of which by the United States Senate led to the adoption of a joint resolution by Congress for the admission of that State into the Union and thus paved the way to the Mexican war.

During all these years, affairs in the Spanish American provinces had not been at a standstill. In 1824, Mexico revolted from Spain, and in 1836, Texas, following the example thus set her, declared herself independent of Mexico. Of the causes that prompted her to this course it is not my place to speak. All that it concerns us to know is that on the bloody field of San Jacinto she showed, beyond the possibility of a doubt, that she was abundantly able to maintain her position, and that in consequence of the signal victory which she gained on this occasion her independence was recognized by the United States. This action, it is true, has been criticised as being premature, and wanting in comity to a sister republic, but it was in accordance with the traditional policy of the government; and its propriety can hardly be questioned in view of the fact that England and France made haste to do the same thing, and that Mexico was never in a position to reassert her authority over any portion of the revolted province by force of arms — the only way in which such an assertion could have been made effectual.

Being thus left to herself, with her independence acknowledged by three of the leading powers of the world, and with no enemy strong enough to dispute her right to self-government, it was certainly competent for Texas to enter into any engagements that she might think conducive to her future welfare, and with any power with which she might see fit to treat. It was a matter in which she possessed freedom of action by virtue of her position as a sovereign State ; and as the United States had recognized her right to this position when they acknowledged her independence in 1837, it followed necessarily that there was no valid reason, either in law or morals, why they should not become a party to any such treaty, provided they chose to do so. Accordingly, when, in 1844, the treaty of annexation came before the Senate of the United States for ratification, the question to be decided was not one of international morality, for that had been settled some seven years before, but of expediency, and of this they were the sole judges. In other words, they were called upon to say whether the acquisition of the magnificent empire which they were then offered was worth the war which Mexico had foolishly threatened [1] in the event of its acceptance, and the internal struggle and consequent strain upon the Union which the acquisition of additional slave territory would inevitably cause. Other objections there may have been, of more or less weight, but these were the chief, and it may be added that they were decisive, for in April of this year the treaty was

[1] On the 3d of November, 1843, General Almonte, the Mexican minister in Washington, notified the state department that if the United States should commit the " inaudito atentado " of appropriating to themselves an integral portion of the Mexican territory, he would demand his passports, and his country would declare war. Bancroft, *History of the Pacific States,* vol. viii. p. 335. San Francisco, 1885.

rejected by a vote of 35 to 16, a number of those who were in favor of annexation voting against the treaty on account of certain objectionable features which it contained.

This action of the Senate, while it effectually disposed of this particular measure, was so far from putting a stop to the agitation for the acquisition of Texas that it merely transferred it to another and a larger field. It now became the principal issue in the presidential election that came off a few months later ; and it was, no doubt, the position of seeming hostility to this measure which Clay, as leader of the Whigs, was made to assume that led to his defeat and the success of the Democrats. Instead of coming out openly in favor of the acquisition of this region, as from his course in 1819, and again in 1837, it was to have been expected that he would do, he seems to have been driven by the logic of events into a position in which it became necessary to sacrifice something of his freedom of opinion to the necessities of his party, and to what he certainly believed to be the good of the country at large. Thus, for example, when questioned as to his views upon this subject, he answered that, " so far from having any personal objection to the annexation of Texas, he would be glad to see it, without dishonor, without war, with the common consent of the Union, and upon just and fair terms." He also added that he did not think that " the subject of slavery ought to affect the question one way or the other." That he was sincere in returning this Delphic answer, and that his course was dictated by praiseworthy motives, do not admit of a doubt. As an abstract proposition he would unquestionably have been in favor of annexation, as would nine tenths of the people of his State and of the South and West; but during his entire career, devotion to the Union had been his controlling principle of action, and so great was his dread of the consequences that would follow the acquisition of additional slave territory that he was betrayed into a position which committed him to nothing definite, and which, perhaps for this very reason, weakened him in the South and West, whilst it failed to strengthen him in the North. Polk, on the other hand, the Democratic candidate, was pledged to immediate annexation, and his friends were united and aggressive. They knew what they wanted, and as there were no considerations of party policy to qualify their action, they were at liberty to work for it determinedly and with enthusiasm. In the end they were successful, as they deserved to be, whether the cause for which they contended be judged upon its merits, or whether we simply take into consideration the frankness with which they avowed their purpose and the energy with which they carried on the contest.

In this election the people of Missouri, by a very decided majority, recorded their votes in favor of the policy of annexation and against the great Kentuckian, though, in 1824, they had given the electoral vote of the State first to him, and then to the younger Adams, whose election was thus secured. In pursuing this course they were actuated by the sentiment of national pride which finds its expression in the spread of American ideas and institutions, and they were also largely influenced by that faith in themselves and in the future of their country which led them to look upon it as the "manifest destiny" of every contiguous bit of territory to gravitate, sooner or later, into the Union. These sentiments were more or less general, and though by a sort of poetic license they are sometimes said to have been due to the Viking blood that is supposed to course through the veins of every Anglo-American, yet, in reality, under the less attractive name of a passion for territorial aggrandizement, they are common to every growing power, to whatever race it may belong. They are also sufficient, when taken in connection with the sympathy that was felt for the cause of Texas and the horror inspired by the massacres of defenseless prisoners at Goliad and the Alamo, to account for the movement on the part of the people of the Southwest to throw a protecting shield over their weaker neighbor, without attributing their conduct to any such recondite motive as a desire to increase the voting strength of their section by the acquisition of territory which might be ultimately cut up into slave States. This is, no doubt, contrary to the impression that has been assiduously propagated, and possibly, in regard to a few extremists from the far South, the statement may not hold good, but with these exceptions it is believed to be substantially true. Certainly, so far as the people of Missouri were concerned, the extension of the slave area was so little thought of at this time that but for the prominence given to it by the opponents of annexation, it would not have entered into their calculations. Upon this point there is not room for an argument. The recollection of the fierce struggle that had attended the admission of Missouri into the Union, not less than the necessities of her position on the border line between freedom and slavery, had inspired her people with a healthy spirit of conservatism ; and although they had very decided ideas as to the propriety and expediency of " recovering "

Texas, yet they were not prepared to do so in the interest or at the behest of the so-called slave power, if by so doing they were to endanger the stability of the Union. This position they made manifest in a series of resolutions, which was adopted by the legislature for the guidance of their members of Congress, and which was laid before the Senate at Washington, in February, 1845. In it, they express the opinion that the decision of the question as to the existence of slavery " ought to be left to the people who now, or may hereafter, occupy the territory that may be annexed ;" but at the same time they declare that " so essential do they regard the annexation of Texas to the interests of the State and of the United States that, rather than fail in the consummation of this object, they will consent to such just and reasonable compromises . . . as may be indispensably necessary to secure the accomplishment of the measure and preserve the peace and harmony of the Union." In sentiments like these all true patriots can unite, and it would have been well for the peace of the country if they had been more general. They indicate a proper appreciation of the principle of concession which is necessary to the success of representative government, and they breathe a spirit of moderation and loyalty that is in refreshing contrast to the threats of disunion in which at this time, Massachusetts, not less than South Carolina, so freely indulged, provided their respective ideas were not carried out.

But besides the desire for territorial increase and the interest which they, not unnaturally, felt in the effort of their neighbors to maintain their independence, the people of Missouri were closely connected with those of Texas by ties of blood ; and it was the fact of this kinship, the actual personal interest which it gave them in the individual well-being of their friends and relatives over the border, that largely influenced their action at this time, just as during the earlier years of the struggle with Mexico it had led them to make the cause of Texas their own. To understand how this close relationship had grown up, it is necessary to bear in mind that soon after the treaty which gave Spain the undisputed possession of all this region, emigration began to flow into it from Missouri. The stream was never, perhaps, very strong, at least not when compared with the current of population that poured into the older State, but it was steady, and for twenty years or more it rolled in without let or hindrance. At first, these emigrants were drawn thither by the boundless " range " which the plains of Texas promised ; and it may well be that not a few of them, as for instance the Austins, Browns, and others, were attracted by the stories with which they must have been familiar of " the happy days " when, under Spanish rule, land could be had for the asking and taxes were unknown. At all events, similar inducements had brought their fathers across the Mississippi into what was then Spanish Louisiana ; and as they are quite sufficient to account for the desire which, we are told,[1] prevailed among the Missourians of that day to emigrate to Texas, it will not be necessary to seek further for the explanation of a movement which any one familiar with border life will recognize as being perfectly natural.

[1] " It is curious to observe with how much ardor they recur to the recollection of those happy days. And these recollections are the cause that those people and their descendants have still a strong predilection for the French and Spanish governments, and one great reason of their wish to emigrate to Texas." — Flint's *Travels*, p. 209. Boston, 1826.

Some ten or fifteen years later, after the Texan struggle for independence had been begun and when it became evident that Mexico intended, if possible, to crush the movement by force of arms, a new and important element was introduced into the contest. The sympathy which the people of Missouri and the Southwest felt for their friends and relatives in Texas, and which had hitherto been theoretical rather than personal, now lost its passive character and became at once an active moving force. They could not look upon the people of Texas as strangers and foreigners, and it was impossible to sit quietly by and see them engaged in what appeared to be a hopeless struggle with a people of alien race. Accordingly when, in her hour of need, a cry went up from Texas for aid, it met with a quick and effectual response. " Blood " proved to be " thicker than water," and the recognition of this fact led, as it must always do with a people in whom the race feeling is as strong as it is among the Anglo-Americans, to results that can hardly be justified under the law of nations. International boundaries were overstepped as if they had been obsolete lines ; neutrality proclamations and hostile manifestoes were treated as so much waste paper, and, in short, the emigrant now moved with a musket in his hands instead of a plough. In company with their neighbors the people of Missouri had taken the matter into their own hands, and as individuals they did not hesitate to do that which was interdicted to them as a State, and from which in their national capacity they would probably have shrunk. Of the number of them that flocked into Texas during her colonial days and in the anxious years that preceded and followed her declaration of independence, it is impossible to form any-

thing like a correct idea, but it is probably within bounds
to assert that between 1822 and 1836 there were few
prominent Missouri families that were not at some time
represented in the life of the new State.

Such being the feeling in Missouri when the question
of the annexation of Texas became a living issue, the
result could not long be doubtful. Annexation was
carried by a majority of ten thousand against the strong-
est candidate the Whigs could put up, and it would have
been larger, had it not been for the well-settled belief
that Clay was at heart as much in favor of the measure
as was his Democratic opponent, and that really the only
difference between them on this point was in the way in
which they expected and desired to see it accomplished.
That this belief was not without a solid foundation was
shown by the action of Congress, which met in December,
1844, hard on the heels of the presidential election. It
was the same body that had rejected the treaty of annexation, and yet, at this session, they passed a joint
resolution which accomplished the same purpose in a far
more summary manner. On the 4th of July, 1845, Texas
acceded to the terms offered her, and in the December
following she was formally admitted into the Union by
an overwhelming vote, over two thirds of the members
of each house being in favor of the measure.

A few days after the adoption of the joint resolution,
in March, 1845, General Almonte, the Mexican minister
at Washington, closed his legation, as he had said he
would do, and in due time the American representative
at the city of Mexico received his passports. This was
certainly ominous, but President Polk, who was now in
power, unwilling to abandon all hopes of peace, proposed
through the American consul to send an envoy to Mexico,

clothed with powers to settle all the questions that were in dispute between the two countries. This proposition was at first favorably received, and John Slidell was sent out on that errand. He arrived at Vera Cruz in the following December, only to find that the policy of the Mexican authorities had undergone a change. They now refused to receive him, and in so doing they effectually shut the door upon all prospects of peace. Soon after, on the 24th of April, 1846, General Arista, the Mexican commander on the Texas border, notified General Taylor that he considered hostilities to have begun, and the next day the collision took place which gave occasion to the declaration on the part of Congress that "war existed by the act of Mexico."

Whether this war could have been averted by the adoption of some less summary method of annexation is a matter that may well be doubted. On more than one occasion Mexico had officially declared that the incorporation of Texas into the United States would be regarded as a cause of war, and there is no reason for supposing that she did not intend to abide by her declaration. At all events this is precisely what she did ; and, whatever may have been the provocation, it is clear that in the attack which her troops made upon Captain Thornton's small command near the town of Matamoras, but on the east side of the Rio Grande and therefore within the limits claimed by Texas, she committed the first overt act of the war.

When the news of this skirmish reached New Orleans, General E. P. Gaines, a veteran of the war of 1812, who was in command of that military department, became alarmed for the safety of General Taylor's army and made a requisition upon several of the neighboring States for volunteers, in addition to the four regiments asked for by Taylor himself from Texas and Louisiana respectively. Missouri was one of the States thus called upon, and so prompt was her response that, in two weeks from the receipt of the governor's order in St. Louis, a regiment six hundred and fifty strong was on its way to the seat of war. They did not remain long in the field, nor did they see any actual service ; for General Gaines' course was disavowed at Washington, and as the troops raised under his call, owing to the short time for which they were enlisted, were an embarrassment rather than an assistance, they were disbanded and sent home at the end of three months.

With the return of this regiment and its discharge from the service, Missouri's part in the military operations along this portion of the frontier was brought to a close. Her troops were needed in another field, and to this end they were ordered to rendezvous at Fort Leavenworth, a government post on the western border of the State, where a force was being assembled preparatory to a march on New Mexico and California. This little band, known by the pretentious name of the "Army of the West," consisted of one regiment of horse, one battalion of infantry and one of artillery, all volunteers, with six companies — about three hundred — of the first (regular) dragoons, the whole amounting to some sixteen hundred and fifty men. With the exception of the regulars all of these troops were from Missouri, their commander, Colonel, afterwards General Kearney, himself, being a citizen of the State. In the latter part of June, 1846, they set out from Fort Leavenworth, and taking the well known "Santa Fé trail" they reached that town on the 18th of August, having made the journey of nine hundred miles through an uninhabited region in less than fifty days, and with but little loss in men or animals, though there were times when they suffered for want of water and from a scarcity of provisions. Upon their approach Governor Armijo abandoned the place and retreated southwards, — the result, it is said, of an intrigue in which he and Don Diego Archuleta, his second in command, were bribed, — so that when the Americans arrived before the town they had nothing to do but to enter and take possession. This they did, " without firing a gun or shedding a drop of blood."

Compared with the storming of Monterey or the capture of the city of Mexico, the unresisted occupation of this village can hardly be called a brilliant achievement; and yet in the end it led to results that have proved to be quite as momentous, and far more permanent, than any that followed those successes, signal as they were. At that date Santa Fé proper contained a population of about three thousand souls, who lived in badly furnished houses, built of adobe, in the usual New Mexican fashion, and only one story high. Poor and mean as the village was, it had a certain importance, growing out of the circumstance that for twenty years or more it had been the *entrepôt* of the overland trade with Missouri, and a sort of distributing point for all the goods imported into this and the neighboring departments of northern Mexico. From a small beginning in 1822 this trade had gone on, increasing year by year, until in 1843 it was estimated at four hundred and fifty thousand dollars, necessitating the employment of two hundred and thirty wagons and three hundred and fifty men. Even in 1845, after the adoption of the joint resolution for the annexation of Texas, and when the relations between the United States and Mexico were consequently in a high state of tension, the value of the goods brought into Santa Fé over this route is said to have been about three hundred and fifty thousand dollars; and it is a curious fact, indicative perhaps of the sentiments with which the merchants, native as well as foreign, regarded the occupation of this department, that there was at this time a large caravan of traders' wagons, following in the wake of the American troops.

Aside from the importance which this place possessed as a port of entry, it was the political capital of the department, which is divided into two parts by the Rio Grande. It was also situated some miles to the eastward of this stream and therefore within the limits claimed by Texas, though in justice it must be admitted that she had never been able to extend her sway thus far, the effort which she made in 1841 to do so having resulted in a disastrous failure.

On the day after he took possession of Santa Fé, General Kearney issued a proclamation, in which, among other things, he absolved the people of New Mexico from all allegiance to their constituted authorities,' and by a stroke of the pen transformed them into citizens of the United States. This was certainly a very high-handed measure; but it were easily defended, if, as was the case with the proclamation issued August 2d from Bent's Fort, its effect had been limited to so much of the department as was situated east of the Del Norte, as the Rio Grande is here called, though the ultimate ownership of the tract would have depended upon the fate of the war. General Kearney, however, was not disposed to wait upon the slow march of military events, nor did he have the slightest intention of abandoning one foot of the territory upon which he had seized. So far was he from it that on the 22d of August, only three days after the officials at Santa Fé had been required to take the oath of allegiance to the United States, he announced his purpose of holding the entire department " with its original boundaries (on both sides of the Del Norte) ; " and as if to to leave no doubt as to his intentions, he caused a constitution and code of laws to be prepared which changed New Mexico, in name and in fact, from a province of Mexico into a territory of the United States.

In seeking for the authority under which Kearney acted in making these radical changes, we are obliged to fall back upon the confidential instructions sent him June 3, 1846, though, carefully worded and elastic as they are, they can hardly be said to justify his course. Unquestionably, they authorize him to take possession of New Mexico and " establish a temporary civil government therein ; " and there can be no doubt that they also require him to assure the people of this province that " it is the wish and design of the United States to provide for them a free government . . . similar to that which exists in our territories ; " but beyond this they do not go. Nowhere, not even by implication, do they confer upon him the power to annex this or any other region that he might conquer. Indeed, it could not well have been otherwise, for this was a power which the President himself did not possess, and which, consequently, he could not delegate to another. But whilst this is clear, it is difficult to believe that Kearney, soldier that he was and therefore accustomed to obey orders, would, in a matter of this importance, have taken the responsibility of acting as he did, unless he had been assured of sympathy and support from Washington. Of course, this is conjecture and must be taken for what it is worth, though it is but fair to add that it receives a certain amount of confirmation from the fact that President Polk, when communicating the account of these proceedings to Congress, refers to what, he says, may have been "the exercise of an excess of power," and excuses it on the ground that it was "the offspring of a patriotic desire to give to the inhabitants the privileges and immunities so cherished by the people of our own country."

However, let the responsibility for this wholesale seizure of foreign territory be where it may, it is very evident that Kearney was never troubled by any doubts as to what was required of him. On the contrary, he always moved resolutely, without hesitation, and as if sure of his ground. When the constitution and laws, the preparation of which had been committed to Colonel Doniphan and Private W. P. Hall, of the Missouri volunteers, were submitted to him, he at once ordered them to be promulgated and obeyed ; and on the very same day he completed the civil organization of the territory by the appointment of another Missourian, Charles Bent, of Bent's Fort, as governor, with a full complement of judges and other officials, among whom we recognize the well-known name of Francis P. Blair, Jr., as attorney general. Having thus set the wheels of government in motion, he felt that his work in New Mexico was done, and on the 25th of September, but little more than a month from the date of his arrival at Santa Fé, he set out for California.

On the 26th, the day after his departure, Colonel Sterling Price, of the 2d Missouri mounted volunteers, arrived in Santa Fé and relieved Colonel Doniphan, who began to prepare for his march on Chihuahua, where it was supposed he would find General Wool, to whom he had been ordered to report. Before he was ready to move, the Navajo Indians had become so troublesome that an order was sent back by General Kearney, directing him to march against them and put a stop to their depredations. Dividing his command, he sent a column under Major Gilpin up the Chama and across the mountains into the valley of the little Colorado; with another he marched up the valley of the Puerco; while a third party, numbering only thirty men, under command of Captain John W. Reid, took a middle route and thus penetrated into the very heart of the Indian country. By means of these several expeditions all the different bands of the Navajos were visited, and it resulted in bringing a large number of their chiefs and warriors to the Ojo del Oso, — Bear Spring, — a well-known watering-place sixty miles northwest of Zuni and not far from the Moqui villages. Here the council was held and peace was finally concluded, though Colonel Doniphan seems to have had some difficulty in making the Navajos understand how it was that he now appeared as the defender of the people whom he had come out to fight. Thus, when the Navajos were told that they would no longer be permitted to continue their hostile incursions into the territory, one of their chiefs is said to have answered: "Americans, you have a strange cause of war against the Navajos. We have waged war against the New Mexicans for several years. We have plundered their villages, and killed many of their people, and made many prisoners. We had just cause for all this. You have lately commenced a war against the same people. You are powerful. You have great guns and many brave soldiers. You have therefore conquered them, the very thing we have been attempting to do for so many years. You now turn upon us for attempting to do what you have done yourselves. We cannot see why you have cause of quarrel with us for fighting the New Mexicans on the west, while you do the same thing on the east. Look how matters stand. This is our war. We have more right to complain of you for interfering in our war, than you have to quarrel with us for continuing a war we had begun long before you got here. If you will act justly, you will allow us to settle our own differences."

In reply to this statement, which is not without its force, Colonel Doniphan explained that the "New Mexicans had surrendered; that the whole country and everything in it had become ours; that when the Indians now *stole* property from the New Mexicans they were stealing from us; and that when they killed them they were killing our people, and that this could not be suffered any longer." Satisfied with this explanation, or, as is far more probable, intimidated by the display of force and the energy with which the Americans had followed them over snow - covered regions into their mountain fastnesses, the Navajos agreed to a treaty of peace, which, by a special article, was made to include the New Mexicans and also the Pueblo Indians.

Having arranged this matter satisfactorily, Colonel Doniphan was now at liberty to take up his line of march for Chihuahua, and, accordingly, he retraced his steps to the valley of the Del Norte, where he established his headquarters at the town of Valverde, which had been made the depot for his supplies and the rendezvous for the different detachments of his regiment. Here the weary soldiers were allowed a few days of rest, before they were called upon to start on that long and toilsome march which, beginning with Chihuahua as the objective point, only ended on the shores of the Mexican gulf. On the 14th of December, all things being in readiness, the first battalion, consisting of three hundred men under Major Gilpin, set out, the regiment moving in separate divisions for the convenience of crossing the *Jornada del muerto*, a sandy waste of ninety miles, without wood or water. On the 16th Lieutenant Colonel Jackson followed with two hundred men, and on the 19th Doniphan brought up the rear with the rest of the regiment, the principal part of the baggage train, and Lieutenant Colonel Mitchell and ninety men of the 2d Missouri — Price's regiment. A hard march of three days brought them across the desert, and on the 22d the command was concentrated at the little village of Donna Ana, where they found an abundance of supplies of all kinds, with streams of running water. Continuing their journey down the valley, they came, on the afternoon of the 25th, — Christmas Day, — to a place called Bracito ("little arm" of the river), where they pitched their camp and began to make themselves comfortable for the night. Whilst they were scattered about, engaged in gathering forage for their horses, and fuel and water for their own needs, they were attacked by a superior force of Mexicans, nearly half of which was cavalry. Rapidly forming on foot, the Americans held their fire until the enemy came within easy range, when they opened upon them with destructive effect. At the same time Captain Reid, who had succeeded in mounting some fifteen or twenty of his men, broke through the Mexican ranks and threw them into confusion. In less than half an hour the skirmish was over and the Mexicans were in full retreat, " leaving sixty-three killed, one hundred and fifty wounded, and one howitzer, the only piece of artillery in the engagement on either side." The loss of the Americans was eight wounded, none killed.

Resuming their march, the Americans entered El Paso on the 27th without opposition, and there they learned from prisoners and others of the change that had been made in General Wool's movements, and that so far from being in possession of the city of Chihuahua he had not even " marched upon the state." This was not very encouraging, but Doniphan determined to press on, though Chihuahua was still two hundred and twenty-five miles distant, and not a little of the route lay through a desert waste. Under the circumstances, he did not think it prudent to adventure further without artillery, and he ordered down from Santa Fé Captain Weightman's company, with a battery of six guns, under command of Major M. L. Clark.

This involved a delay of some weeks, but the 8th of February found him once more on the march, at the head of nine hundred and twenty-four effective men, and singularly enough with a caravan of over three hundred traders' wagons, which he was supposed to be escorting. On the 28th, at the pass of the Sacramento, fifteen miles from Chihuahua, " the enemy was discovered strongly posted on high ground, fortified by entrenchments and well supplied with artillery." After an effective cannonade, Colonel Doniphan advanced to the attack with seven dismounted companies in line and three mounted ; but the battle was decided by the charge of two twelve-pound howitzers, under Captain Weightman, supported by the cavalry and followed up by the dismounted troops and the rest of the artillery. In this charge the howitzers were not unlimbered until they were within fifty yards of the enemy's redoubts, and the cavalry riding up to the brink of the entrenchments drove the Mexican gunners from their pieces. Unable to withstand this onset, the Mexicans retreated, closely followed by the Americans, until night put an end to the conflict. In this engagement the Mexicans had about four thousand men, of whom some fifteen hundred were rancheros, badly armed with lassos, lances, and *machetes* or corn-knives, and their loss is given at three hundred killed, as many wounded, and forty prisoners. The Americans, as has been said, had nine hundred and twenty-four effective men, to which number must be added two companies of teamsters, under Samuel C. Owens, of Missouri, and a few amateur soldiers, which carried the total force up to eleven hundred and sixty-four men. Of this number but one, Owens, was killed, though eleven were wounded, three of whom subsequently died.

On the 1st of March, 1847, the day after the battle, Doniphan took possession of Chihuahua, and here he remained until the 28th of April, when, in obedience to orders from General Taylor, he set out for Saltillo and Matamoras, nine hundred miles distant, but not until he had provided, as far as it was possible to do so, for the safety of the traders whom he now left behind. The march to Saltillo was a hard one owing to the want of transportation and the scarcity of water, but it was successfully accomplished, and would, perhaps, have passed without incident had it not been for the severe punishment which Captain Reid and a detachment of thirty-five Americans inflicted upon a marauding band of Indians at the request of the people of Parras, and in grateful recognition of the kindness which they had shown to the sick of General Wool's command. Take it all in all, this rescue of eighteen Mexican boys and girls from a captivity worse than death by a party of Missouri troopers was a novel and pleasing episode ; and as it was, in its origin and ending, as creditable to the Mexicans as to the Americans, and was, moreover, a fair illustration of Western character, it is here given in the words of Jose Ignacio Arabe, the prefect of Parras. Under date of May 18th he thus addresses Captain Reid : —

"At the first notice that the barbarians, after killing many and taking captives, were returning to their haunts, you generously and bravely offered . . . to fight them on their crossing by the Pozo, executing this enterprise with celerity, address, and bravery worthy of all eulogy, and worthy of the brilliant issue which all celebrate. You recovered many animals and much plundered property, and eighteen captives were restored to liberty and to social enjoyments, their souls overflowing with a lively sentiment of joy and gratitude which all the inhabitants of this town equally breathe in favor of their generous deliverers and their valiant chief. The half of the Indians killed in the combat, and those which fly wounded, do not calm the pain which all feel for the wound which Your Excellency received defending Christians and civilized beings against the rage and brutality of savages. All desire the speedy reëstablishment of your health, and although they know that in your own noble soul will be found the best reward of your conduct, they desire also to address you the expression of their gratitude and high esteem. I am honored in being the organ of the public sentiment, and pray you to accept it, with the assurance of my most distinguished esteem."

On the 22d of May the Missourians, "rough, ragged, and ready," reached General Wool's lines near Saltillo; and the next day, as the term of their enlistment was rapidly drawing to a close and there was no prospect of further need of their services, Captain Weightman turned over the battery which he had so worthily commanded to the officer who was appointed to receive it. The ten guns which had been captured at Sacramento were, by permission of General Taylor, conveyed to Missouri and deposited with the state authorities at Jefferson City, subject to the action of the War Department at Washington.

Leaving Saltillo, the Missourians proceeded by relatively slow and easy marches to Brazos Island, at the mouth of the Rio Grande, where they arrived on the 9th of June; and the following day they embarked for New Orleans and home. With their arrival on the shores of the gulf this extraordinary march came to an end. Including the Navajo expedition, it had extended over a distance of three thousand miles, through an uninhabited or a hostile country, often without water or supplies of any kind; and it had been made in the face of difficulties which tested to the utmost the endurance of those who took part in it. That they were able to accomplish it with a loss of less than fifty men, counting those who fell in the sharply contested action at Sacramento, speaks volumes for the material of the command, and justly entitled them to the enthusiastic welcome which they received on their return. Considered, however, as a factor in the military problem, assuming this to have been the capture of the city of Mexico, the work performed

by this column loses much of its importance, owing to
the adoption of the route by way of Vera Cruz instead
of that by way of Zacatecas and San Luis Potosi, over
which Taylor had proposed to advance ; but if we estimate it by its final results, we shall have to admit that
the conquest and occupation of New Mexico simplified
the task of the American commissioner when negotiating
the treaty of Guadalupe Hidalgo, and made it possible
for him so to perfect the title to the territory which we
then gained that, compared with that by which Germany
now holds Alsace and Lorraine, it may be said to be
without a flaw either in law or morals.

But whilst we have been following the march of
Doniphan and his men, New Mexico was the scene
of a bloody uprising, which led to the death of Governor Charles Bent, and threatened the supremacy of
the Americans.   Benton tells us that it was due to the
machinations of a certain Diego Archuleta, the second
in command under Governor Armijo, and intimates
that Archuleta's course was dictated by the conviction
that he had been cheated in the intrigue to which he
is said to have been a party, by virtue of which he
was to have been permitted to make himself master of
so much of the province as lay to the west of the Rio
Grande, in consideration of the surrender of Santa Fé
to the Americans.   So far as Archuleta was concerned
this may well have been true.   Certainly, if the story
of the intrigue be accepted, and if, furthermore, it be
admitted that he was led to believe that Magoffin, who
seems to have been the tempter in this case, was acting
by the authority of the United States, it will be easy to
understand why, having fulfilled his part of the iniquitous bargain, he should have regarded Kearney's procla-

mation annexing the whole of New Mexico as an attempt to get rid of him without paying him for his services. But even if all this were true, we must not forget that Archuleta was only one of the prime-movers in this revolt, and apparently not the ruling spirit among them; and base and sordid as may have been the motives that governed his conduct, there is not the slightest ground for supposing that the co-conspirators were influenced by any such considerations. Their course may have been dictated by high patriotic motives. In fact the evidence all seems to point that way, for Colonel Price, of the 2d Missouri, who was left in command of the troops stationed in the territory, writing under date of July, 1847, speaks of "the deadly hostility" with which the New Mexicans regarded the Americans, and it is not probable that the feeling was any less bitter in the months immediately succeeding the occupation, or whilst the so-called revolt was in progress.

Under any circumstances the dismemberment of a nation or the forcible annexation of one people by another, especially when they differ in race and religion, is not a gentle process; and when it is attended, as was the case in the present instance, by radical changes in their mode of government and in their laws and customs, it inevitably gives rise to a deep-seated feeling of hostility which may be suppressed by the strong hand, but which only awaits a favorable opportunity to burst forth into acts of open, and, we may add, justifiable warfare. When an outbreak of this character is successful, or if, perchance, the story be told of ourselves, the movement is always ascribed to patriotic ardor; but if, on the other hand, it result in failure, or if we happen to be the sufferers, then it is characterized by other and less high-sounding terms. In a struggle of this kind, the losers, like the absent, are always in the wrong, and such seems to have been the case with the New Mexicans in the effort which they made to throw off the yoke that had been imposed on them. Evidently they had never accepted the situation, and although the conditions were not favorable to a reënactment on this distant field and at this late day of the "Sicilian Vespers," yet they gallantly made the attempt; and but for the promptness of the American commander in attacking the insurrectionary force before it had perfected its organization, the result might have been different.

According to the vague and somewhat incomplete accounts that have come down to us, the first mutterings of the storm were heard about the middle of December, only four months after the occupation of Santa Fé, during which period the plans of the conspirators had been so far matured that the 25th of the month, the day on which Doniphan fought the skirmish at Bracito, was chosen for the uprising. Colonel Price, however, had received an intimation of the impending danger, and he at once took measures to meet and counteract it. Several arrests were made, and for the time being the progress of the movement seemed to have been checked. The affair, however, had gone too far to admit of any other mode of settlement than by an appeal to the sword, and for this the Americans were not yet prepared. Indeed so secure did they feel that Governor Bent, on the 14th of January, 1847, left Santa Fé on a visit to his family at Taos, distant about seventy miles; and here he was when, on the 19th, a revolutionary force took possession of the place, and murdered him and several other government officials, among whom was Cornelio

Vigil, the prefect, a native of New Mexico. Similar outbreaks took place at Arroyo Hondo, Mora, and other places in this portion of the territory, during which a number of Americans, and of those who were supposed to be favorable to them, lost their lives.

The news of the uprising at Taos and the murder of Governor Bent was brought to Colonel Price on the day after it occurred, and he immediately sent orders to Major Edmonson of his regiment, at Albuquerque, to move up to Santa Fé and take command there, whilst he himself marched against the insurgents, who were reported to be advancing and rapidly gaining in strength. On the 23d, he set out at the head of only three hundred and fifty men, consisting in great part of the dismounted troopers of his own regiment, and on the next day he encountered the enemy near the village of Canada, where they were posted on heights commanding the road, and in some strong adobe houses at the foot of the hills. After a sharp skirmish, in which the brunt of the fight seems to have been borne by Captain Angney's battalion of (Missouri) infantry, and St. Vrain's company of volunteers from Santa Fé, the enemy were driven from every position, and retreated, leaving thirty-six of their number dead on the field, while the Americans had to lament the loss of two killed and seven wounded. Following up his success, Price reached Luceros on the 28th, where he was joined by Captain Burgwin, with one company of the first dragoons and a six-pound cannon. This increased the number of his available men to four hundred and eighty, and with this force he marched on Taos, whither the enemy fled after a second skirmish, which took place at Embudo. After a hard march of several days, during a portion of which the snow was so deep that the soldiers were obliged to break the way for the artillery and baggage wagons, he reached the village of San Fernando de Taos, through which he passed on his way to the pueblo of the same name, where the insurgents had taken refuge. This place was " inclosed by formidable walls and strong pickets, within which were two large buildings of irregular pyramidal form, seven or eight stories in height. Besides these dwelling-houses, each capable of sheltering five or six hundred men, there was a large church situated in the north-west angle of the inclosure, with a narrow passage between it and the outer wall." All these buildings were of adobe, — sun-dried bricks, — and it was no doubt owing to this fact, to the thickness of these walls, and to their singularly defensive form, pierced as they were for rifles, that the besieged were able to resist, during the better part of two days, an attack in which the guns, under Lieutenants Dyer (afterwards chief of ordnance) and Wilson, were served at unusually short range.

Into the details of this siege we do not propose to enter, though some idea may be formed of the difficulty of the undertaking and the obstinacy of the defense from the fact that at eleven o'clock on the morning of the second day, Price, finding that it was impossible to breach the walls of the church with his cannon, ordered the building to be stormed. At a given signal Captain Burgwin, with his own company and one of the 2d Missouri, " charged upon the western flank of the church ; " while Captain Angney, with his battalion of infantry and another company of the 2d Missouri, attacked the northern wall. As soon as the troops under Captain Burgwin had established themselves on their side of the church, they began to cut their way through the wall with axes.

After some hours of this kind of work, during which Capt. Burgwin was mortally wounded, " the six-pounder was run up within sixty yards of the church, and after ten rounds, one of the holes which had been cut with axes was widened into a practicable breach." Through this the stormers entered, and the building was carried without further resistance.

This virtually put an end to the conflict; for the enemy, in their haste to escape, either fled to the neighboring mountains, or took refuge in the large communal houses in other parts of the village. The next morning, in answer to their supplications, Colonel Price agreed to a peace on condition that they would deliver up Tomas, one of their leading men, who was said to have been actively engaged in the murder of Governor Bent. This was done, and Tomas was taken to San Fernando de Taos and confined in the guard-house, where he was shortly afterwards shot by a private soldier. The number of the enemy, Mexicans and Pueblo Indians, engaged in this battle was estimated by Colonel Price at between six and seven hundred, of whom one hundred and fifty were reported killed. On the side of the Americans the loss was seven killed and forty-five wounded, many of whom died.

With the fall of this pueblo the revolt may be said to have been brought to an end. Of those who were prominently concerned in it, a few died in action, while others, among whom was Archuleta, took time by the forelock and escaped. Fifteen, seven of whom were Pueblo Indians, were accused of treason, — a crime of which, under the circumstances, they could not have been guilty, — and having been tried and convicted by a court which had no jurisdiction in the matter, they were promptly executed. This was but little better than a judicial murder; and that such was the opinion of the cabinet at Washington is evident from the way in which President Polk treated those cases that were recommended to him for mercy. To have pardoned them would have been to acknowledge the legality of the sentence under which they were to suffer, while, on the other hand, to have refused to do so would have been to make himself, in a measure, responsible for the outrage upon law and justice by which they were condemned; and so, if we may trust Benton's account, he solved the difficulty by instructing the authorities in New Mexico quietly to turn them loose.

Notwithstanding the severity of the measures taken for the suppression of the uprising, affairs within the territory continued for some months to be in a very unsettled condition, and intercourse between Santa Fé and Missouri became very unsafe. Trains were captured and pillaged, distant grazing camps were attacked and the animals stampeded, and not unfrequently cases of the murder of isolated parties of Americans occurred. These outrages, it is true, were not the result of a concerted attempt on the part of the Mexicans to drive out the invaders, but were the work of individual bands of marauders, red as well as white, who were bent on robbery; and although the perpetrators when caught met with a short shrift, yet they were so numerous, and their depredations so daring, that, joined to the rumors of another insurrection and of the approach of a large hostile force from the South, Colonel Price was led, in the letter to which we have already referred, to ask for additional troops to take the place of those whose terms of service were about to expire.

These were promptly furnished, his call for reinforcements having been anticipated, and by autumn the available force in New Mexico was raised to three thousand men by the arrival of fresh regiments, which, with but one exception, were from Missouri. With this force, about twice as large as that which had originally taken possession of the province, Colonel or as he must now be called General Price, found no difficulty in restoring order and in maintaining the advantages which had already been gained. In an incredibly short time the people of New Mexico submitted to the situation, and the treaty of Guadalupe Hidalgo, concluded in February, 1848, so far from effecting any change in their condition, merely gave a legal sanction to what was an accomplished fact. New Mexico to all intents and purposes was already a territory of the United States; and if we except the few companies of the first dragoons, whose gallant services there is no wish to disparage, it was made so by Missouri volunteers. Of the seven thousand men whom she sent to the war, over six thousand were employed in the conquest and pacification of this province; and there can be no question that it was the thoroughness with which they did their work that made it relatively an easy matter for the Mexican authorities to part with all this region in return for the very handsome monetary consideration which they received.

CHAPTER XI.

THE acquisition of California and New Mexico was made the occasion for reviving the slavery issue, though it assumed a different form from that which it had worn in 1820, when the adoption of the Missouri Compromise put a stop, temporarily, to the agitation of the question. At that time, it will be remembered, slavery existed in all the territory west of the Mississippi owned by the United States ; and the effect of the compromise then adopted was to transform the northern portion of that vast region from possible slave to actual free territory. Now the conditions were reversed. California and New Mexico, so far as negro slavery was concerned, were free — made so by the law of Mexico ; and to extend the line of thirty-six degrees and thirty minutes north latitude through them and on to the Pacific Ocean, as the Southern representatives insisted upon doing, was to transfer the southern portions of those territories from actual freedom to possible slavery. In other words, in the one instance slavery was excluded from a region in which it legally existed, whilst in the other it was in contemplation to make it legally possible in territories where it had been prohibited by the laws of the country to which they had belonged. This a large majority of the people of the

North were anxious to prevent; and to this end they not only opposed the extension of the line of the Missouri Compromise into the newly acquired territories, but their representatives in Washington endeavored so to shape the action of Congress as to prohibit, by legislative enactments, the introduction of slavery into any part of this region.

To all such legislation the people of Missouri were opposed; not that they were necessarily in favor of the extension of the area of slavery, but for the reason that they either did not believe that Congress had the power, under the Constitution, to legislate upon the subject, or because, admitting that Congress had the power, they did not deem its exercise advisable, believing as they did that the people of a territory, when framing their State Constitution, ought to be left free to decide as to the institutions under which they were to live. Upon this point their ideas were very clear, and in January, 1849, the legislature of the State embodied them in a series of resolutions intended for the guidance of their members of Congress. In local history, these resolutions are known as the "Jackson resolutions" from the fact that Governor C. F. Jackson was chairman of the committee that reported them; though they were introduced into the Senate by Carty Wells, of Marion County, and were originally drawn up, so it was said, by Judge W. B. Napton, of the supreme court, a learned lawyer, an upright judge, and a most estimable citizen.

After a stormy debate, which was but a prelude to the heated political contest that was to follow, the entire series was adopted, the Whigs opposing, while the Democrats, who had a large majority in both branches of the General Assembly, were, with few exceptions, in favor of it. Notwithstanding the almost unanimous vote which they had given to these resolutions, the Democrats soon found that instead of being a bond of union and a source of strength, they were a cause of discord and an element of weakness. Benton, in open Senate, refused to be bound by them on the ground that, like Calhoun's resolutions, of which they were to some extent a copy, they contemplated secession and did not truly represent the opinions of the people of the State ; and it was this refusal that led to the split in his party and brought about his defeat after a service of thirty years in the Senate of the United States.

So far as these resolutions can be said to have threatened disunion, there can be no question that Benton was right, and that they did not reflect the sentiments of the people of the State ; but whether, admitting that they did contemplate secession, he was equally correct in charging that all who supported them were aiming at such a result is a point about which opinions may well differ. At this time there was probably not a handful of people in the State who believed that matters would ever be carried to such an extreme as to lead to secession ; and to understand these resolutions aright it is necessary to bear in mind that they are to be interpreted, not by the events which subsequently took place, but by the opinions that were current among those by whom they were adopted. Tried by this standard, the vague threat or warning which they contain may be said to have been a mere bit of stage thunder, meaning anything or nothing, according to the fancy of the person who used it, and therefore harmless so long as there was no attempt made to carry it into execution. Neither then, nor at any subsequent period, did any considerable number of the people of Missouri ever look to the secession of their State as a remedy for the injustice of which they felt they had a right to complain. Not even by the most ardent supporters of these resolutions was such an idea generally entertained; for among them are to be found not only some of those who afterwards followed the fortunes of Benton, but also others who, like Governor Robert M. Stewart, did what they could to defeat him, though when the crisis came, ten years later, they were among the stanchest defenders of the Union. But this is not a matter upon which it is necessary to enlarge. All that we are interested in knowing is that these resolutions proved to be the wedge that split the Democratic party, and gave the Whigs a Senator in place of Benton. For this reason, and because of the important part which they played in the political affairs of the State during the next few years, they are here given in full: —

"*Resolved by the General Assembly of the State of Missouri:* That the federal Constitution was the result of a compromise between the conflicting interests of the States which formed it, and in no part of that instrument is to be found any delegation of power to Congress to legislate on the subject of slavery, excepting some special provisions having in view the prospective abolition of the African slave trade and for the recovery of fugitive slaves. Any attempt, therefore, on the part of Congress to legislate on the subject, so as to affect the institution of slavery in the States, in the District of Columbia, or in the Territories, is, to say the least, a violation of the principles upon which that instrument was founded.

" 2. That the territories, acquired by the blood and treasure of the whole nation, ought to be governed for the common benefit of the people of all the States, and any organization of the territorial government, excluding the citizens of any part of the Union from removing to such territories with their property, would be an exercise of power by Congress inconsistent with the spirit upon which our federal compact was based, insulting to the sovereignty and dignity of the States thus affected, calculated to alienate one portion of the Union from another, and tending ultimately to disunion.

" 3. That this General Assembly regard the conduct of the Northern States on the subject of slavery as releasing the slaveholding States from all further adherence to the basis of compromise fixed on by the act of Congress of March 6, 1820, even if such act ever did impose any obligation upon the slaveholding States, and authorizes them to insist upon their rights under the Constitution ; but for the sake of harmony, and for the preservation of our federal Union, they will still sanction the application of the principles of the Missouri Compromise to the recent territorial acquisitions, if by such concession future aggressions upon the equal rights of the States may be arrested, and the spirit of anti-slavery fanaticism be extinguished.

" 4. That the right to prohibit slavery in any territory belongs exclusively to the people thereof, and can only be exercised by them in forming their constitution for a state government, or in their sovereign capacity as an independent State.

" 5. That in the event of the passage of any act of Congress conflicting with the principles herein expressed, Missouri will be found in hearty coöperation with the slaveholding States, in such measures as may be deemed necessary for our mutual protection against the encroachments of Northern fanaticism."

Leaving out of consideration the covert threat and the somewhat truculent language in which these resolutions are couched, and regarding slaves simply as property, as they were subsequently decided to be by the highest tribunal in the land, it is difficult to find anything in the positions here taken to which a fair-minded person can reasonably object. Benton, however, as has been said, refused to abide by them, and appealed from the legislature to the people of the State. His reasons have been briefly indicated, though it is proper to add that back of them, and lying far deeper, was his belief in the evil of slavery. Upon this point, his position cannot be mistaken ; and it is worthy of note that it was his conviction as to the difficulty of getting rid of the evil when it was once firmly established — a conviction shared by many thoughtful men in the State — that made him all the more determined in his opposition to any measure that made its extension possible. "The incurability of the evil," he said, on a subsequent occasion, "is the greatest objection to the extension of slavery. If it is wrong for the legislature to inflict an evil which can be cured, how much more to inflict one that is incurable and against the will of the people who are to endure it forever. I quarrel with no one for deeming slavery a blessing ; I deem it an evil, and would neither adopt it, nor impose it upon others." How the problem was finally to be solved in regions where slavery existed seemed to him, as he frankly confessed, to be beyond the reach of human wisdom; but, added he, " there is a wisdom above human, and to that we must look. In the mean time do not extend the evil."

This is certainly a strong presentation of the case ; and if it had been made in opposition to an attempt on the part of Congress to legislate slavery into a region where it had not previously existed, it would not have been easy to frame a satisfactory reply. But, in point of fact, Congress was not asked or expected to do anything of the kind. All that these resolutions demanded was that Congress should not interfere in the matter, save, perhaps, in the way of compromise. What was wanted was that the question should be left open, so that the people of the slaveholding States might go into any of the territories which they had helped to acquire, taking their slave property with them in case they so desired, upon the same footing as that upon which the people of the free North were permitted to move into these same territories with their horses, or any other articles of personal property that they might possess. Of course, in such an event it was possible that the people in some of these territories, when framing their state constitutions, might see fit to sanction slavery, though this was by no means certain. But even if it had been, it would hardly have afforded any just grounds for opposing the policy of " non-interference," as it was called, since the question was not whether Congress should or should not legislate slavery into the territories, but whether it should leave the people of each territory free to decide that matter for themselves. Between these two courses there was a wide difference ; and whilst in the former case Benton's argument would have been perfectly relevant, in the latter it was out of place, for the reason that there was no necessary connection between a desire to extend slavery into the new territories and a denial of the power of Congress to legislate upon the subject. Indeed, the very reverse of this was true, since it was possible to be a believer in the constitutionality of the doctrine of " non-interference," and to be opposed to the extension of the slave area. In other words, a person might be in favor of transforming a territory into a free State, when the time came to make the change, though he denied the power of Congress to prevent the introduction of slaves into that territory, as long as it remained in that condition. So far from involving any inconsistency, this position was perfectly logical; and as subsequent events abundantly showed, it was the position held by a large proportion of the people of the State, including some of those who voted for the resolutions, and who were known as anti-Benton Democrats, or " Softs."

Benton did not recognize this fact, or, what is far more probable, he did not think it necessary to take advantage of it; otherwise it would have been easy for him, without any very great sacrifice of opinion, so to shape his course as to conciliate those of the malcontents in his own party who, whilst differing with him as to the means by which they hoped to attain a certain end, fully agreed with him as to the end itself. Unfortunately for the success of his candidacy, a spirit of conciliation formed no part of Benton's disposition, and the experience of a quarter of a century and more, during which he had been the acknowledged leader of the party that controlled the political destinies of the State, had not been of such a character as to lead him to cultivate that virtue. Gifted with superb courage, physical as well as moral, and possessed of an imperious will, he was probably never more at home than when engaged in one of those fierce political contests in which quarter was neither given nor expected. In all such cases his practice had been to crush, not placate; and in the present instance his natural tendency to deal with his opponents in this summary fashion was no doubt strengthened by the conviction that those who supported these resolutions were secretly aiming at disunion. With all such, or with those whom he only suspected of such a purpose, Benton held no terms. Devotion to the Union had come to be with him the one ruling idea, and thus it may have happened to him, as it not unfrequently does to strong natures, when similarly placed, that he mistook the individual prejudices and animosities that had sprung from the stormy debates in which he had participated, for the dictates of reason and patriotism. Such, in fact, appears to have been the case. By some inexplicable process he had satisfied himself that Calhoun's object was to bring about a separation of the States, and as these resolutions which he was called on to obey embodied the South Carolinian's views as to the power of Congress to legislate upon the subject of slavery, he not unnaturally transferred to those who had been instrumental in securing their adoption a portion of the personal hostility with which he appears to have regarded that greatly misrepresented and much-abused man and every measure with which he was prominently identified.

The circumstances, however, were very different, now, from what they had been during the earlier portion of Benton's career. A generation of voters had grown up who "knew not Joseph," and among them were a number of comparatively young men, who were ambitious of political preferment, and who afterwards attained and wore worthily the highest honors within the gift of the people of the State. As a rule, they were men who, in the expressive idiom of the time, were accustomed to do their own thinking ; and as they regarded the political situation through an altogether different medium from that which enveloped the Capitol at Washington, they may be excused if they failed to see in these resolutions the evidence of a purpose to break up the Union. They had yet to learn that the assertion of the rights to which they believed they were entitled under the Constitution was a political crime ; and they were not ready to admit that the declaration of their intention to make common cause with the other slaveholding States in case of a refusal on the part of the free and populous North to grant these rights was proof of disloyalty. It did not need the authority of Webster to convince them that " a bargain broken on one side is broken on all sides."

When, therefore, Benton, in the course of the tremendous struggle which he now made for the retention of his political power, asserted that an adherence to these resolutions would inevitably lead to secession, and contended that those who knowingly supported them were endeavoring to bring about such a result, the charge was met by an indignant denial. It was all the answer to which it was entitled ; for, like so many other attempts that have been made to impeach the motives of an entire party on the strength of an induction, it was based upon a false premise, the exceptions being too numerous to justify the conclusion. But even if this had not been so, and his opponents had been as disloyal as he painted them, it would not have helped his cause, for the reason that the people of the State could not be made to believe that the political situation was as urgent as he insisted that it was. So far were they from sharing in his apprehensions that there never was a time when they were more actively engaged in advancing their private interests and pushing forward those measures upon which the future welfare and prosperity of the State were thought to depend. Hence it was that almost the only effect of the appeal, and of the fierce personal element which he introduced into the canvass, was to make the breach between his former friends and adherents practically irreparable.

In this factional fight the Whigs took no immediate part. They had no love for Benton ; and whilst it is probable that a majority of them would, if put to the test, have sympathized with him in his opposition to the extension of slavery into territory then free, as they certainly did in his denunciation of everything that savored of secession, yet they did not regard the situation as being serious enough to call upon them to forget old party affiliations so far as to aid in giving him a new lease of power. For thirty years, during much of which time they had been taught to look upon him as the embodiment of all that was politically evil, they had steadily but unsuccessfully opposed him and his methods, and they were not prepared to abandon the contest now, when they saw the prize of victory almost within their grasp. Accordingly, they kept their organization intact ; and the result of the election which occurred in the summer of 1850 fully justified this policy. In the triangular contest which then took place, they succeeded in returning sixty-four members to the General Assembly, one of whose duties it was to choose a United States

Senator in place of Benton. This gave them a plurality in that body, as the Benton men, who came next in point of numbers, were only able to elect fifty-five, and the anti-Benton men, or "Softs," had to be content with thirty-eight.[1] On the 10th of January, 1851, the legislature met in joint session, but failed to elect, neither party having a majority of all the votes cast. Finally, after some ten or twelve days spent in voting by day and caucussing by night, a break occurred in the ranks of the anti-Benton men, and on the fortieth ballot enough of them, under the lead of Senator Robert M. Stewart, went over to Henry S. Geyer, the Whig candidate, to secure his election, the vote being, for Geyer 80, Benton 55, Stringfellow (anti-Benton Democrat) 18, and 5 anti-Benton men scattering.

With this defeat Benton's official career may be said to have been brought to a close; for although he represented the St. Louis district in the Congress of 1852–54, during which the Kansas-Nebraska bill was passed, and was conspicuous in his opposition to that measure, yet in his own State he was steadily losing ground. The principle of non-interference by Congress in the domestic affairs of a territory which was then formally announced, and the consequent abrogation, in specific terms, of the Missouri Compromise, had come to be regarded as a cardinal doctrine by one wing of the Democratic party, and the current of opinion in its favor was too strong to be successfully resisted. At the next election Benton was beaten by Luther M. Kennett, formerly a Whig, but who now ran as a Native American, or "Know Nothing," the Whigs, as a party, having disappeared from

[1] This was the first vote given for senator on January 10, 1851, but there were two members absent and one had died.

the field of Missouri politics. In 1856 he again came
before the public for their suffrages, this time as a
candidate for the office of governor. Although sev-
enty-four years of age, and suffering from an incurable
disease, yet, in the course of the canvass which he then
made, he traveled over the entire State, a distance of
some twelve hundred miles, and made forty speeches,
each one of which was one or two hours in length. Under the circumstances this was, as his biographer well
says, "a remarkable feat," but it was without avail.
His star was on the wane, and in the poll which then
took place he was third, receiving less than twenty-eight
thousand votes, out of a total of one hundred and fifteen
thousand. In the senatorial election, or elections, for,
owing to a failure to elect at the previous session, two
of them came off during the ensuing winter, his friends
once more brought him forward, but with no better success.

This was his last appearance in the political arena,
though in the autumn of 1856 " he made, by request, a
lecturing tour in New England, speaking on the danger
of the political situation and the imperative necessity of
preserving the Union, which he now saw to be gravely
threatened." In April, 1858, he quietly passed away at
his house in Washington, busy to the last upon the literary work to which he devoted himself when he first lost
his seat in Congress, and which is, after all, the foundation upon which his claims to remembrance must rest.
As a Senator and in matters of national concern he was
overshadowed by some of his compeers; and in bringing forward and advocating measures like the bills to
repeal the salt tax, to graduate the price of the public
lands, and, perhaps, some others that were of special

service to the State and section, and which could hardly
have been carried without his support, he cannot justly
be credited with originality, since he was but following
in paths that were by no means new. The one measure
which may be said to have been peculiarly his own, and
upon which he certainly prided himself, was the " Ex-
punging Resolution," as it was called ; and this, to say
the least, was a piece of child's play, unworthy of Benton,
and beneath the consideration of any deliberative body
that aimed at official dignity.

Amid the turmoil and excitement attending these
political contests it is a satisfaction to be able to say that
the material and educational interests of the State were
not neglected. In February, 1849, shortly after the
adoption of the Jackson resolutions, the legislature authorized the construction of the Missouri Pacific Railroad
from the city of St. Louis to the western border of the
State. The preliminary surveys were at once begun,
and in July, 1850, " ground was formally broken " at
the eastern end of the line. It was the first permanent
work of the kind done within the State, though it was
not by any means the first essay which the people of
Missouri had made in the field of internal improvements.
As early as 1836, they had awoke to the fact that the
Missouri, the Mississippi, and their tributaries did not
afford all the means of intercommunication necessary to
the development of the different sections of the State.
Centres of population had sprung up at a distance from
these great commercial highways, and it was a matter of
the first importance to provide them with outlets for their
surplus products. The dirt roads on which the people
had hitherto been dependent were often impassable, and
the mode of transportation which they afforded was felt

to be too slow to suit the fast increasing wants of the age. Accordingly, the legislature which met in that year chartered a number of roads, though it is evident from an examination of these charters that the people of the State had not yet formed any very clear ideas as to the relative value of steam or horses as a motive power, and were, in fact, somewhat undecided as to what sort of road they really wanted, whether of plank, rail, or simple macadam. But whilst they may be said to have been in doubt upon this important point, they appear to have had no misgivings as to the possible earnings of these roads. At least, this is the not unnatural inference from the fact that upon some of them the prospective dividends were, by the terms of their charters, limited to twenty per cent. — a wise precaution no doubt under certain contingencies, but needless in the present case. Fortunately for Missouri, her legislators were not so far dazzled by visions of the golden harvest that was to follow upon the completion of these roads, as to lead them to commit the State to the task of carrying out the system of internal improvements which they had authorized. Charters they were willing to grant — any number of them, and containing the most liberal provisions ; but when it came to engaging the State in the work of building these roads, they wisely called a halt. Under the circumstances this course, involving, as it did, a certain self-denial, was as wise as it was unusual ; and if Missouri, during the next few years, escaped a portion of the pecuniary troubles that bore so heavily upon some of her sister States, it was owing to the conservative spirit which then ruled in her legislative councils.

In the fourteen years that elapsed between 1836 and 1850, there was a notable growth in the wealth and

population of the State, and with it came a change in
the opinions of those who had succeeded to the management of her finances. To a certain extent, the departure which now took place from the conservative
methods that had hitherto prevailed can be justified.
The State was virtually out of debt ; her revenue had
largely increased, and granting that it is ever right or
prudent for a State to engage in a work of internal improvements, or " developing her resources," as enterprises of this kind were called, it is safe to say that the
time had now come when the people of Missouri could
afford to indulge in such an undertaking. The trouble,
however, when a State once embarks in a business of this
kind, is to find a stopping place. The doors of the public
treasury having been thrown open, local interests at once
step in, and as each section of the State has an undoubted
claim to recognition, it often ends in a general scramble
for the spoils. Such seems to have been the case in the
present instance. No sooner was it understood that the
Missouri Pacific road was to receive a subvention from
the public purse than there arose the demand for other
trunk roads, to each of which the State was expected to
lend assistance. In quick succession the Southwest
Branch, as the St. Louis and San Francisco was then
called, the Iron Mountain, and the North Missouri roads
were chartered ; and in the short space of eight years,
including the sums voted to the Hannibal and St. Joseph, these different roads received from the State,
in the shape of guaranteed bonds, loans amounting, in
the aggregate, to about twenty-four millions of dollars.
Upon this sum the roads were expected to pay the
interest ; but inasmuch as with but one exception they
failed to do so, the State became bound for the entire

sum upon which default was made, amounting to some twenty millions of dollars. At the time, this was a heavy load, especially when supplemented, as it was soon afterwards, by the large sums which the State was called upon to pay out during the war of the rebellion. However, by judicious management and a willingness on the part of her citizens to meet these additional expenditures by a corresponding increase in the rate of taxation, a goodly portion of this debt has already been discharged, and the balance, amounting in 1887 to fourteen million dollars, has been so placed that it can be met without causing any undue hardship. To a great extent this result has been brought about by the very development these roads were intended to effect; and to grieve, therefore, over the amount which they have cost, or which is yet due is as idle as would be " the lamentations of a boy over the loss of the bait with which he had caught the fish."

Simultaneously with the adoption of these plans of internal improvement, measures were taken for extending and improving the school system of the State and establishing it upon a broader financial basis. Hitherto these " free schools," as the institutions organized under this system were called, depended for their support upon the income derived from certain funds which belonged to the State, the county, and the township respectively, and upon the voluntary contributions of those who were in a condition and were willing to avail themselves of the advantages which the system offered. The sums received from these several sources were small, that from the State amounting in the most prosperous year to less than seventy thousand dollars,— a mere drop in the bucket when compared with what might have been usefully expended. For this reason, and perhaps owing, also, in some degree to the sparseness of population and to a feeling of prejudice which still lingered in certain quarters against the use of schools that were wrongly called "free," the cause of public education was in anything but a flourishing condition. In some portions of the State, especially in the remote and thinly populated districts, schoolhouses were necessarily few and far apart; and in those regions where they were more common, they were often "nothing more than log huts, unplastered and unceiled, with chimneys constructed of sticks, mud, and straw, and without school furniture, unless long, backless benches, made of inverted puncheons, and wide planks fastened to the wall for a writing desk, can be called furniture." Rude and unsuitable as these buildings would now be considered, they were all that could then be afforded, and not unfrequently, it is to be feared, they were in keeping with the qualifications of the teachers and the elementary character of the instruction given. Webster's Speller and Pike's Arithmetic were the text-books in general use, and when a boy had "been through" these, and was able to write "fine hand," his education, so far as these primitive institutions were concerned, may be said to have been completed.

Such, in brief, seems to have been the condition of public instruction throughout the State of Missouri during the earlier years of her existence. In a few favored localities, as for instance in St. Louis and in some of the other wealthy and populous counties, a better state of affairs might have been found; but this was the result of local causes, and was in nowise due to any action on the part of the State, considered as such. Indeed, when regarded from this point of view, it must be confessed that Missouri, despite the positive injunctions of her constitution to the contrary, had done but little to forward the cause of popular education. Even the small sums which, from 1842 to 1854, were annually apportioned, for this purpose, among the children of the State, were derived from a fund, the principal of which she had received, at different times, from the general government in the shape of gifts in money and land.

Fortunately, all this was now to be changed. The growth of the State in wealth and population, and the diversification of interests that had followed in its train, made a higher standard of education necessary, and lent additional force to the demand which came up for an increase in the facilities with which such an education was to be obtained. The great mass of the people were no longer content with an occasional schoolhouse of logs, or with the rudimentary branches in which they had hitherto been instructed; and although the wisdom of a policy which permits any part of the school fund to be " wasted in bricks and mortar," or allows one portion of the community to be taxed in order to teach another music and German, may well be questioned, yet it cannot be denied that a long step forward was necessary, if the State was to be kept abreast of her neighbors in matters of education. This fact was duly recognized, and at the session of 1852–53 the General Assembly passed a law requiring twenty-five per cent. of the annual revenue of the State to be set apart and divided between the different counties, according to the number of children of school age in each. The first full apportionment under this law took place in 1855. With the exception of the seven years between A. D. 1861 and 1867 inclusive, it has been regularly continued ever since, and so satisfactory have been the results produced, that in 1875, when a new constitution was adopted, a provision continuing and perpetuating this appropriation was made part of the organic law, thus fixing, so far as it was possible to do so, the policy of the State.

Liberal as was this provision, it is by no means all that the people of Missouri have done for the cause of popular education. From various sources the State, county, and township funds have been increased, until they now amount to ten million five hundred thousand dollars, a good part of which is invested in the bonds of the State. The interest upon this sum is all that can be used, but it has reached an amount which, added to the annual appropriation and to the receipts from tuition fees and the voluntarily imposed local taxes, swelled the grand total, for the year ending June 30, 1886, to the magnificent proportions of five millions of dollars.

In disposing of these amounts as from year to year they became available, care has been taken to add to the number of primary as distinguished from high schools, experience having shown that they are relatively of greater importance, owing to the number of pupils who attend them and do not advance any farther. Institutions for dispensing a higher education, however, are by no means ignored. " In the larger cities and towns, and in many of the smaller towns and villages, prosperous graded schools are maintained for eight, nine, or ten months in the year; and nearly all support a high school," with a curriculum extending through two, three, or four years. Besides these institutions of a higher class, there are in the State four normal schools, one of which is intended to furnish teachers for the colored schools, and a State University, to which are attached a school of mines and an agricultural and mechanical department. To the support of all these the State contributes liberally, the amount of each appropriation varying with the necessities of the case. Of the benevolent institutions, the asylums for the blind, the deaf and dumb, and the insane, it is unnecessary to speak at length. In number and thoroughness of equipment they have kept pace with the demands of the time, and they are maintained upon a scale of liberality befitting the State.

CHAPTER XII.

KANSAS TROUBLES : PROGRESS OF THE STATE :
ELECTION OF 1860.

FROM considerations of this pleasant and peaceful
character, the people of Missouri were recalled by the
adoption, in May, 1854, of the Kansas bill and the
struggle to which it gave rise between freedom and slavery for the possession of that fair land. As has already
been intimated, the region which it was proposed, under
this act, to organize into a territory, was a part of the
Louisiana Purchase, and as it was situated north of
the line of thirty-six degrees and thirty minutes north
latitude, it of course came within the limits within which
slavery was prohibited by the terms of the Missouri
Compromise. This measure, it was then contended, was
no longer binding, having been superseded by the compromise of 1850 ; and that there might be no doubt as
to the opinion of Congress upon this point, a clause was
inserted into the Kansas bill, by virtue of which the
Missouri Compromise was expressly repealed, and the
people of the newly organized territory were left to decide whether they would or would not sanction the existence of slavery within its limits, just as had lately been
done in the cases of New Mexico and Utah, and as had
been the custom in the early days of the Republic.

To any one not wedded to an idea, or not blinded by

political prejudices, this return to the policy of the fathers seems like a fair and equitable settlement of the question. The Missouri Compromise had been tried and found wanting, and in abrogating it, as it undoubtedly had the right to do, Congress not only performed a tardy act of justice to the South, but it anticipated by some three years the decision of the supreme court, which pronounced this same compromise to be unconstitutional, and therefore null and void. In taking this action, then, Congress certainly gave no grounds for supposing that it was actuated by a wish to legislate slavery into the territory, neither, on the other hand, did it show any evidence of an intention to exclude it therefrom; but in throwing open this region to settlement by the people alike of the slave and free States, and declaring that its object in so doing was to leave them " perfectly free to form and regulate their domestic institutions in their own way, subject only to the Constitution of the United States," it furnished the best possible proof of its desire to eliminate, as far as it could be done, " the dangerous and exciting question of slavery " from the field of national legislation, and confine it to the people who were directly interested in solving it. That such would have been the result if the settlement of the territory had been permitted to go forward in the usual way, without any outside interference, there is every reason to believe; but the experiment was never tried, owing to the course which the anti-slavery faction of the North now thought proper to pursue. They were determined to prevent the formation of any more slave States; and to this end they began, even before the Kansas bill became a law, the organization of Emigrant Aid companies, the object of which was to flood the territory with voters [1] who should control it in the interest of freedom. In this they ultimately succeeded; and whilst it is not possible to approve of the revolutionary measures to which they and their agents in Kansas were obliged to resort in order to effect this purpose, yet there are, to-day, but few who will regret the result.

As might have been expected this course added not a little to the excitement which the discussion of the question of slavery in the territories had created among the people of the Southern States. They regarded it as an effort on the part of the North to evade the evident spirit and intent of the law, and it led to the formation of counter associations and "blue lodges," which were intended to perform in behalf of slavery the same kind of work that was expected of the aid societies in the cause of freedom. Especially was this the case in Missouri, which, being coterminous along its western border with the new territory, was supposed to be in a position to be more seriously affected by the result than was any other portion of the South. Evidently, if Kansas were to become a free State it would make of Missouri a huge

[1] The character of much of this emigration may be gathered from the fact that " the Kansas societies, leagues, and committees . . sent out men only," and that in some of their bands Sharps' rifles were more numerous than agricultural implements. Mining camps, we may remark, are peopled on this principle, but *bonâ fide* settlers in a farming country do not emigrate in this one-sided fashion, — a truth of which the Hon. Eli Thayer seems to have caught a glimpse, when he tells us that " when the Missourians went into Kansas to settle, they took their families with them." So far as the Blue Lodges of Missouri and the Emigrant Aid companies of Massachusetts were concerned, their object was the same and their methods identical. The only difference was that the Missourians were more open and above-board in their efforts to capture the State.

slave peninsula jutting up into free territory, and it was assumed, whether rightly or wrongly it matters not, that this fact would lessen, if it did not practically destroy, the value of the slaves owned in the State, by rendering their possession insecure. At this time, Missouri contained, on a rough calculation, about one hundred thousand of these unfortunate people, worth, perhaps, some thirty-five millions of dollars. Probably one half of this number were to be found in the western half of the State; and though there was no reason to suppose that they would escape into Kansas any more than they had done into Illinois, Iowa, or the Indian country, yet the possibility of such a contingency, and the feeling of alarm which it created as to the safety of this kind of property, were seized upon by the small but active band of slavery propagandists who lived in the State, and made to do duty as a reason why those who wished to preserve the "peculiar institution" should cross the border and endeavor to fasten it upon Kansas. "If," said Senator Atchison, on the eve of the territorial election in November, 1854, "a set of fanatics and demagogues, a thousand miles off, can afford to advance their money and exert every nerve to abolitionize the territory and exclude the slaveholders when they have not the least personal interest" in so doing, how much more is it the duty of those who live within a day's journey of the territory, and whose peace, quiet, and property depend on the result, to meet and counteract these efforts by sending some hundreds of their young men over the border to vote for their institutions. "Should each county in the State only do its duty," the question, he thought, "would be decided quietly and peaceably at the ballot-box;" but if they failed and the territory was lost to slavery, then, he added, " Missouri and the other Southern States would have shown themselves recreant to their interests and would deserve their fate."

From a Southern point of view, this is perhaps as strong a statement of the case as can be made, though it is in the nature of a *tu quoque* argument, and cannot be considered as justifying the course of the pro-slavery men, so far as this can be shown to have been contrary to law. It is well, however, when condemning crimes against the ballot-box, no matter by whom committed, to remember that in a newly organized territory the conditions of citizenship are different from those that prevail in old established communities. Tomahawk claims and such like devices, according to the unwritten law of the frontier, have always been held to convey certain rights as to property, and inferentially as to citizenship ; and bearing this fact in mind, and having due regard for the saving effect of a few days' presence in the territory, it must often have been a difficult matter to know whether a given person was or was not a citizen within the purview of the law. Certainly, if a company of so-called northern emigrants, in which there were two hundred and twenty-five men and only five women, whose " wagons contained no visible furniture, agricultural implements or mechanical tools," but " abounded in all the requisite articles for camping and campaigning purposes," were considered as *bonâ fide* settlers and permitted to vote, there could not have been a sufficient reason for ruling out any band of Missourians who ever crossed the border and declared their intention of remaining, even though they left the next day.

Another consideration, but of a purely political nature, and having for its object the restoration of the equilibrium between the free and slave States which had been disturbed by the admission of California, was not without its weight. Its influence, it is true, was but limited, for, as yet, the circle of those who recognized the full significance of the struggle for the possession of Kansas was small. To the great mass of the American people, North as well as South, it was a mere incident in the contest for political power which had been going on for fifty years and more ; and like all former incidents of the same kind, it was regarded as important only so far as it might give a temporary advantage to one or the other of the political parties into which the country was divided. To shrewd, far-seeing politicians like Senator Atchinson and B. F. Stringfellow, it meant much more. They saw in it the last peaceful struggle that the South could make upon this issue, with any prospect of success ; for they knew, as only one " to the manner born " could know, that upon the result in Kansas depended not only the future of New Mexico and Utah, but also of all the rest of that vast region which the repeal of the Missouri Compromise had thrown open to the Southern slaveholder upon the same terms as those upon which it was open to the Northern free-soiler. If, with all the advantages which the proximity of Missouri to Kansas gave them, they could not secure that territory to their interest, it needed no prophet to tell them that the prize for which they had so long contended was lost ; that as parties were then constituted, the struggle for political supremacy was ended ; and that hereafter, so far as slavery was concerned, they would have to fight not for its extension into new territories, but for its existence even in those States in which it had the sanction of law.

Powerful as these considerations must have been with a certain class, and influential as that class confessedly was, by reason of its wealth and intelligence, they do not enable us to account for the number and political complexion of the Missourians who crossed over into Kansas during the year or two succeeding its organization as a territory, and in good faith sought to make a home there. To do this we shall have to trust to an entirely different order of facts, — to one that is not only disconnected with the question of slavery, but which is at once general in its application and immediate in its effects. Thus, for instance, assuming with the census of February, 1855, that the number of qualified voters then in the territory (a majority of whom are admitted to have been of Southern birth) was about three thousand, it is probably safe to say that from one third to one half of them had come from Missouri, though they may not all have been natives of that State. They were not slaveholders, or if they were, they evidently had not taken their slaves with them, for to have done so would have been to incur the very risk which, as owners of this kind of property, they were anxious to avoid; but they were, as a class, small farmers, — men who were not above the necessity of doing their own work with their own hands, though with a genuine Anglo-Saxon greed for land, they either owned or expected to own the farms upon which they lived. To state the character of the emigration in this fashion is to suggest the motives of those who took part in it. Obviously, their object was none other than that which had led their fathers across the Mississippi; and to any one familiar with frontier life, it is needless to say that this was the very general though somewhat prosaic desire of improving their condition. In the older communities, much of the desirable farming land had been taken up, and was either in cultivation, or held for speculation; whilst Kansas was, as yet, a virgin field, a sort of promised land, where farms could be had at government prices, and the range was practically boundless. Considerations of this character have ever been irresistible with a certain class of borderers, and tempted by them now, numbers of Missouri farmers, following in the footsteps of their fathers, joined the long caravan of movers, and pitched their tents a day's march farther west.

Not being slave-owners even in the restricted sense in which that term was used in the border States, they cannot be accused of having any direct pecuniary interest in the extension of the " peculiar institution " to their new home. In fact, upon economic grounds it would seem as if they ought to have been the natural political allies of the free-State men ; and yet such had been the effect produced by the agitation of the slavery question, and the short-sighted action of the more violent among the Northern abolitionists in running off slaves and abusing all who were interested in the institution, even those who only tolerated it, that they were, as a rule, changed from possible friends to actual enemies. From their ranks came not a few of those who were most determined to make Kansas in all respects like Missouri.

Of the details of the struggle which took place when these two opposing currents met it is not necessary to speak. That task has been committed to another hand, and from the account which Mr. Spring [1] has given of those stirring times, it is evident that the sins were not all on the side of those who wished to make Kansas a slave

[1] See *Kansas*, in " American Commonwealths," by L. W. Spring.

State. To any one conversant with the facts, this assurance is not necessary, and yet so generally and persistently have the occurrences of this period been misrepresented that it may not be out of place to intimate that if all that was ever charged against the so-called border ruffians in the way of illegal voting be admitted, it would not justify the course which the friends of freedom thought proper to pursue at this juncture. The remedy for the evils of which they complained was to be found at the ballot-box, and not in revolution. Without going into the particulars of this long and bloody struggle, it will be sufficient for my purpose to state that whilst, as a matter of fact, both parties were engaged in the disreputable business of colonizing the territory with voters, the legality of the first election — the one held in November, 1854 — was not only not contested, but the pro-slavery delegate to Congress, then chosen, was permitted to take and hold his seat without opposition. At the next election, in March, 1855, things were very different. It was attended with more or less violence and intimidation, and there seems to be no doubt that, in this case, the Missourians or pro-slavery men were the chief, but not the only sinners. At all events they polled the most votes, more it is said than there were voters in the territory, and elected an overwhelming majority of their candidates to the territorial legislature, even after ruling out the six whose seats were contested, and two others, against whose election there was no protest, but to whom Governor Reeder also refused certificates. This purgation, sweeping as it was, did not satisfy the free-State men. On second thoughts, and for obvious reasons, they now wished the whole election to be set aside ; but to this neither the territorial authorities nor Congress were willing to accede.[1] Failing in their efforts to bring this about, the anti-slavery party set up an opposition legislature, and endeavored, by force and usurpation, to overthrow the government which had been regularly established over them. In taking this course, instead of submitting their cause to the arbitrament of the ballot-box, they not only gave good grounds for doubting the truth of their oft-repeated statement as to the preponderance of population in their favor, but they placed themselves outside of the law, and therefore clearly and hopelessly in the wrong. Had they succeeded, it would have resulted, as President Buchanan well and truly said, in establishing a revolutionary government in place of the one " prescribed and recognized by Congress," [2] and would have been " a usurpation of the same character as it would be if a portion of the people of a State were to undertake to establish a separate government within its chartered limits, for the purpose of redressing any grievance, real or imaginary," of which they thought they had a right to complain. "Such a principle," he added, "if carried into execution, would destroy all lawful authority and produce universal anarchy," and yet, new as the fact may be to some of us, this is precisely what the free-State men of Kansas and their friends and allies in the North tried to accomplish.

[1] . . . At the time I entered upon my official duties " (March 1857), " Congress had recognized this legislature in different forms and by different enactments. The delegate elected to the House of Representatives, under a territorial law, had just completed his term of service on the day previous to my inauguration. In fact, I found the government of Kansas as well established as that of any other territory." — *Buchanan's Administration*, p. 31. New York, 1866.

[2] *Buchanan's Administration*, chapter ii. New York, 1866.

With such a beginning, it was inevitable that evil should follow. The difficulty, not to say impossibility, of enforcing the processes of the courts, United States as well as territorial, in Lawrence and other portions of the territory where the friends of freedom held sway, naturally gave rise to an era of lawlessness; and in the saturnalia that then prevailed, the "jayhawkers," as those who took to robbery in the interest of anti-slavery were called, are said to have been "the superior devils." [1] In the long list of crimes attributed to them, illegal voting, the one offense of which the free-State men complained most bitterly, and which it was therefore natural to suppose they would have avoided, certainly holds a place; and it was reserved for John Brown to inaugurate the system of murder for opinion's sake, by the assassination of five peaceable settlers on the Pottowatamie, apparently for no better reason than because they differed from him upon the question of slavery, and he thought an example necessary.[2]

[1] *Kansas*, by Leverett W. Spring, p. 256. Boston, 1885.

[2] "Measured by the scale of the times, the five squatters on whom he laid a tiger's paw were not exceptionally bad men." — Spring's *Kansas*, p. 147. "I became satisfied from new and conclusive evidence that these men were innocent of all crime or threatened crime, and that their taking off was not intended for the protection of free-State men from their outrages and such as theirs, but was intended by Brown as an act of offensive war." — Governor Charles Robinson, in a letter dated Lawrence, July 22, 1884, and published in the *Boston Transcript* of August 15th. Any one desirous of further information upon this point, or as to Brown's career in Kansas, will do well to consult *Reminiscences of Old John Brown*, a pamphlet published at Rockford, Ill., in 1880. The author, Dr. George W. Brown, was the editor of the *Kansas Herald of Freedom*, and one of the most active men of that time on that side. The *Life of John Brown*, by F. B. Sanborn, may also be read to advantage.

During all these troublous years, it is a noteworthy fact that the pro-slavery men of the territory, whatever may have been their sins as individuals, were, as a party, uniformly to be found supporting the government.[1]   Even upon those occasions when, reinforced by their friends and neighbors from Missouri, they are said to have invested, or beleaguered, or sacked Lawrence, they were serving as a *posse comitatus*, summoned by the regularly constituted authorities of the territory [2] to aid in enforcing the laws.

With Kansas in a state of anarchy, it was impossible that the people in the adjoining counties of Missouri should not suffer.   Compared with their neighbors on the other side of the border, they were old settlers, and as they had accumulated more or less property they of course had something to lose, which is more than can be truthfully said of most of the new-comers.   This fact the "jayhawkers" were not slow to learn, and as they cared as little for state lines as they did for law, they soon began their freebooting inroads into the more thinly populated counties south of the Missouri, taking whatever they could conveniently carry off.   One of these raids was headed by John Brown, and it is memorable as being his last appearance in Kansas affairs.   It took place in December, 1858, and resulted in the destruction of considerable property, the liberation of eleven slaves, and the death, but not by the hands of Brown's immediate party, of a slave-owner, who seems to have ob-

[1] " Whilst the pro-slavery party in the territory sustained the government in all its branches which had been established over it by Congress, the anti-slavery party repudiated it." — *Buchanan's Administration*, p. 29.   New York, 1866.

[2] Spring's *Kansas*, pp. 91, 118, 189, 197; Sanborn's *Life of John Brown*, pp. 216, 234.

jected to the way in which it was proposed to dispossess him of his property. This raid, coming as it did soon after the joint attempt of the governors of Missouri and Kansas to bring about a pacification of the frontier, created great excitement in the former State, where it was made the basis of legislative action at the meeting of the General Assembly, which took place in the January following. During the course of that session, Governor Stewart sent in several messages, in which he called attention to this outrage and urged that measures be taken to protect the people of that portion of the State from further trouble. Accompanying one of these messages were memorials from thirty-five citizens of Bates and Vernon counties, in which they gave accounts of crimes that had been perpetrated in their neighborhoods by organized bands of robbers from Kansas, and asked that a sufficient force be sent to the border to defend " peaceable and law-abiding citizens from insult, outrage, and lawless violence."

In accordance with this request, a bill was prepared and introduced into the Senate, where it was favorably received. When the measure came up in the House, it was referred to the committee on federal relations, and in due time it elicited from that body a report, which is well described by a recent writer as being a "singularly dispassionate and sensible document." In it, the committee, after referring to the delicate relations that must exist between States which are separated only by an imaginary line, and to the fact that the borders of counties, so separated, are the favorite resorts of banditti and desperadoes, go on to say : —

"We do not doubt that at least ninety-nine out of every hundred of the citizens of Kansas deplore the events under consideration. . . . The people of Kansas and Missouri are most intimately connected, not only by geographical lines, but by the tender cords of kindred. We are the same people, impelled by the same interest, and bound by the same manifest destiny. . . . Even if this difficulty be winked at by Kansas . . . we would earnestly recommend the trial of every honorable means of reconciliation before a resort to extreme measures. . . . If . . . an army be stationed along the line of our frontier for the avowed purpose of protecting our border from incursions from a neighboring territory . . . Missouri . . . might well expect other States on our border to act on the line of the same suicidal policy . . . and the fraternal feeling that is not now circumscribed by state lines, would be rent asunder, and we would meet our brothers from our sister States as aliens and enemies."

" This bill," it was further objected, " provides that these troops are to be raised from the counties on the border ; taken from the midst of a people already exasperated by the murder and robbing of their kindred and neighbors. Companies formed out of such material would be hard to restrain from acts of summary punishment, should any of these desperadoes fall into their hands ; and it would likewise be difficult to teach such troops the line of our jurisdiction, and, in the excitement of inflicting a merited punishment on some offender, it would be hard for them to comprehend the deplorable evils attending an armed invasion of a sister territory by the militia of a State. . . . Your committee," it is added, " are not insensible of the obligations of the State to protect all her citizens, . . . but . . . we are most unwilling that the State should

run wild in the remedies applied   We have evidence of
the most satisfactory character that outrages, almost
without a parallel in America, at least, have been perpetrated upon the persons and property of unoffending
citizens of Bates and Vernon counties, — their houses
plundered and then burned, their negroes kidnapped in
droves, citizens wounded and murdered in cold blood,
— which evils demand at our hands the best remedy the
wisdom of the legislature can apply."   In conclusion,
they decline to recommend the use of a military force,
but they advise that rewards should be offered for the
arrest of the jayhawking leaders, and that circuit judges
should hold special terms in the disturbed districts, for
the purpose of investigating grievances and adopting
measures for the arrest of all offenders.   A bill to this
effect was accordingly passed ; and by way of affording
additional security to the people of the threatened counties, the governor was authorized to use his discretion
in the adoption of such measures as he might deem necessary for their protection, and a special appropriation
of thirty thousand dollars was made to enable him to
carry out this purpose. In accordance with this law, a reward of three thousand dollars was offered for the arrest
of Brown, but it was of no avail. He succeeded in pilot-
ing his little band of fugitive slaves to a place of safety
in Canada, and then returned to Ohio, where he sold the
horses he had stolen, though we are told, with what may
be an attempt at humor, that he " warned the purchasers
of a possible defect in the title." [1]

With this successful foray, John Brown's career in
Kansas and on the border came to an end. On each
of his visits to the territory, his path had been marked

[1] Sanborn's *Life of John Brown*, p. 494.

with blood ; and yet, except in the little town of Tabor,
Iowa, which had been one of his favorite haunts when
Kansas became " too hot to hold him," his course does not
appear to have called forth a word of protest from his
Northern admirers.   Instead of meting out to him the
treatment due to a monomaniac or a fugitive from justice, they received him as a sort of popular hero.   His
murders were either denied or justified ; the attempts
which he and his friends successfully made to resist arrest were characterized as battles, and philanthropic
gentlemen were found in Boston and elsewhere, who did
not hesitate to supply him with "material aid," though
they must have known that in the schemes in which he
was engaged, robbery certainly, and probably murder,
were essential to success.   In their sympathy for "bleed-
ing " Kansas — made so by crimes for which they were
largely responsible — they seem to have forgotten that
even in as good a cause as a crusade to prevent the formation of another slave State, the end did not justify the
means.[1]

For some time after this action of the Missouri officials, and in consequence, also, of the exertions of the
federal and territorial authorities, a condition of comparative peace was established on the frontier.   It did

[1] Some idea of the state of feeling that prevailed in certain
quarters may be inferred from the following statement of Mr.
F. B. Sanborn, published in the *Boston Transcript* of December
6, 1884 : " I myself heard a Massachusetts man, high in the confidence of Mr. Lawrence, propose (in the rooms of the Emigrant
Aid Company in Winter Street, Boston, a few days after Buchanan's election, November, 1856), that men should be sent out to
dispatch Stringfellow and Atchison, leaders of the border ruffians
in Missouri.   No one responded to the suggestion, but it was
seriously made."

not last long, as the decline of guerilla life was apparent rather than real. In November, 1860, another outbreak occurred, in which the United States court for the third Kansas district was broken up by a band of "jayhawkers," under the lead of Montgomery, and the United States officers, including the judge himself, "were obliged to fly for their lives." A grand juror by the name of Moore was murdered, as were Samuel Scott and Russell Hindes, the latter a citizen of Missouri.

The crime of which they were accused, according to a paper found in Hindes' pocket after death, consisted in being engaged (in) hunting and kidnapping negroes in 1859. In other words, they were hung because they had aided in capturing a runaway slave, as it was clearly their right to do under a law which, however objectionable in some of its features, did not differ in its end and aim from one that had been passed in 1793, and had received the approving signature of Washington himself. Naturally enough these proceedings caused much alarm along the border, and more particularly as they were indorsed by a so-called convention of Linn and Bourbon counties, Kansas, and were backed by the declaration of Montgomery that he intended " to keep possession of Fort Scott and other places near the state line, to prevent ' a fire in the rear,' while he cleaned out southern Missouri of its slaves." [1]

When the report of these proceedings, somewhat exaggerated, perhaps, so far as it related to the invasion

[1] Our authority, Judge Williams of the United States District Court, adds that " *so far*, he has carried out *literally* his declared programme," and " the citizens of Missouri on the Osage, Marmaton, and in Bates and Vernon, are flying from their homes into the interior."

of the State, reached Jefferson City, Governor Stewart ordered Brigadier-General D. M. Frost to proceed at once to the border with men enough to end the difficulty. This order reached St. Louis on the 23d of November, 1860, and in less than forty-eight hours a force of six hundred and thirty men was on the way to the scene of the out-break. Upon reaching the frontier, which they did early in December, they found that General Harney of the regular army had already arrived at Fort Scott; and when Montgomery saw himself threatened by both federal and state troops, he abandoned his fort, disbanded his men, and temporarily left the county. In a report made after his return to St. Louis, General Frost submitted a number of affidavits, from which it appears that "Hindes was taken from the midst of an indigent and dependent family . . . and hanged to death for no other crime, than that he had been faithful to the laws and institutions of his State." General Frost further states "that the deserted and charred remains of once happy homes, combined with the general terror that prevailed amongst the citizens who still clung to their possessions, gave but too certain proof of the persecution to which they had all been subjected, and which they would again have to endure, with renewed violence, so soon as armed protection should be withdrawn." In view of this condition of affairs, and in order to carry out fully Governor Stewart's order " to repel invasions and restore peace to the border," Frost determined to leave a considerable force in the threatened district. Accordingly, a battalion of volunteers, consisting of three companies of rangers and one of artillery, was enlisted, and Lieutenant-Colonel John S. Bowen, who afterwards rose to high rank in the Confederate service, was chosen to the command.

With the organization of this force, and perhaps owing also, in some degree, to the inclemency of the season, "jayhawking," as such, came to an end, though the thing itself, during the first two or three years of the civil war, and, in fact, as long as there was anything left on the Missouri side of the border worth taking, flourished more vigorously than ever. The old jayhawking leaders, however, now came with United States commissions in their pockets and at the head of regularly enlisted troops, in which guise they carried on a system of robbery and murder that left a good portion of the frontier south of the Missouri River as perfect a waste as Germany was at the end of the Thirty Years' War.

Notwithstanding the condition of semi-hostility that prevailed upon her western border during a great part of the time, the progress of Missouri in wealth and population during the ten years that intervened between 1850 and 1860 was satisfactory. From being the thirteenth in the sisterhood of States, in point of numbers, she had grown to be the eighth, and in this respect, at least, she was at the head of the Southern States. In other words, she now had within her borders a population of one million one hundred and eighty-two thousand as against six hundred and eighty-two thousand in 1850 ; a rate of increase, we may remark in passing, which is hardly reconcilable with the theory that emigration always shunned the regions where slavery existed. Of this whole population one hundred and fifteen thousand were slaves, about twenty-seven thousand more than were reported in the census of 1850. Assuming these two enumerations to have been correct, it will give an increase of about thirty-one per cent. for the ten years, a fraction over three per cent. per annum, only about one third the rate at which the whites had advanced during the same period. Under the circumstances this increase in the number of blacks is a noteworthy fact, not so much on account of the percentage of growth which it indicates, as for the insight which it gives us into the condition of public opinion in the State. Thus, for instance, if we compare this rate of increase with the progress in numbers made by this ill-fated people during the several decades that had elapsed since the organization of Missouri as a territory, it will be seen that there is a marked falling off. This has been construed, and no doubt correctly, as foreshadowing the fate that would ultimately have befallen the " peculiar institution " if it had been left to the action of natural causes. It may even be taken as an indication that the process of its gradual extinction in the State was already well under way ; but if, on the other hand, we limit ourselves to the consideration of the actual increase in the number of slaves during this interval, without reference to any previous period, it will be found to suggest a different order of facts. Viewed in this light, it tells us in no doubtful terms that, up to this time, but few of these people had been sent South, as they would have been if such a course had been deemed necessary to their retention as slaves, and it justifies the inference that the great mass of the people of the State still looked forward to a peaceable solution of the difficulties between the North and the South, which now began to take a most portentous shape.

Another fact of much economic and, as we shall see later on, of no little political importance that may be gathered from a study of the census returns is to be found in the number of foreign-born emigrants that

were then in the State. According to the reports of
1860, they amounted to one hundred and sixty thousand
— almost a seventh of the entire population; and of
this number eighty-eight thousand were Germans, whilst
the Irish, who came next, had but forty-three thousand.
The revolutions of 1848 and the unsettled condition of
continental Europe for some years afterwards, taken in
connection with the failure of the potato crops in 1846–47
and the consequent famine in Ireland, will no doubt account for much of the emigration that took place during this period; and when once these new-comers had
landed on our shores, the central position and temperate
climate, to say nothing of the agricultural and commercial advantages which Missouri held out to those in
search of a home and a livelihood, will go far towards
explaining the favor with which the State was generally
regarded. Although not in receipt of the heaviest contingent of these new arrivals, yet she had no reason to
be dissatisfied with the number or character of those of
them who found homes within her hospitable borders.
Compared with Ohio, Illinois, or even Wisconsin, she
certainly lagged behind, but among the other States of
the West and Northwest she was easily first.

Contrary to the practice of immigrants generally, a
number of these new-comers, especially among the Germans, turned their attention to farming and market-
gardening, and established themselves on small hold-
ings near the cities and towns; or else, going into the
country, they might have been found on little farms, and
usually in isolated communities, whole townships in portions of the State being taken up with their settlements.
Being industrious and frugal, they soon came to own
the farms on which they lived, and were thus pecu-

niarily independent. To this extent, and so far as they proved themselves to be law-abiding and, when the crisis came, patriotic, they may be said to have been a valuable addition to the population. From a political point of view, however, it may well be questioned whether they did not show themselves to be possessed of certain characteristics which made them less desirable as citizens than were the emigrants from other portions of Europe, who were not gifted with their prudent foresight, but who were more easily assimilated. Leading the isolated lives they did, they were not open to outside influences, and this, of course, had a tendency to keep them separate and apart from the rest of the community, and it also aggravated the natural tenacity with which they clung to the language, the manners and customs, and habits of thought which they brought from the " fatherland." Indeed, they may be said to have had in an eminent degree, as they still have, the defects of their virtues. The very strength of race which has made the Anglo-Saxon the virtual owner of a large part of the habitable globe, and which he inherited from his German ancestors, may upon occasion prove a source of discord and an element of danger in so far as it prevents the German emigrant of to-day from becoming thoroughly and speedily Americanized.

Great as was the progress of the State in population, it was more than equaled by her increase in wealth. According to the official reports, the estimated value of the property, real and personal, for the year 1860 was $501,214,398 as against $137,247,707 in 1850, an increase of about 265 per cent. This is believed to be too great, as the valuation of 1850 was low ; but even if we add to that estimate fifty millions of dollars, it will still give very satisfactory results. Of the whole amount, the farms are put down as being worth some two hundred and thirty millions, and this is probably not far from their actual value, as, up to that date, twenty-one millions of acres had been taken up, over six millions of which were in cultivation. On the other hand, the manufactured products were estimated at only about forty-two millions of dollars, the original plants, or capital invested, being rated at half that sum.

Of this latter amount but a small fraction was employed in mining and kindred pursuits, though the geological survey of the State had shown that her stores of mineral wealth were practically inexhaustible, and that they were so situated with reference to each other and to a market as to promise favorable returns upon any efforts that might be made to develop them. This survey, it is true, was not yet finished, but enough had been done to show that of the sixty-nine thousand square miles composing the total area of the State, fourteen thousand were underlaid by workable beds of coal; that more than one thousand valuable veins of lead, and half as many of iron, had been discovered and partly traced, besides many of zinc, copper, hydraulic limestones, and mineral paints.

It had also been demonstrated that "that portion of the State south of the Osage River, once considered by the superficial observer as almost worthless, has a soil (rocky and broken as it is) and a climate wonderfully adapted to the grape and other valuable fruits." Of the forty-four millions of acres of land in the State, there were only about three millions, and these mainly in the swamp region of the southeast, that did not promise plenteous returns to careful and intelligent hus-

bandry. All the grains, grasses, fruits, and vegetables
that are adapted to a fertile soil and temperate climate,
to say nothing of such products as tobacco, hemp, and
even cotton, were cultivated to advantage ; and upon
the broad prairies and in the fertile valleys of the State
countless herds and droves of domestic animals found
abundant food and shelter.

Such, in fine, was the condition of Missouri on the
31st of December, 1860, when the twenty-first General
Assembly of the State began its first session at Jefferson
City. This body, consisting in the Senate of twenty-
five Democrats, seven Bell-Everett (Compromise Union)
men, and one Republican, and, in the House, of eighty-
three Democrats, thirty-seven Bell-Everett men, and
twelve Republicans, had been chosen at the election
which took place in the preceding August ; and, speaking without reference to the question of secession, it
may be said to have been fairly representative of the
political parties in the State as they had shown themselves to be at the presidential election in November of
that year. Of the 165,000 votes then cast, Lincoln received 17,028 ; Bell and Everett, 58,372 ; and the
Democrats had the rest. Their vote, however, was divided between Breckinridge and Douglas, the former of
whom received 31,317 votes, whilst the latter, with a following of 58,801, obtained the electoral vote of the State.
In attempting to carry our classification still further, and
distinguish between the two wings of the Democratic
party, the Breckinridge men, or rather those who afterwards became such (for at the time of their election
this issue was not sharply drawn), may be set down as
being States' rights men, and there can be no doubt
that, when the time came for a decision, the leaders

amongst them, and not a few of the rank and file, cast their lot in with the South ; but to speak of them as being secessionists, meaning thereby that they were in favor of an immediate dissolution of the Union at any and every cost, would be gross injustice. Probably at this time, although it was ten days after South Carolina had seceded, there was not a handful of people in the State who did not believe, with Senators Crittenden and Douglas, that the difficulty would be settled by a compromise of some sort, and without an appeal to arms. Of secessionists proper, using the term in the sense we have given to it, there was not a corporal's guard in the whole State.

But whilst this statement is believed to be substantially true, it would be a grave mistake to suppose that the people of Missouri were in sympathy with the position which the triumphant Republicans of the North now occupied, or with the long course of action, legislative and otherwise, that had led to it. So far were they from anything of the kind, that they held the Republican party responsible for the condition in which the country was placed, and in proof of it they referred to the continued interference, in Congress and out of it, with the institution of slavery ; to the repeated attempts to deprive the people of the South of their constitutional rights in and to the territories that should have been common to all ; and they pointed to the fact that, at this very time, fourteen out of the seventeen free States had upon their statute-books laws which were intended not only to nullify the act of Congress for the return of fugitive slaves, but were in direct violation of an express mandate of the Constitution.

With such facts staring them in the face, it was not

possible for the people of the State to shut their eyes to the aggressive spirit which the North — except, perhaps, in the one case of the repeal of the Missouri Compromise — had manifested when dealing with any proposition that looked to an increase in the number of slave States; nor could they forget the declarations of Lincoln and other leaders of the Republican party that " a house divided against itself must fall," and that "this country could not permanently endure half slave and half free." Clearly, if these were the sentiments of the Northern people, it was their duty as patriots, now that they had control of the executive department of the government, to do what they could to remove the last vestige of slavery from the country; and, conceding to them the same honesty and sincerity which they claimed for themselves, the people of the Southern States had no reason to doubt that such would be their course. In view, then, of these declarations, and of the success in the presidential election of the party that indorsed them, the people of Missouri may be excused for thinking that the South had a right to demand additional guaranties against Northern aggression. Exactly what these guaranties were to be was never clearly formulated. In a vague sort of way it was said that they must be embodied in a constitutional provision, though how that provision was to be enforced, or made any more binding than were the mandates of the Constitution under which they now lived and of the violation of which they complained, is a point upon which we are left to conjecture.

CHAPTER XIII.

ALTHOUGH the Breckenridge, or Southern rights men,
were in a minority in the State even when compared with
the supporters of Douglas, in the legislature they outnumbered either of the other parties. Not being numerous
enough, however, to effect an organization by themselves,
they united with the Douglas men, and by this means
they secured the election of their candidate for speaker.
The newly chosen President of the Senate, too, Lieutenant-Governor Thomas C. Reynolds, belonged to their
wing of the party, as did the governor-elect, Claiborne F.
Jackson, so that the Southern rights Democrats were in
possession of the chief places in the legislative and executive departments of the State; and but for the fact that
they voluntarily relinquished their power into the hands
of a constitutional convention, it was possible for them to
have given the course of legislation a very different direction from that which it was eventually made to take.

The retiring governor, Robert M. Stewart, belonged
to a different school of politics. He was a Northern
man by birth and no friend to slavery, though he
" believed that the Southern people had the right to
take their slaves into all the territories and hold them
there, under the protection of the Constitution." He
was, moreover, a staunch Union man; and in the valedic-

tory message which he sent in on the meeting of the
General Assembly, he denounced the heresy of secession,
and took the ground that, no matter what the other slave
States might do, it was the duty of Missouri, as it was
her interest, to remain within the Union. But whilst
his opinions upon this point were very decided, he was
not blind to the scant measure of justice which the
South had received, or to the dangers that might come
to her institutions from hostile legislation ; and he believed that the only way to maintain the Union was for
the North to give the South guaranties against the
threatened aggressions, — " not such ephemeral contracts
as are enacted by Congress to-day and repealed to-mor-
row, but a compromise assuring all the just rights of the
States, and agreed to in solemn convention of all the
parties interested. Upon this subject," he continued,
" Missouri has the right to speak, because she has suffered. Bounded on three sides by free territory, her
border counties have been the frequent scenes of kidnapping and violence, and this State has probably lost as
much in the last two years, in the abduction of slaves, as
all the rest of the Southern States. At this moment
several of the western counties are desolated, and almost depopulated, from fear of a bandit horde who
have been committing depredation — arson, theft, and
foul murder — upon her adjacent border. Missouri
has a right, too, by reason of her present position and
power, as well as from the great calamities which a hasty
dissolution of the Union would bring upon her. She
has already a larger voting population than any of the
slave States, with prospective power and wealth far beyond any of her sister States. . . . Indeed, Missouri
and her sister border States should be the first, instead

of the last, to speak on a subject of this kind. They have suffered the evil and the wrong, and should be the first to demand redress. Is it quite proper that those who have suffered no pecuniary loss should initiate a proceeding of this kind, and say to us, by their premature action, that we do not know when to redress our wrongs or defend our honor? Our people would feel more sympathy with the movement if it had originated amongst those who, like ourselves, had suffered severe loss and constant annoyance from the interference and depredations of outsiders.

" As matters are at present, Missouri will . . . hold to the Union so long as it is worth an effort to preserve it. So long as there is hope of success, she will seek for justice within the Union. She cannot be frightened from her propriety by the past unfriendly legislation of the North, nor be dragooned into secession by the extreme South. If those who should be our friends and allies undertake to . . . reduce us to the position of an humble sentinel to watch over and protect their interests, receiving all of the blows and none of the benefits, Missouri will hesitate long before sanctioning such an arrangement. She will rather take the high position of armed neutrality. . . .

" If South Carolina and other cotton States persist in secession, she will desire to see them go in peace, with the hope that a short experience at separate government, and an honorable adjustment of the federal compact, will induce them to return to their former position. In the mean time Missouri will hold herself in readiness at any moment to defend her soil from pollution and her property from plunder by fanatics and marauders, come from what quarter they may."

In this vein he continued for some time longer, and then, after painting in glowing colors the benefits that had flowed from the establishment of the Union, and the evils that must necessarily follow its dissolution, he concluded with an impassioned appeal for its preservation, in the course of which he said that, "whilst recommending the adoption of all proper measures and influences to secure the just acknowledgment and protection of our rights, and, in final failure of this, a resort to the last painful remedy of separation; yet, regarding . . . the American confederacy as the source of a thousand blessings, pecuniary, social, and moral, and its destruction as fraught with incalculable loss, suffering, and crime, I would here, in my last public official act as governor of Missouri, record my solemn protest against unwise and hasty action, and my unalterable devotion to the Union, so long as it can be made the protector of equal rights."

This message was received on the 3d of January, and on the same day Governor Jackson was sworn into office and delivered his inaugural address.

Born in Kentucky of Virginia parentage, Jackson had come to Missouri in his boyhood, and found employment in a country store. By the time he was thirty years of age he had accumulated enough of this world's goods to enable him to retire from business and devote himself to politics, "for which he had a natural aptitude and great fondness." In 1836, he was first elected to the legislature, and from that time until his death in 1862 he was steadily in public life. In 1849 he was a member of the state senate, and, as chairman of the committee on federal relations, he reported the resolutions of instructions which bear his name, and which, as we have seen, led to Benton's appeal from the decision of the legislature to the people of the State. In the fierce struggle that ensued, Jackson was a conspicuous figure, and it was the readiness he showed in debate, and the skill he displayed in the management of men, that gave him the leading position which he then took in the councils of his party, and which he ever afterwards maintained.

He was at this time fifty-five years of age, and is described by one who knew him well as being " tall, erect, and dignified ; a vigorous thinker, and a fluent and forcible speaker, always interesting, and often eloquent ; a well-informed man, thoroughly conversant with the politics of Missouri and of the Union ; with positive opinions on all public questions, and the courage to express and uphold them ; courteous in his bearing towards all men, for he was kind-hearted, and by nature a democrat ; and a truthful, honest, and honorable gentleman. He loved the Union, but not with the love with which he loved Missouri, which had been his home for forty years, nor as he loved the South, where he was born and where his kindred lived." [1]

Called to the high position which he now occupied at a moment of unparalleled excitement, he is said to have " assumed the office with becoming modesty, but with an unshakable determination to defend the honor and the interests of Missouri against all assailants whatsoever."

In the course of his address, after commenting on the rise of the Republican party, he went on to say that it

---

[1] For these facts, and many others in the course of this and the succeeding chapter, I am indebted to Colonel Thomas L. Snead, whose *Fight for Missouri* must be carefully studied by any one who wishes to arrive at a correct understanding of the course of events in Missouri at this critical period.

was purely sectional, and that its one principle was hostility to slavery. Its object was, "not merely to confine slavery within its present limits ; not merely to exclude it from the territories, and prevent the formation and admission of any slaveholding States, . . . but to strike down its existence everywhere. . . . The triumph of such an organization is not the victory of a political party, but the domination of a section. It proclaims in significant tones the destruction of that equality among the States which is the vital cement of our federal Union."

The destiny of the slaveholding States was one and the same, and Missouri, he thought, would "best consult her own interests, and the interests of the whole country, by a timely declaration of her determination to stand by her sister slaveholding States, in whose wrongs she participates, and with whose institutions and people she sympathizes. These views," he said, "are advanced, not upon a belief that all hope of the present Union is lost, but upon a conviction that the time has arrived when a further postponement of their consideration would be unwise and unsafe. . . . So far as Missouri is concerned, her citizens have ever been devoted to the Union, and she will remain in it so long as there is any hope that it will maintain the spirit and guaranties of the Constitution.

" But if the Northern States have determined to put the slaveholding States on a footing of inequality by interdicting them from all share in the territories acquired by the common blood and treasure of all ; if they have resolved to admit no more slaveholding States into the Union ; and if they mean to persist in nullifying that provision of the Constitution which secures to the slaveholder his property when found within the limits of States which do not recognize it or have abolished it, — then *they* have themselves practically abandoned the Union. . . .

" We hear it suggested in some quarters," he continued, " that the Union is to be maintained by the sword," but this, he urged, would lead to consolidation or despotism, not to union. " That stands upon the basis of justice and equality, and its existence cannot be prolonged by coercion.

" As the ultimate fate of all the slaveholding States is necessarily the same, their determination and action . . . should be the result of a general consultation," and should be in the nature of a demand for a constitutional guaranty and not a congressional compromise, " as experience had shown that such compromises only lay the foundation for additional agitation. Being but laws, they are, like all other laws, liable to be repealed ; and their duration depends altogether upon the fluctuations of public opinion, operating through the representatives of that opinion at Washington." In conclusion he said that he was " not without hope that an adjustment alike honorable to both sections may be effected, . . . but in the present unfavorable aspect of affairs it is our duty to prepare for the worst. We cannot avoid danger by closing our eyes to it. The magnitude of the interests now in jeopardy demands a prompt but deliberate consideration ; and in order that the will of the people may be ascertained and effectuated, a State convention should . . . be called." He also advised, " in view of the marauding forays which continue to harass our borders, as well as of the general unsettled condition of our political relations," that the militia of the State should be thoroughly organized.

Upon a comparison of these two messages it will be found that up to a certain point they are in full accord, and there can be no question that to that extent they reflected the sentiments of an overwhelming majority of the people of the State. It was only in the event of the attempt on the part of the North to coerce the seceding States back into the Union, that the paths recommended by Stewart and Jackson began to diverge. In such a contingency the former thought the true policy of Missouri was to adhere to the Union, whilst the latter held that the honor as well as the interest of the State required her to make common cause with the South. As yet, this issue was in abeyance, and there were, comparatively speaking, but few who imagined that she would ever be called upon to make the decision. Among these few, though, was Francis Preston Blair, Jr., the leader of the unconditional Union men of the State. With rare foresight, he had already grasped the situation, and even now he was busy organizing the force which, when the moment of action came, enabled him to lay an iron hand upon the city of St. Louis, and by a movement necessary, perhaps, but none the less revolutionary, drive the regularly constituted authorities of the State away from the capital and into exile.

Blair was then forty years of age, having been born in Lexington, Kentucky, in February, 1821, of Virginia parentage. When but a lad, his father, upon the invitation of General Jackson, removed to Washington city, and took the editorial control of the administration organ; and it was in this school and under such teachers that "Frank Blair," as he was familiarly called, learned his first lessons in politics. In due time he was sent to Princeton College, and soon after he came to

St. Louis, where, in 1843, we find him studying law in the office of his brother, Judge Montgomery Blair, afterwards postmaster-general under President Lincoln. In 1845, on the outbreak of the Mexican war, he was in Sante Fé, whither he had gone for his health; and when Kearney took possession of that territory and annexed it to the United States, he appointed him attorney general in the provisional government which was then established, and of which Charles Bent was the head. Returning to St. Louis in 1847, young Blair made his first appearance in the political field in the presidential election of 1848, when he championed the cause of Van Buren, the unsuccessful candidate of the free-soilers. In the following year, he supported Colonel Benton on the occasion of his appeal from the legislature to the people of the State; and when death removed that doughty warrior from the field of Missouri politics, Blair, by common consent, took his place, and became the leader of the anti-slavery men of the State. In 1852 and again in 1854 he was elected to the legislature upon the Benton ticket; and in 1856 he was transferred to the national House of Representatives at Washington, of which body he was a member-elect, having been returned, for the second time, at the preceding election.

During all this portion of his career, and in fact until slavery was stricken down by the strong hand of arbitrary power, Blair was its steady and consistent opponent, though he was by no means an abolitionist in the sense in which that term was then used. He did, it is true, wish to get rid of the negroes in Missouri, and his efforts were no doubt directed to this end. He was also in favor of keeping them out of all territory not

yet cursed by the presence of slavery; but in taking
this course he was governed by economic considerations,
and " not by a sentimental regard for the blacks, or a de-
lusion as to their equality with the whites."   In a word,
he approached the subject as a statesman, rather than as a
moralist, and he wished to abolish the system in Missouri
because he saw that it was a burden upon the State, and
must inevitably retard her development in wealth and
population.

For advocating these views, he was often called an
abolitionist, which troubled him but little; and it is possible, though Colonel Benton did not find it so, that
there may have been portions of the State in which it
would not have been safe for him to speak his sentiments on this subject; but this was evidently not the
case in St. Louis, where his friends were in the majority, where his personal popularity, even among those
who differed from him politically, was very great, and
where his high social position was unquestioned.   Indeed, it may well be doubted whether Blair himself
thought so, for in those days, as some of us can remember, there was no surer way of leading him to make a
fierce attack upon slavery, no matter how unpalatable
his speech may have been to some of his hearers, than by
assuring him that its delivery would be attended with
personal danger.   In the pursuit of an object which he
had once marked out for himself as desirable and proper,
he knew no such thing as fear, and it is but just to add
that in moral courage he was equally grand.

Such was the man to whom the Union men of Missouri now turned, and not in vain, for counsel and en-
couragement.   As has already been intimated, he was
one of the few who realized the full significance of the

impending struggle, and he never deluded himself with the hope that it might be peaceably settled. From the first, he seems to have felt instinctively that it was one of those questions that could only be decided by an appeal to the sword, and, acting on the maxim that "God fights on the side of the heaviest battalions," he began at once to make ready for the part which he intended to play in the bloody drama.

These preparations, it is proper to say, were not carried on with any very great amount of secrecy, and in fact there was no particular reason why they should have been, though the contrary has been asserted. The semi-military associations, composed chiefly of Germans, which, under the name of Wide-Awakes, had done good service for Lincoln in the election of 1860, had a perfect right to continue their organization as Union clubs, home guards, or under any other name that they might think proper to adopt, and that they were doing so, was well understood. The use, too, to which they were to be put in case an effort was made to detach Missouri from the Union, was never doubted by any one who knew Blair; and yet, despite this fact, so reluctant were Governor Jackson and the Southern sympathizers in the legislature to take any steps that would bring the State into conflict with the federal government, without the previously expressed approval of the people, that, although they were fully alive to the necessities of the situation, they failed to take advantage of the only opportunity they ever had of securing such a supply of arms as would have enabled them to meet Blair, upon anything like equal terms, in the fight which he was evidently determined to make for Missouri. Had they shown as little hesitation in making war upon the federal govern-

ment as, some four months later, the federal government
showed in making war upon Missouri, they would have
seized the arsenal, as there is reason to believe they
might have done at almost any time during the first
three weeks of January, 1861, and as it was clearly
their policy to do, with or without law, in case they had
resolved upon secession, and had the power to carry
their resolution into effect. Instead of doing so, they
contented themselves with adopting a measure, which
not only committed them to a course of delay when instant action was necessary to the success of their cause,
but which involved, on their part, a relinquishment of
the power of legislation upon the very question that
was at issue. By the terms of this act, which was
approved on the 21st of January, it was provided that
an election should be held on the 18th of February
for members of a convention who were "to consider
the relations between the government of the United
States . . . and the government and people of the State
of Missouri ; and to adopt such measures for vindicating the sovereignty of the State, and the protection of
its institutions, as shall appear to them to be demanded."
By way of safeguard, it was added that "no act, ordinance, or resolution of said convention shall be deemed
to be valid to change or dissolve the political relations
of this State to the government of the United States,
or any other State, until a majority of the qualified voters of this State, voting upon the question, shall ratify
the same."

So far as the action of Blair and the Wide-Awakes
was concerned, the adoption of this measure was without any practical effect. He had made up his mind
that, in a certain contingency, he would wage war upon

his State, and, as in that event it would make but little difference what laws or how many of them stood in the way, he did not consider it necessary to pretermit his exertions to arm and equip the recruits that were flocking to his standard.

Not so, in regard to the Southern sympathizers, or secessionists, as, for the sake of brevity, we shall now call them. To them, and the cause they had so much at heart, this measure was full of serious consequences. As has been said, it amounted practically to an abdication by the legislature of certain powers, and, although in all probability not so intended, yet, in so far as it gave occasion to the exhibition of Union sentiment which took place at the February election, it was fraught with disaster to the cause of the South. No matter from what point of view we approach it, the effect will be found to have been the same. Regarded as a political measure, it checked at once the drift of Missouri secessionward, and later on, by a vote that admitted of no dispute, it fixed her position firmly in and with the Union. By the same token, it placed her vast resources in men and quartermasters' stores at the service of the Union, and, speaking militarily, it may be roughly said to have thrown back the Confederate line of battle from the Missouri to the Arkansas.

Curiously enough, although this measure brought with it an Iliad of woes to the cause of the South, yet so little were its consequences foreseen, that at the time of its adoption it was regarded by the Southern sympathizers as a triumph. In a certain sense this was perhaps true, for it enabled them to appeal to the people of the State upon an issue upon which they could not carry the legislature, but from any other point of view it was a mistake. The times were revolutionary, and whilst the Southern rights men in the legislature may have had every confidence in the result of the appeal to the people, they do not appear to have realized the fact that every moment of delay strengthened Blair and weakened them. Indeed, when we reflect that the very measure, which they welcomed as a harbinger of success, not only tied the hands of their friends at a time when instant action could alone have saved their cause, but that it also resulted in the total annihilation of their party at the succeeding election, it would seem as if the irony of fate could scarcely have reached further.

To understand the influences that combined to bring about the adoption of this measure, it is necessary to bear in mind that the three leading parties in the legislature, consisting respectively of the followers of Breckinridge, Douglas, and Bell, were so evenly divided that they served as checks upon one another. The Southern sympathizers, whose main support was drawn from the Breckinridge men, were not strong enough to carry a resolution in favor of secession, even if they had been disposed to do so; and the Union men, though united upon one point, differed among themselves to such an extent upon certain ulterior issues that it was difficult for them to find any ground which they could occupy in common. Moreover, at the time of the election, the question of secession had not entered into the canvass, and consequently there was no certainty as to what was the prevailing sentiment of the people of the State in regard to it. For these reasons, among others, the members of the legislature, unwilling to assume the responsibility of committing the State to a line of action that might prove unacceptable, and hopeful, perhaps, of the success of their respective views, joined, almost without distinction of party, in referring the question back to the people. In the Senate there were but two votes against the measure, and in the House but eighteen, eleven of whom were Republicans from St. Louis. In fact, it may be said that the Republicans alone opposed it; and yet, by an unexpected turn of the wheel, their wing of the Union party was the only one that derived a permanent benefit from it. Probably no more striking instance can be given of the changes that were now going on in the opinions of the people of the border States, or of the certainty with which the Union men were gradually coming up to the position to which they were logically committed.

With the adoption of this measure all political legislation came, for the time being, to an end. Resolutions, it is true, were adopted which denounced coercion in vigorous terms, and pledged Missouri to resist it by force; but except in so far as they may be taken as indicating the opinions of the individual members of the legislature, they amounted to nothing. The power to decide upon the course which Missouri was to follow was now in the hands of the convention, placed there by the act of the legislature itself, and so long as this act was unrepealed, any attempt on the part of the legislature to shape that course was a mere waste of time.

In the canvass which now took place for the choice of delegates to the convention, the best men in the State came to the front. The rights of the States and the authority of the federal government to coerce a State; the relations of Missouri to the Union, to the seceded States, and her duty in the premises to them and to herself, — in a word, the whole question of secession, so far as it bore upon the future of the State, was thoroughly discussed, and with an earnestness and an absence of excitement that showed how deeply impressed the great mass of the people were with the gravity of the situation.

Among those who were most prominent on the side of the South, we may mention the governor of the State, Senators James S. Green and Trusten Polk, ex-Senator and ex-Vice-President David R. Atchison, with Vest, Parsons, Claiborne, Churchill, and others in the General Assembly. Their organ was the "St. Louis Bulletin," of which J. W. Tucker and Thomas L. Snead were the editors. From the latter, whose position as a chosen counselor of Governor Jackson, and subsequently as a trusted officer on General Price's staff, enabled him to speak with authority as to the motives of his party friends, we learn that there were but few of them who were primarily secessionists or believed in the right of secession. They deplored the precipitate action of South Carolina and the other seceding States, and would gladly have persuaded them to return to the Union and trust to peaceful methods for the protection of their rights. They were not particularly devoted to the institution of slavery, nor were they deeply interested in the maintenance of that system. They were secessionists *only* because they believed that the Union had been dissolved, that its reconstruction was impossible, that war was inevitable, and that in war the place of Missouri was by the side of the Southern States. Opposed to them were the Union men, who were divided among themselves, according to the degree of their loyalty, into conditional and uncon-

ditional Union men, but who upon this occasion, thanks
to the adroit management of Blair, voted together. Of
these two subdivisions, the former was composed almost
altogether of those who had supported Douglas and
Bell at the presidential election, and, as events subsequently proved, they constituted a large majority of
the people of the State. They did not believe in secession as a remedy for the evils of which the South
complained, and in their speeches and writings they
avowed their attachment to the Union, and declared
their intention of standing by it so long as there was a
hope of preserving it. Some plan of adjustment, they
felt certain, would be adopted, and they referred to
the Crittenden proposition, which had been declared
satisfactory by those representative Southern senators,
Toombs of Georgia, and Davis of Mississippi, as affording a basis of settlement upon which all could agree.
If, however, the North should refuse to listen to the
just demand of the South for additional guaranties
against aggressive legislation, it would then, they
thought and said, be the duty of Missouri to unite with
the Southern States for the protection of their common
interests, including, of course, slavery. They also declared that " if the North, pending the attempt to adjust
matters peaceably, should make war upon any Southern
State, Missouri would take up arms in its defense."

The position of the unconditional Union men differed
from this in one very important particular. As their
name indicated, they took the ground that they would
support the government in any and every measure that
might be deemed necessary to preserve the Union and
enforce the laws. They were recruited from the ranks
of the Republicans, or supporters of Lincoln, and, natu-

rally enough, they were elated at their success at the late election, and provoked at what seemed to them to be the refusal of the secessionists to abide by the result of that election. In St. Louis, where, alone in the State, they could expect to form an appreciable factor in the political problem, a large majority of them were Germans, though their leaders were Anglo-Americans, and, with but few exceptions, men of Southern birth and lineage. Between them and the conditional Union men there was but little sympathy; in fact, not much could have been expected when one party held the other responsible for the deplorable condition in which affairs then were, and the other recriminated by charging their *quasi* friends and allies with being but little better than secessionists in disguise. So bitter was the feeling that it required all of Blair's tact and management to induce the two wings of the party to work together against the common enemy. "I don't believe," said a Republican partisan, "in breaking up the Republican party just to please these tender-footed Unionists. I believe in sticking to the party." "Let us have a COUNTRY first," responded Blair, "and then we can talk about parties."

This was sound advice, and backed as it was by the full weight of Blair's personal influence, it resulted, in St. Louis, in the formation of a ticket composed of seven Douglas, three Bell, and four Lincoln men, which swept the county by a majority of over five thousand. In the State at large the victory of the Union men was not less complete. By a majority of eighty thousand the people of Missouri decided against secession. Not a single member of that party was returned to the convention; though there were a number of the delegates who were believers in the doctrine of states-rights, or as it is now termed, local self-government. Of the whole number of members eighty-one were born in the slave States, fourteen in the North, three in Europe, and one in the District of Columbia.

To speak of the result of the election as being a surprise and a disappointment to the secessionist leaders is but faintly to describe the feelings with which they witnessed the overthrow of their air-built castles. They had worked themselves into the belief that Missouri was ready to follow South Carolina and the rest of the cotton States into the secessionist camp, and was only waiting for the forthcoming election in order to do so; and so satisfied were they of it that they did not hesitate to counsel delay to a small and gallant band of their friends, who were anxious to attempt the seizure of the arsenal. "Wait," said they in effect, "until the people shall, at the forthcoming election, declare their intention of siding with the South! Then the governor will order General Frost to seize the arsenal in the name of the State, and he with his brigade and the minute men and the thousands" who it was supposed would flock to his aid, could easily do it.

From these dreams, as they are now known to have been, the secessionist members of the General Assembly were rudely awakened by the result of the election. It was a verdict that admitted of no misinterpretation, and as such it was accepted. The military bill, as it was called, which was intended to arm and equip the militia, and was supposed, in some quarters, to cloak a project for forcing the State into secession, was accordingly shelved, and Missouri prepared of her own free will, and by the votes of her chosen delegates, eighty per cent. of whom were southern born, to take her place with the loyal North.

On the 28th of February, agreeably to the law which called it into existence, the convention met at Jefferson City. Sterling Price, a decided Union man, who had been member of Congress, governor of the State, and had played a conspicuous part in the conquest and occupation of New Mexico, was chosen president, the vote being seventy-five for Price, to fifteen for Nathaniel W. Watkins, a half-brother of Henry Clay. As soon as the organization was complete, an adjournment was had to St. Louis, whose loyal atmosphere is said to have been preferable to that of the capital, though it is probable that the comfort and convenience of the members, to say nothing of the desirability of having a suitable hall for their deliberations, may have had something to do with the change. On the 4th of March, the day of Lincoln's inauguration, the convention reassembled in St. Louis, and by an ominous conjunction it was on the afternoon of this day that, by special invitation, Luther J. Glenn, commissioner from the State of Georgia, appeared before the convention for the purpose of making the communication with which he was charged. In a few well-chosen sentences he announced the secession of Georgia from the Union, with the reasons therefor, and in the name of his State he asked the people of Missouri to adopt a similar course, and unite with their kinsmen in Georgia in forming a Southern confederacy. His message was not favorably received, though the able adverse report of John B. Henderson was not acted upon, the necessity for such a proceeding having been superseded by the adoption of the report of the committee on federal relations which virtually covered the same ground.

This most important committee, appointed for the

purpose of considering "the relations now existing between the government of the United States, the government and people of the different States, and the government and people of this State," consisted of Hamilton R. Gamble, chairman, John B. Henderson, John T. Redd, William A. Hall, Jacob T. Tindall, Alexander W. Doniphan, Nathaniel W. Watkins, Willard P. Hall, Harrison Hough, Samuel L. Sawyer, William Douglass, John R. Chenault, and William J. Pomeroy. It was a picked body, fairly representative of the different shades of opinion that were to be found in the convention ; and in the list of its members will be found the names of a number of those whom the State delighted to honor, and to whom their fellow-citizens now looked for counsel.

On the 9th of March this committee made a report, which is a model of clear, compact statement and close, dispassionate reasoning. In it, they very properly draw a distinction between the action of individual Northern States and of the federal government ; and whilst admitting that the people of the South had just cause of dissatisfaction with many of the former, they take occasion to say that, thus far, there had been no intimation that the latter had ever violated any of the rights of the Southern States, or had any intention of doing so. They also deemed it a subject of congratulation that, although " a spirit of insubordination to law, unequaled, perhaps, in any other civilized country, reigned throughout the land, yet the judicial tribunals of the federal government had not failed, in any case that had been brought before them, to maintain the rights of Southern citizens, and to punish the violators of these rights." The cause, then, of the present condition of affairs, they continued, was to be found in "the alienated feelings existing between the Northern and Southern sections of the country, rather than in the actual injury suffered by either; in the anticipation of future evils, rather than in the pressure of any now actually endured."

In regard to the hostile legislation, which in almost all of the Northern States had taken the shape of personal liberty bills, and was intended to nullify the act of Congress for the return of fugitive slaves, the committee held, and very justly, that it was unconstitutional. The remedy for it, they maintained with equal justice, was provided by the Constitution, and was to be found not in secession, or "its equivalent, revolution," but in an appeal to the supreme court. This tribunal was the recognized arbiter in all such cases, and there was no reason to suppose that it would not vindicate the supremacy of the Constitution in this instance, as it had done in all others which had been submitted to it for adjudication.

Other points of law and fact which we must dismiss with a bare mention, were discussed with equal clearness. In conclusion, the committee, in a few pregnant paragraphs, refer to the destructive effect which secession, or as they prefer to call it "revolution," would entail upon the best interests of the State, including slavery itself, and they ask what under the circumstances is the position Missouri ought to assume? To this they answer: "Evidently that of a State whose interests are bound up in the maintenance of the Union, and whose kind feelings and strong sympathies are with the people of the Southern States, with whom we are connected by ties of friendship and blood. We want the peace and harmony of the country restored, and we want them with us. To go with them as they are now . . . is to ruin ourselves without doing them any good. We cannot now follow them ; we cannot now give up the Union ; yet we will do all in our power to induce them to take their places with us in the family from which they have attempted to separate themselves. For this purpose we will not only recommend a compromise " (the Crittenden proposition), " with which they ought to be satisfied, but we will unite in the endeavor to procure an assemblage of the whole family of States, in order that in a General Convention such amendments to the Constitution may be agreed upon as shall permanently restore harmony to the whole nation." Such a recommendation, it was thought, would come with appropriateness and effect from Missouri, for she " was brought forth in a storm, and cradled in a compromise."

Accompanying this report was a series of resolutions which was adopted, but not without debate. Among them, the first and most important was the one which declared that there was " no adequate cause to impel Missouri to dissolve her connection with the Federal Union." Upon this, there was practically no disagreement, the vote upon its adoption being eighty-nine to one — Mr. Bast of Montgomery. The others were of less moment, though among them were one or two that were possessed of a certain interest, not so much on account of any effect which they had in " stilling the tempest," as from the fact that they showed how tenaciously the people of the State clung to the fast-disappearing hope of a compromise, and how surely the loose and shifting Union sentiment was crystallizing into unconditional loyalty.

This latter fact was made especially manifest in the course of the debate which took place upon an amendment declaring what Missouri would do in case the North should attempt to coerce the seceding States back into the Union. Thus, for instance, when it was said that she would never furnish a regiment for any such purpose, William A. Hall tersely replied that Missouri was in the Union, and it was her duty to respond to all demands that the federal government might constitutionally make upon her. This was certainly plain enough; and what was more to the point, it admitted, logically, of no satisfactory answer. Nor was this all. Events outside of the convention had moved rapidly of late, and the question now, among those who knew whereof they spoke, was not what Missouri would or would not do, but what she was to be permitted to do. "Missouri has not the power to go out of the Union if she would," said James O. Broadhead of St. Louis, a Virginian by birth and one of Blair's most trusted advisers, in the course of a speech in which he pictured the State as standing in the pathway to the Pacific, and urged this as a reason why the North would never consent to her secession. "Missouri has not the power to go out of the Union if she would," he repeated, and little as the truth of the statement was then suspected, it was soon seen to be fraught with meaning. Read in the light of subsequent events, it meant that the arsenal was safe, that Blair was ready to strike, and only bided his time.

The adoption of this report virtually closed the proceedings of the convention, and on the 22d of March it adjourned to the third Monday in December, but not until a committee had been appointed with power to call it together at an earlier date, should such a course be deemed necessary. On the 28th of the same month the General Assembly, which of late had been chiefly engaged in local legislation, also adjourned.

CHAPTER XIV.

THE ARSENAL, CAMP JACKSON, AND THE SECOND MEETING OF THE CONVENTION.

THE refusal of President Buchanan to withdraw the Federal troops from Charleston, and his evident determination to regain possession of the forts which had been surrendered to South Carolina, and to reinforce those which still held out, hastened the action of Georgia and the Gulf States, and led them, early in January, 1861, even before they had formally seceded, to seize the arsenals and such other public property as were within their limits. This proceeding, which was epigrammatically described by Blair as " stealing empty forts and full treasuries," but which was nothing more than the practical application of the doctrine, then quite common, of state sovereignty, naturally directed the attention of the leaders of the different political parties in Missouri to the arsenal in St. Louis, and set them to work planning how they might get control of the forty thousand muskets and other munitions of war which it was known to contain. They felt that upon the success or failure of their efforts to accomplish this purpose depended the future of the State; for let the result be what it might, they knew the party that obtained those guns would be able to hold St. Louis and Missouri, by virtue of its ability to arm its adherents.

Impressed with this belief, and satisfied that move-

ments were on foot among irresponsible parties, Union-
ist as well as Secessionist, to take possession of this
post, General D. M. Frost, of the Missouri state militia,
a graduate of West Point and a thorough soldier, is said
to have called Governor Jackson's attention to the necessity of "looking after" it, so that the State might be in
a condition to arm her troops, as he was satisfied she
would, sooner or later, have to do, whether she fought
for the Union or against it, or whether, having declared
for neutrality, she simply wished to make her position
respected.   Jackson, however, needed no prompting.
The secession of the cotton States had, he thought, made
disunion an accomplished fact; and as he had long since
come to the conclusion that, in such an event, Missouri's
place would be with the South, and as, moreover, he had
no doubt that this was the sentiment of the people of the
State generally, he did not hesitate to give Frost authority to seize the arsenal, whenever in his judgment it
might become necessary to do so.   Meanwhile he was
to assist in protecting it against mob violence of any
kind or from any source.   In the discharge of this
duty, Frost called upon Major William H. Bell, the
commandant of the arsenal, who gave him to understand
that whilst he was determined to defend the post against
any and all irresponsible mobs, come from whence they
might, he would not attempt to defend it against the
proper State authorities, as he was of the opinion that,
whenever the time came, the State had the right to claim
it as being on her soil.   He also promised that he would
not suffer any arms to be removed from the place
without giving notice of the fact.   In return, Frost
engaged to use the force at his command to protect the
arsenal from the assaults of all persons whatsoever,

though he frankly avowed that, in view of the present defenseless condition of the place, and in order to carry out this purpose, it might become necessary for him to come down and quarter troops there, to which Major Bell assented. These assurances were satisfactory to Frost, as they were, of necessity, to the small but active band of secessionists which had been organized in the city, and which, as we have seen, was held in check by the advice of friends at Jefferson City ; and they fully justified Frost, who had every confidence in Major Bell's word, in declaring that he should now rest easy, though he intended to be " prepared with the proper force to act as emergency might require."

Frost, however, was not the only person in St. Louis who had his eyes fixed upon the arsenal and its contents. Frank Blair was looking longingly in the same direction, and was already busily engaged in organizing the bands which, supplied with guns from this very storehouse, enabled him, some four months later, to lay such a heavy hand upon Missouri. Just then, it is true, he could not arm them, for except the few muskets furnished by the liberality of his friends and through the instrumentality of Governor Yates of Illinois, he was without the necessary means ; but he did not permit this to interfere with the work of recruiting and drilling. That went on steadily, and as a consequence, when the moment came for action, Blair was able to appear at the decisive point with a well-armed force, ten times as numerous as that which his opponents could bring against him.

In the mean time, whilst these two, or rather three, parties (for Frost can hardly be termed a secessionist, though as an officer in the service of the State he was willing to obey the orders of his commander) were watching each other, the federal government awoke from its lethargy, and began to concentrate troops in St. Louis for the protection of its property. The first arrival, consisting of a detachment of forty-seven men, occurred on the 11th of January; on the 24th, the very day that Frost reported to the governor the result of his visit to the arsenal, Major Bell was relieved from command and Major Hagner put in his place; and by the 18th of February, the day of the election of delegates to the convention which pronounced so decidedly against secession, there were between four and five hundred men behind the arsenal walls, and under the command of officers who would not have hesitated to use them in defense of the property intrusted to their care. With such a force, properly handled as this unquestionably would have been, the place was now so far from being in need of "protection," either by secessionists or Union men, that it was abundantly able to take care of itself; and General Harney, who was in command of the department and presumably familiar with its condition, under date of February 19, notified the authorities at Washington that there was no danger of an attack, and never had been. "If," added he, "one should be made, the garrison would be promptly rescued by an overwhelming force from the city."

Such was not the opinion of Captain Nathaniel Lyon, who had arrived at the arsenal on the 6th of February, and who was destined, in the short space of the coming six months, to write his name indelibly in the history of the State. He was at this time forty-three years of age, having been born at Ashford, Connecticut, in July, 1818. In personal appearance he is described as having been "of less than medium height;

slender and angular; with abundant hair of a sandy color, and a coarse, reddish-brown beard. He had deep-set blue eyes; features that were rough and homely; and the weather-beaten aspect of a man who had seen much hard service on the frontier," as, in truth, he had. Indeed, it is quite probable that it was his service in Kansas during the troublous days of which we have spoken, the scenes which he had then witnessed and in some of which he had been an actor, that had so intensified his dislike of slavery and slaveholders as to make him forgetful, at times, of the distinction which should be drawn between the sin and the sinner. In his inability, too, to see more than one side of a question, and in the terrible earnestness with which he saw that, he betrayed the puritanical bent of his mind, as he also did in his impatience of control, and in the spirit of intolerance that made it impossible for him to understand how there could be two opinions upon a subject upon which he had made up his mind, and that caused him to attribute incapacity, or unworthy and improper motives, to any one who ventured to differ from him, or who failed to approve of the extreme measures to which he naturally inclined. This last characteristic is especially noticeable in his political writings and in his treatment of Major Hagner, whose refusal to act upon his suggestions for strengthening the arsenal is said to have been the result of "imbecility or d—d villainy." It may also be seen in his denunciation of General Scott's decision awarding the command of the arsenal to Hagner and not to him, which we are told was made " in his usual sordid spirit of partisanship and favoritism to pets, and personal associates, and toadies; " and it led him to question Lincoln's " resolution to grapple with treason, and to put it down forever," and to express the fear that " he was not the man for the hour," and that " our political triumph had been in vain."

Qualities like these are hardly of a character to commend their possessor to men of moderate views, and hence we find that in the efforts that were made in St. Louis and at Washington to effect Hagner's removal and Lyon's installment in his place, the latter gentleman received but little aid from men of a conservative stamp. Even after the accession of Lincoln and the capture of Camp Jackson, his advancement was opposed by such Union men as Attorney General Edward Bates, Hamilton R. Gamble, the president of the convention, and James E. Yeatman, afterwards so well known as the efficient head of the Western Sanitary Commission. On the other hand he was possessed of certain soldierly qualities, and had withal a military way of untying political and legal knots that appealed at once to men of action, like Blair and Broadhead and the other members of the Union Safety Committee. Through all this trying period they supported him bravely and steadfastly ; and it was due in great part to their ceaseless efforts that he finally succeeded in obtaining the appointment which gave him the command of the arsenal and made him the master of St. Louis.

As yet all this was in the future. President Buchanan's term of office still had a month to run, and so long as he remained in power neither Blair nor Lyon could hope for any special favor. All that they or any one could expect was that he would take care that the public property was properly defended, and this he was evidently determined to do, whether the attack came from Union men or secessionists. In fact, it was owing to this very determination, and the consequent concentration of troops at the arsenal, that Lyon now found himself in St. Louis, and engaged in the congenial occupation of drilling and disciplining the home guards, thereby transforming them from an unarmed mob of civilians into a band of trained soldiers, ready to defend, or if need be take the arsenal, and prepared at all times to fight for the Union.

For this work he was well fitted, not only by his military training, but also by his tireless energy and his devotion to the Union. It was to him a labor of love, and such was the zeal he brought to bear in its prosecution, the cheerful courage with which he bore up under the depressing influence of hope deferred, and the confidence that he manifested in the righteousness of the cause in which he was engaged and in its ultimate success, that he became a tower of strength to the weak and timid, and even among the strong and courageous he was speedily recognized as a leader. Under the stimulating influence of two such spirits as Blair and himself, the work of preparation went bravely on. By the middle of April, four regiments had been enlisted, and Lyon, who was now in command of the arsenal, though not of the department, proceeded to arm them in accordance with an order which Blair had procured from Washington.

Backed by this force, Blair felt strong enough to set up an opposition to the state government, and accordingly, when Jackson refused to furnish the quota of troops assigned to Missouri under President Lincoln's call of April 15, 1861, he telegraphed to Washington that if an order to muster the men into the service was sent to Captain Lyon, " the requisition would be filled in

two days." The order was duly forwarded, and five
regiments having been sworn in instead of four, as called
for, Blair was offered the command. This he declined,
and, on his recommendation, Lyon was elected in his
place. On the 7th and 8th of May another brigade was
organized, and Captain Thomas W. Sweeny, of the 2d
Infantry, was elected commander. This made ten regiments of volunteers, besides several companies of regulars and a battery of artillery, that were now ready for
service; and as General Harney, whose relatives and
associates were suspected of disloyalty, had been ordered
to Washington to explain his position, Lyon was virtually
in command of the department. The wished-for opportunity had come at last; and Blair and Lyon, no longer
trammeled by higher authority, and determined that
Missouri should be made to fight for the Union instead
of occupying the merely negative position which she had
taken upon the question of secession, were now at liberty
to carry out their plans.

Meanwhile the February election had passed off without disturbance, and resulted, as has already been said,
in an overwhelming defeat of the secessionists. It was
a fatal blow to their cause, for it led the General Assembly to adjourn without taking any measures to put the
State in a position either to fight or to defend her neutrality. This, of course, left Governor Jackson powerless, and, as Snead says, "turned Missouri over, unarmed
and defenseless, to Frank Blair and his home guards."
In St. Louis, it is true, a small and gallant band of young
men, under the lead of Basil W. Duke and Colton
Greene, both of whom afterwards held high command in
the Confederate service, showed a disposition to contest
the prize with him, but their efforts came to naught.

For some unexplained reason, although possessed of admirable recruiting grounds, they never numbered over three hundred men — not a tenth of the force with which Blair stood ready to overwhelm them ; and in the end they wisely dropped their organization as minute men, and formed a battalion, which was assigned to Frost's brigade of the state militia.

Jackson, too, though possessed of but little actual power, was unwilling to give up the contest without an effort. He did not accept the decision of the February election as final, and as his views in regard to the position that Missouri should take in the impending struggle had undergone no change, he showed in this supreme moment of his life that he did not lack the courage of his convictions. Repairing to St. Louis as soon as the adjournment of the General Assembly had left him free, he began at once, in conjunction with certain leading secessionists, to concert measures for arming the militia of the State, and thus putting her in a condition to make her action, whatever it might be, effective. To this end, the seizure of the arsenal was held to be a prerequisite, and General Frost was preparing a memorial showing how this could best be done, when the surrender of Fort Sumter and the President's consequent call for troops hurried Jackson into a position of antagonism to the federal government, though no one knew better than he how inadequate the resources of the State were to maintain the defiant attitude which he assumed. However, he was not dismayed. To the requisition made upon Missouri for four regiments to suppress combinations, maintain the Union, and repossess the forts which had been seized, he answered that she would not send a man for the purpose of carrying on an unholy crusade against the people of the seceded States. Under the circumstances, this was a rash declaration, for, as events subsequently proved, the matter had already passed beyond the control of the state authorities, though Jackson knew it not; and if he had, it is questionable whether it would have made any difference in his official action, as he was determined, if possible, to place Missouri where he thought she belonged, on the side of the South. Accordingly he sent messengers to the Confederate authorities at Montgomery, Alabama, asking them to supply him with the guns that were needed for the proposed attack on the arsenal; and he summoned the General Assembly to meet at Jefferson City on the 2d of May, to deliberate upon such measures as might be deemed necessary for placing the State in a position to defend herself. He also ordered, as he was authorized to do under the law, the commanders of the several military districts to hold the regular yearly encampments for the purpose of instructing their men in drill and discipline. And here it is worthy of note, as indicating the motives of the people of the State, that the law under which this order was issued was introduced into the state senate by General Frost in 1855, and was intended, as he then said, to provide the means for raising a volunteer force of fifty thousand men, which was to be used in " preventing our Northern and Southern brethren from flying at each other's throats, as they will probably do at the next presidential election in 1856, or passing that, then certainly in 1860, unless the border States take action such as this to keep the peace." The bill, we are told, was passed, but not until it was shorn of the appropriation which alone could give it force, though General Simon B. Buckner of Kentucky, who " shared in these fears and views as to the means of preventing their realization," seems to have had better success, as he is said to have " obtained a copy of the law and passed it in better shape through the legislature of his State." For this curious bit of unwritten history we are indebted to General Frost, and chimerical as the project may have been, it is of interest as showing that the idea of neutrality was by no means of recent origin in the border States, and it may help to explain the hold which that idea had taken upon a people as combative as those of Kentucky and Missouri showed themselves to be.

Returning now to the order for the encampment, we find that it was general, though practically its effect was limited to the first or Frost's brigade, as that was the only one that had been organized under the law. On the 3d of May, this little band, numbering less than seven hundred men, pitched their tents in a wooded valley in the outskirts of the city of St. Louis, and named it Camp Jackson, in honor of the governor. It is described as being surrounded on all sides, at short range, by commanding hills ; it was, moreover, open to a charge of cavalry in any and every direction, and the men were supplied with but five rounds of ammunition each, hardly enough for guard purposes. In a word, it was defenseless, and this fact is believed to be conclusive in regard to the peaceful character of the camp as it was organized. Whatever, then, may have been Jackson's motives when he ordered its formation, and there is but little doubt that he intended to take advantage of any favorable opportunity that might have occurred for seizing the arsenal, it is evident that Frost did not, now, contemplate any such action. Independently of the fact that the removal of the arms to a place of safety in Illinois had taken away the occasion for such a course, he was too good a soldier, had he intended any such movement, or had he anticipated an attack from Lyon, to have brought his small command within easy striking distance of ten times their number of well-armed men ; nor would he have encamped in a position in which, from the nature of the ground, it was impossible to make a successful defense.

All this was, of course, well known to Lyon, but it did not satisfy him of the peaceful character of the camp. On the contrary, we are told by his biographer that he regarded it as a " fearful menace, which by prompt action would amount to no more than bravado, but if suffered to continue and grow, would become very shortly a source of serious trouble, and might result in terrible conflicts in the very streets of the city." These gloomy anticipations may or may not have been well founded, but in either case it is difficult to understand why Lyon should have concerned himself about the matter, since he was not a guardian of the peace in St. Louis, and, moreover, he was even then engaged in maturing a plan that certainly threatened the peace which he seemed so anxious to preserve. The times, however, were revolutionary, as General Scott said when approving of an order that gave the Safety Committee power to declare martial law in St. Louis ; and in view of the tremendous stake for which Blair and Lyon were playing, it would have been too much to expect that they could or would square their conduct by the rules of logic any more than they did by the laws of the State. In their judgment, the hour had come when the interests of the Union demanded that they should strike down the legally constituted authorities of the State, and revolutionary as was the proceeding, they set about it in a fashion that left no doubt as to the thoroughness with which they proposed to do the work.

As a preliminary step, it was determined to seize Camp Jackson and every man in it, and hold them as prisoners of war. At a meeting of the Safety Committee Lyon unfolded this plan, and gave as a reason for thinking this course necessary, that a longer delay might enable the camp to assume proportions so formidable as to endanger the safety of the State. Blair, Broadhead, O. D. Filley, and J. J. Witzig agreed with him; but Samuel T. Glover and John How, the remaining members of the committee, though desiring the capture of the place, objected to the time and manner in which it was proposed to take it. The camp, they said, had a legal existence but for a week, five days of which had already elapsed, and they did not think it ought to be attacked during that period. Besides, the officers in command of it recognized the government of the United States, and had in no instance disturbed the peace. True, there was property there, believed to have been wrongly taken from the government arsenal at Baton Rouge, but the way to reach that was by a writ of replevin. If General Frost refused to respect the writ, the marshal might then call upon General Lyon for assistance, and thus the object would be gained.

In reply to this, Lyon urged the impropriety of allowing Frost to prepare for resistance when the whole enterprise could be managed without the firing of a gun. He knew, he said, the camp to be a nest of traitors; that the legislature was in secret session, and even then a new military law might be in operation, or, if not, it would

certainly be in a day or so. Advices from all parts of
the State, he added, were discouraging to the Union
men, and the rebels were gathering in strength, and he
closed with the significant warning that General Harney
would arrive on Sunday (it was now Thursday) and be
once more in command, and no one could tell what he
would do.

The mention of Harney's return and the fear as to
the effect of his peaceful policy are said to have decided
Glover, who thereupon agreed to the necessity of breaking up the camp, though he still held to the opinion that
it would be best to have the United States marshal at
the head of the attacking column, and let him first make
a demand for the arms which the Confederate authorities had forwarded at Jackson's request, and which were
now, by Frost's permission, and at the earnest solicitation of Mayor Taylor, deposited outside the front entrance to the camp. Lyon opposed this plan as being
in the nature of a subterfuge, and in a private consultation with Blair he announced his intention of seizing the
entire force at the camp, without any ceremony other
than a demand for its surrender. "This demand he
would make with his men in line of battle and his guns
in position, and if it was not complied with at once, he
would fight for it." [1] The next day — the last of the
encampment — Frost, who had heard of the proposed
attack, sent a letter to Lyon, in which he denied that he
or any part of his command were actuated by hostile
intentions towards the federal government; but that

[1] For this account of the meetings of the Safety Committee,
and for many other facts connected with this most eventful
period, I am indebted to *General Nathaniel Lyon and Missouri in
1861*, by James Peckham. New York, 1866.

officer, having matured his plans for taking the camp, refused to receive it. Frost also notified Glover, How, and other members of the Safety Committee, that he knew nothing and cared nothing about the arms said to have been taken from Baton Rouge and now deposited at the entrance to his camp; that he had no claim on them and no orders regarding them, and that if the United States marshal wanted them he was welcome to come and take them away. These protestations were of no avail, as Lyon had made up his mind that the time had come for action. He seems to have thought, as was said by Blair in his letter to the President, that to seize Camp Jackson and follow it up "by blows struck at the enemy in other parts of the State would speedily and effectually, and at small cost of life and treasure," crush the rebellion in the State. In this he was no doubt correct, though it is probable that the result, when achieved, would have been due not so much to the "blows" which he proposed to strike, as to the fact that except Governor Jackson and his adherents or "clique," as Postmaster General Blair styled them, there were no rebels in the State. Missouri, it will be remembered, had just given a majority of eighty thousand against secession, and to suppose that the Union men of the State could have been duped or driven into an opposite course by less than one fourth of their number is preposterous, and it was so considered by those who may be said to have been most directly interested.

Lyon, however, was not to be turned from his purpose by such considerations, any more than he was by peaceful protestations or legal obstacles. Putting his troops in motion early in the morning of the 10th of May, he surrounded Camp Jackson and demanded its surrender.

As Frost could make no defense against the overwhelming odds brought against him, he was of course obliged to comply; and his men, having been disarmed, were marched to the arsenal, where they were paroled — all except Captain Emmett McDonald, who refused to accept his release upon the terms offered, and was finally set free by the action of the courts.

After the surrender, and whilst the prisoners were standing in line, waiting for the order to march, a crowd of men, women, and children collected and began to abuse the home guards, attacking them with stones and other missiles. It is even said that several shots were fired at them, but this lacks confirmation. According to Frost, who was at the head of the column of prisoners, the first intimation of firing was given by a single shot, followed almost immediately by volley firing, which is said to have been executed with precision considering the rawness of the troops. When the fusillade was checked, it was found that twenty-eight persons had been killed or mortally wounded, among whom were three of the prisoners, two women, and one child. In justice to the federal troops, it must be added that one of them was killed; and if we may credit Peckham, Captain Blandowski, of the third (Sigel's) regiment, whose company began the shooting, died the next day from the effect of a wound received at the hands of the excited crowd before he gave the order to fire.

Judging this action by the reasons assigned for it, and by its effect throughout the State, it must be pronounced a blunder. So far from intimidating the secessionists, it served only to exasperate them; and it drove not a few Union men, among them General Sterling Price, into the ranks of the opposition and ultimately into the

Confederate army. That Blair and Lyon were honest
and sincere in what they said is not, for a moment,
doubted; but this can hardly be considered as a full
justification of their conduct. Even after admitting all
that can be brought forward in their favor and against
Jackson, there will remain the fact that in seizing the
camp they were actuated not so much by anything that
had taken place, as by their fears of what might hereafter be done. Such an explanation is but a phase of
the tyrant's plea of necessity, and whilst there are times
when it is satisfactory, it is not in the present instance,
for the reason that Blair and Lyon both knew that one
effort had already been made to detach Missouri from
the Union, and had failed; and they had no reason to
suppose that a second attempt would be any more successful. In taking the course they did, then, they were
in open, flagrant revolt against the State; and so far as
their action was dictated or sanctioned by the authorities
at Washington, the capture of Camp Jackson was an act
of war perpetrated by the federal government upon a
State which was as much a part of the Union as was
Illinois or Iowa.

When the news of the seizure reached Jefferson City
the General Assembly was in secret session; and if a
proof of its ill-effect upon the people of the State, or a
measure of it, be needed, it will be found in the influence it exerted upon the members of that body and the
legislation to which it led. Thus we find that the military bill, as it was called, was then under consideration,
and that its opponents were contesting its passage, striv-
ing by every device known to parliamentary warfare to
deprive it of the features that made it objectionable to
the Union men. It was the same measure that had

been rejected at the previous session of the legislature; the men who defeated it then were opposing it now, and there was no reason to believe that the result would have been different; and yet, such was the revulsion of feeling caused by the ill-advised attack upon the state troops, that in less than fifteen minutes from the time that the news was received, the bill was rushed through both branches of the General Assembly in the shape in which it had been originally introduced, the amendments that were intended to render it less objectionable having been rescinded. Resolutions denouncing the conduct of Blair and Lyon were also passed, and the governor was unanimously requested to call out the militia for the purpose of defending the State. Other and more extreme measures were also adopted, but it is unnecessary to specify them, as, owing to the rapid march of events, this General Assembly soon ceased to be a factor in Missouri politics, and these enactments died with it.

Fortunately for the State, and perhaps for the Union, the question of secession was not one of those upon which the legislature could take action. That matter had been referred to the convention; and the wisdom that led this body, when its ostensible work was finished, to take a recess instead of adjourning finally, was now fully justified. By adopting this course it was, constructively, still in existence, and so long as this was the case, the question of the secession of Missouri was within its control, and the General Assembly was powerless to act in the matter.

But whilst this was undeniably true, it was equally true that there was no reason why the General Assembly should not arm and equip the state troops, or take any constitutional measures that might be deemed necessary to secure the enforcement of the laws; and this was precisely what it claimed to be doing when it authorized the enlistment of a body of troops to be known as the state guard. Under the terms of this law, the governor was empowered to appoint a major-general, who was to be in command of the entire force, and eight brigadier-generals, who were to have control of the several military districts into which the State was divided. To the first of these positions Sterling Price, the president of the convention, was appointed, and, to the great delight of the secessionists, he accepted. Volunteers at once began to flock to Jefferson City, and in a week from the time that Blair and Lyon had thrown down their gage of battle, a regiment was formed, of which John S. Marmaduke, the late governor of the State, was made colonel.

Meanwhile General Harney had returned to St. Louis and resumed command of the department. He approved of the capture of Camp Jackson, and on the 14th of May he issued a proclamation, in which he announced that the whole power of the United States would, if necessary, be exerted to maintain the State in her present position in the Union. Upon this point he was explicit, but beyond this he seems to have had no other wish than to preserve the peace. To this end he invited General Price to an interview, in which it was agreed that the latter officer should be intrusted with the duty of keeping order within the State, subject to the laws of the general and state governments. If this were done, the people were assured by Harney that he would have no occasion, as he had no wish, to make military movements which might create excitement and jealousies. In accordance with this agreement, Price dismissed the troops which had assembled at Jefferson City, though, in reply to a suggestion of Harney, he is said to have answered that he had no power to suspend the organization of the state guard, as that was carried on under a law of the State which must be obeyed until it was repealed, or decided to be unconstitutional by competent authority.

This agreement which, according to Harney, produced a good effect throughout the State, was by no means satisfactory to Blair and Lyon. They did not want the State to be neutral, nor did they intend that she should be. What they wanted was that she should be made to fight for the Union; and as this could not be effected whilst Jackson was in authority, they determined to depose him and drive him from the State. But before this could be done it was necessary to get rid of Harney; and accordingly they set to work to bring this about. A circular signed by O. D. Filley, one of the safety committee, was sent to loyal men throughout the State, in which they were asked to write frequently to headquarters in St. Louis, and give any information they might have as to the organization of troops under the military law. They were also asked to forward accounts of any outrages of which they had cognizance, that might be perpetrated by secessionists upon Union men; and they were earnestly recommended, in violation, it was claimed, of the Price-Harney agreement, to organize " as fast as possible — with arms, if to be had, if not, without them." In response to this circular, the committee was flooded with letters from all parts of the State; and if we may judge of the whole number from those that were published, they were not of a character

to entitle them to any great amount of credence. They
consisted chiefly of rumors that were afterwards proved
to be false, and inferences based upon them, all of which
were gravely stated as facts. In one case, — and it is
a fair sample of all, — a loyal gentleman, writing from
the southwestern portion of the State, tells us that in
that region " the people are overwhelmed with terror
and fright," though he admits that at that time there
were in the town in which he lived eight hundred home
guards already mustered into service ; and General
Sweeny, writing from the same place, six weeks later,
says that the people in that vicinity were generally loyal,
and that since his arrival he had organized several regiments of Union troops. Stories like these were eagerly
collected, and although General Harney discredited
them, and on more than one occasion bore official testimony to the fidelity with which Price was carrying out
his part of the agreement, yet they had the desired effect
upon Lincoln, to whom they were duly forwarded. In
fact, so impressed was he with their truth, and with the
sufferings and dangers to which the Union men of the
State were said to be exposed, that he issued an order,
or rather a series of instructions, in which Harney was
enjoined to put a stop to " these outrages " by the aid of
the troops under his command, and with such assistance
from Kansas, Iowa, and Illinois as he might require.
He was also told that the state officers were not to be
trusted ; that the authority of the United States was
paramount ; and that whenever it was apparent that a
movement, whether by color of state authority or not,
was hostile, he must put it down. These instructions
indicate very plainly the light in which Missouri was
now regarded at Washington, and the position to which

it was proposed to reduce her; and they are reproduced here simply for that reason, as Harney did not receive them until he was no longer in a situation to carry them out, the order relieving him of the command having been delivered to him by Blair on the 30th of May.

The dismissal of Harney left Lyon once more at the head of the Federal troops in Missouri. As his intentions in regard to the State were well known, both sides began to prepare for war; but before hostilities were begun, an effort was made by Thomas T. Gantt, William A. Hall, and other well-known citizens to bring about an agreement between the rival parties which would give a promise of peace to the State. To this end a meeting was arranged, and took place in St. Louis on the 11th of June, in which Blair, Lyon, and Major Conant represented the federal government, and Price, Jackson, and Colonel Thomas L. Snead appeared for the State, but it came to naught. After some hours spent in a fruitless discussion, Lyon, who was still seated, closed the interview in the following words, spoken "slowly, deliberately, and with peculiar emphasis : ' Rather than concede to the State of Missouri the right to demand that my government shall not enlist troops within her limits, or bring troops into the State whenever it pleases, or move its troops at its own will into, out of, or through the State ; rather than concede to the State of Missouri for one single instant the right to dictate to my government in any matter however unimportant, I would' (rising as he said this, and pointing in turn to every one in the room) 'see you, and you, and you, and you, and you, and every man, woman, and child in the State, dead and buried.' Then turning to the governor he said : ' This means war. In an hour one of my officers will call for you and conduct you out of my lines.' And then," continues Snead, " without another word, without an inclination of the head, without even a look, he turned upon his heel and strode out of the room, rattling his spurs and clanking his sabre, while we, whom he had left, and who had known each other for years, bade farewell to each other courteously and kindly, and separated — Blair and Conant to fight for the Union, we for the land of our birth."

Returning to Jefferson City, Jackson forthwith issued a proclamation in which he announced the result of the interview in St. Louis; spoke of the humiliating concessions he had been willing to make in order to avert the horrors of civil war, of their contemptuous rejection by Lyon, and the declaration that the administration intended to take military possession of the State and reduce it to the condition of Maryland ; and he closed by calling out fifty thousand of the militia for the purpose of repelling the attack that had been made upon the State, and for the protection of the lives, liberties, and property of her citizens. He also sent orders to the commanders of the different military districts to assemble their men and prepare for active service. This done, and warned by the rumors of Lyon's approach, he left on the 13th of June for Boonville, where he found General John B. Clark, with several hundred of the men of Marmaduke's regiment, awaiting his arrival. Here he determined to make a stand, more to give the state troops which had been organized on the north side of the river time to join him, than from any expectation of being able to hold the place permanently. In fact, General Price had already decided that, being without artillery and having his men armed only with shotguns and hunting rifles, it would be impossible for him to defend the line of the Missouri; and consequently he had gone to Lexington, to prepare the troops there for moving to some point near the Arkansas border, where he could organize and equip them under the protection of McCulloch and the Confederates.

In the mean time Lyon was not idle. Having resolved upon war, he lost no time in making such a disposition of his troops as would enable him to carry it on to the best advantage. A brigade, consisting of three regiments of infantry and two batteries of artillery, under the command of General Sweeny, was sent to Springfield, charged with the double duty of watching McCulloch, and of intercepting the retreat of Jackson and the state guard, against whom Lyon proposed to march in person, and whom he intended if possible to drive back, in that direction, out of the State.

In pursuance of the part of the work he had marked out for himself, Lyon set out from St. Louis on the 13th of June, the very day that Jackson left Jefferson City. On the 15th he took peaceable possession of that place, and on the 17th, after a slight skirmish, fought in obedience to Jackson's order, but against the advice of Marmaduke, he captured Boonville, and obliged the state troops to beat a hasty retreat towards the southwestern portion of the State. He was, however, in no condition to follow up his success, and during the two weeks and more that he was detained, reorganizing his command and waiting for transportation, etc., Jackson crossed the Osage and effected a junction with the troops from Lexington, who were also in full retreat, followed by Major Sturgis, with nine hundred regulars and two regiments of Kansas volunteers.

Jackson's force now amounted to between six and seven thousand men — a formidable array as then reckoned, though practically it was but little better than a rabble, being without organization and poorly supplied with arms and equipments. A third, perhaps, of the men were without guns of any kind, but as an offset, they had a surplus of baggage, some of which, as, for example, the feather beds and frying pans, were scarcely suited to a column in light marching order.

Continuing his retreat southward, Jackson, on the morning of the 5th of July, found his further progress barred by a force, consisting of about a thousand men, under Colonel Sigel, who had thrown himself in the way, for the purpose of holding him in check until Lyon and Sturgis could come up and by an attack in the rear complete his destruction. The approach of this new enemy was a surprise to Jackson, but it did not disconcert him. On the contrary, taking a position on the ridge of the prairie, nine miles north of Carthage, he awaited the attack of the Federal troops. This was promptly begun with artillery, to which the batteries of Guibor and Bledsoe replied, apparently without much damage to either side. After an hour of this practice, Jackson ordered certain changes in the position of his troops, which gave Sigel the impression that he was about to be surrounded. To prevent this, he ordered a retreat, which was well conducted, though he did not consider it safe to halt for rest or food until he reached Sarcoxie, a town situated fifteen miles beyond Carthage on the road to Springfield. The day after the battle, Jackson entered Carthage, and here he was met by General Price, who had preceded him to Arkansas, and at whose solicitation McCulloch had crossed the border and come to the rescue, with several regiments of Confederate and Arkansas state troops. Finding that they were not in danger of pursuit, for Lyon and Sturgis had been delayed by high water in the Osage and other streams, McCulloch and Price, who now assumed command of the Missourians, moved slowly back, the former to his old position near Maysfield, Arkansas, whilst the latter pitched his camp on Cowskin Prairie, in the extreme southwestern corner of the State. Here, as we are told by Quartermaster - General James Harding, "prairie grass, lean beef, and water," were plentiful, though there seems to have been a lamentable scarcity of everything else that an army, in active service, is usually supposed to need in the way of food and supplies.

Price now began in earnest the work of organizing and arming his men ; and to any one not familiar with the ready methods of the frontier, it must have appeared a hopeless task. Powder he had, owing to the foresight of Governor Jackson, and the Granby mines furnished him with lead ; but beyond this he had nothing, "neither arms nor military stores of any kind, and no money to buy them, if any had been for sale." Uniforms were, of course, out of the question, but this difficulty he obviated by causing bits of red flannel or white cotton to be tied around the arms of the officers. To add to his perplexities, there were but few trained soldiers with him. Even the officers of his staff, except Colonel Little, who left for Richmond on the 19th of July, were ignorant of their duties. His chief of ordnance, Colonel Snead, who tells the story, "did not know the difference between a siege gun and a howitzer, and had never seen a musket cartridge." Fortunately, he had under him men who had served in Mexico with Price or Doniphan, or who had passed their lives upon the frontier, and were accustomed to meet and overcome such difficulties. Major Thomas H. Price, for instance, knew how to convert the neighboring forest trees into huge bullet moulds, and in a few days his improvised ordnance shop turned out bullets and buckshot enough to satisfy the immediate wants of the command. Guibor, too, whose guns were heard in every battle in which the state guard had a part, soon had an " arsenal of construction " in working order, and with some of Sigel's captured shot as models, was busy making cartridges for his cannon. " A turning-lathe in Carthage supplied sabots ; the owner of a tin-shop contributed straps and canisters ; iron rods which a blacksmith gave and cut into small pieces made good slugs for the canisters ; and a bolt of flannel, with needles and thread, freely donated by a dry-goods man, provided us with material for our cartridge bags. A bayonet made a good candlestick ; and at night . . . the men went to work making cartridges ; strapping shot to the sabots, and filling the bags from a barrel of powder placed some distance from the candle. . . . My first cartridge resembled a turnip rather than the trim cylinders from the Federal arsenals, and would not enter a gun on any terms. But we soon learned the trick, and at the close range at which our next battle was fought, our home-made ammunition proved as effective as the best." [1]

In the quartermaster and commissary departments, things were in an equally crude state. General James

---

[1] Lieutenant Barlow, of Guibor's battery, in the *St. Louis Republican*, of March 1, 1885.

Harding, the present chairman of the board of railroad commissioners of the State, has given an amusing account of the difficulties and perplexities that beset him, during his career as quartermaster-general of the state guard; and speaking of this very period, he tells us with delicious frankness that " we did not have any too much to eat, and at one time rations were very scarce, and much grumbling was heard in consequence. How we got along, I don't know; more by luck than management, probably."

Of course, in such a dearth of the necessaries of army life, and with nothing that could by any possibility be termed a camp chest, the men were obliged to serve without pay. This did not make much difference, for they did not expect any, and consequently they were not disappointed. As a rule, they belonged to the well-to-do class, were above the average in intelligence and education; and they had joined the guard not from any expectation of pay, but from an honest conviction that the State had been wantonly outraged and it was their duty to come to her defense, or else they had been led thereto by the determination to stand by their Southern friends and relatives in their effort to resist invasion. The question of slavery was lost sight of altogether, and Snead was probably not far wrong when he said that among them all there was not a man who would have fired a shot had that been the only issue involved.

Leaving Price to go on with the work of organizing his little army, Jackson, on the 12th of July, left for Memphis, Tennessee, in order to induce the military authorities to send a body of Confederates into Missouri strong enough to take possession of the State. It was not the first time that he had urged such a policy, for early in June, before Lyon's declaration of war, he had sent Captain Colton Greene to McCulloch's headquarters at Fort Smith, requesting him to move into Missouri with his army, for the purpose of encouraging the Southern rights people, and of giving Price time to enlist and organize the state troops. This was certainly a singular request to come from the governor of a State which had decided against secession, though, considered from a military point of view, there can be no doubt as to the advisability of the movement he suggested. In fact, so favorably was it regarded that McCulloch applied to the Confederate War Department for permission to undertake a campaign which was partly based upon it. Before he could get an answer, it became necessary for him to act, and it was therefore upon his own responsibility that, on the 4th of July, he had crossed the border and advanced to the support of Jackson, who was supposed to be in danger of being caught between Lyon and Sigel and so destroyed.

When, at length, after his return to his camp in the Indian Nation, an answer was received to his application, it was found to discourage the idea of a forward movement into Missouri. She had not, it was said, seceded ; and through an absurd adherence, at this most inopportune moment, to the doctrine of states' rights, the authorities at Richmond let slip the opportunity, and failed to make the fight for Missouri at the only time when they could have done so with any prospect of success. To McCulloch's request for permission to occupy Fort Scott, and thereby overawe southern Kansas and encourage the secessionists in that part of Missouri, they answered, under date of July 4th, that " the position of

Missouri as a Southern State still in the Union requires, as you will readily perceive, much prudence and circumspection, and it should only be when necessity and propriety unite that active and direct assistance should be afforded by crossing the boundary and entering the State before communicating with this department." As Richmond was a thousand miles from McCulloch's headquarters, and telegraphic communication between the two points was not continuous, the propriety of such an order may well be questioned.

During the time that Jackson was in Memphis, engaged in what proved to be a fruitless undertaking, the convention which had been called together by the committee appointed for the purpose met at Jefferson City. In the two months and more that had elapsed since the seizure of Camp Jackson, the exasperation caused by that act had measurably subsided, or rather, it had given place to a tardy recognition of the fact that the two sections of the country were at war ; and that divested of extraneous issues, all that Missouri now had to do was to adopt such a course as would make her adherence to the Union effective. This simplification of the issue had necessitated another change of parties, and men who but a few months before had ridiculed the idea of a Federal invasion of the South were now ready to buckle on their swords and take part in such an invasion. Indeed, so rapid had been the development of the Union sentiment that on the 30th of July, the convention went to the extreme length of deposing Governor Jackson and appointing Hamilton R. Gamble in his place. They also declared vacant the seats of the members of the General Assembly, and they formally abrogated the laws which had been passed for the purpose, it was charged, of enabling the governor to carry on a war against the general government.

These were certainly radical measures, but they were necessary steps in the revolution then in progress in the State, and as such they can be justified. Jackson was unquestionably engaged in an attempt to defeat, by force, the will of the people as expressed at the February election, and for this he deserved impeachment and removal. Under the circumstances, however, this was impossible, and consequently the only way to reach him and to put a stop to his intrigues was to depose him. This could only be done by a successful revolution, and in the condition of affairs which then prevailed, it was eminently proper that the convention should take the lead in such a movement. But whilst all this is plain enough to require no argument, it must be confessed that the attempt to invest the proceeding with any legal sanction is not so successful. Certainly, if the convention had the right to pull down and set up state officers who held their positions by the same title as that by which the members of the convention held theirs ; and if, furthermore, they had the right, during three years, to arrogate to themselves the executive and legislative powers of the State, so far as the military authorities permitted them to do so, there can be no good reason why they might not have declared themselves a close corporation, with power to govern the State in perpetuity, and this is absurd.

Moreover, from the necessities of the case, the committee to which was intrusted the task of defending the action of the convention were obliged to rest their argument upon facts which, if carried to a logical conclusion, would have brought the State into armed collision

with the federal government as surely as they had
done in the case of Governor Jackson. Without going
into details, it is sufficient to say that the State was "in-
vaded " by troops from Iowa and Kansas some time before the Confederates crossed the boundary. Regarded
simply as " outrages," the one invasion was as bad as
the other; and if " the duty of vindicating the sovereignty of the State " required the convention, in the one
case, to depose Governor Jackson for inviting the Confederates to enter the State, it is difficult to understand
why the same sense of duty should not, in the other instance, have led these same defenders of the doctrine of
state sovereignty to resent the continued presence of
troops who had come into the State without an invitation from any authoritative quarter, and whose illegal
exactions and arbitrary arrests were the cause of the
unsettled condition which prevailed in portions of the
State otherwise unquestionably loyal.

In thus calling attention to the inconsistency and illegality that characterized some of the acts of the convention, it must not be supposed that the writer under-
rates the importance of the work it performed, or that
he wishes to detract from the meed of praise to which
it is so justly entitled. Undoubtedly, those of its ordinances that partook of a legislative character were illegal and revolutionary, but they were necessary to the
life of the State, and their illegality and revolutionary
nature will be overlooked in view of this fact, and because it was only by usurping legislative and executive
powers that the convention was able to preserve the
machinery of the state government and keep it in motion. When Jackson was driven into exile, the State
was left without a legal official head, and she was in

danger of drifting into anarchy or being reduced to the condition of a conquered province and governed by an appointee from Washington. In this emergency, the convention stepped into the breach, organized a provisional government, and thereby saved her from the threatened dangers. It was a practical and timely assertion of the principle of self-government, for which the convention deserves and should receive the thanks of every Missourian. Unconsciously, perhaps, but none the less surely, it had removed the only excuse that could be found for keeping the State in a condition of military subjection, and in so doing, it saved her from the pit of political degradation into which the States in rebellion were sunk during the period of reconstruction.

CHAPTER XV.

FOR two weeks and more after the occupation of
Boonville, Lyon was unable to move owing to the want
of transportation. Even after he started, he was still
further delayed by high water and the necessity of swerv-
ing from his direct route in order to effect a junction
with Major Sturgis, so that he did not reach Springfield
until the 13th of July. Including Sweeny's command,
he found himself, upon his arrival here, at the head of
about seven thousand men. Of this number, some three
thousand had enlisted for only ninety days, and as their
term of service would expire on or before the middle of
August, they could not be depended upon for a longer
campaign. They were, besides, badly clothed, poorly
fed, and imperfectly supplied with tents ; none of them
had been paid, and the three months' volunteers are said
to have become so disheartened that very few of them
were willing to reënlist. In view of these facts and the
rumored approach of Jackson with " not less than thirty
thousand men," Lyon telegraphed St. Louis, immediately on his arrival at Springfield that he must have
an additional force of ten thousand men or abandon the
position.

For various reasons it was impossible to reinforce
him. In fact not a regiment was ordered forward until

the 4th of August, too late to be of any service ; and though General Fremont, who took command of the department on the 25th of July, has been severely censured for the delay, it is difficult to see how, with the other interests committed to his charge, he could have acted differently. The battle of Bull Run, it will be remembered, had just been fought, and leaving out of consideration the necessity which was then supposed to exist of hurrying every available man to the defense of Washington, it will be sufficient to call attention to the fact that upon his arrival in St. Louis, Fremont, with a limited force and insufficient means, found himself confronted by the problem of defending Cairo and the mouth of the Ohio, whilst according to the testimony of Colonel Chester Harding, Jr., Lyon's adjutant-general, the condition of Missouri was such as to make it unsafe to withdraw any troops from the sections of the State in which they were then stationed. Moreover, Lyon's force was as large as any other separate command in the department; and if we may credit the statement that Fremont, when told that Lyon intended to fight anyway, answered that "he must do it upon his own responsibility," it would appear that he did not approve of the plan of risking a battle when, by a retreat upon Rolla, the safety of the command might be insured. Such too was evidently the opinion of Lyon's subordinates, and was his own, though he afterwards saw fit to change his mind without, however, assigning any satisfactory reason for so doing.

In the mean time, whilst Lyon was detained here, waiting for the reinforcements which it was impossible to furnish, the Confederate authorities at Memphis resolved upon a campaign which embraced the advance of a strong column into southeast Missouri for the purpose either of " taking him in the rear whilst Price and McCulloch attacked him in front, or marching upon St. Louis, capturing that city, and then sweeping up the Missouri." This plan would have been feasible enough if the Confederates had been in a condition to invade the southeastern portion of the State in force. Unfortunately, however, for the success of their plans, they were obliged to convert this proposed movement into a feint; and although it was successful in so far as it prevented Lyon from being reinforced, and thus obliged him to fight a losing battle, yet it deprived Price, in the advance which he subsequently made to the Missouri River, of the advantage which would have accrued to him from a diversion, such as the march of a heavy column upon St. Louis would have caused.

Of the adoption of this plan and of its abandonment, Price and McCulloch were duly informed, but not in time to affect their movements; and being thus left to fight the battle at their end of the line according to their best judgment, they prepared to march upon Lyon without reference to the movement of any corresponding column. On the 25th of July, Price broke camp on Cowskin Prairie and set out for the rendezvous at Cassville, a small town situated about forty miles southwest of Springfield. There he arrived on the 28th. The next day McCulloch came up with 3,200 Confederates, and following close behind him was General Pearce with 2,500 of the Arkansas state troops. These with the 5,000 armed men under Price swelled the entire force available for the march on Springfield to about 11,000, in addition to which there were 2,000 unarmed Missourians, who insisted upon following the army, much to McCulloch's disgust.

Informed of the advance of these different commands and thinking to strike them in detail, Lyon moved out from Springfield on the 1st of August at the head of 5,000 men. The next day, he encountered the advance guard of the Confederates, consisting of a part of Rains' brigade of Missouri troops, which he easily put to flight. It was an insignificant affair, of no material benefit to the victors, and yet it is said to have caused McCulloch to lose all confidence in the fighting qualities of the Missourians. On the morning of the 3d, Lyon advanced still further, and took a position within six miles of McCulloch's camp. Here he remained for twenty-four hours, when fearing lest the Confederates might cut off his communications, he fell back upon Springfield, arriving there on the evening of Monday the 5th.

Meanwhile there was a total want of harmony in the councils of the Confederates, growing out of the fact that Price and the Missourians were determined to bring on a battle, whilst McCulloch was unwilling to assume the offensive, alleging as an excuse that his orders did not permit him to move into Missouri except so far as it might be necessary for the defense of the Indian territory ; and that to advance further into the State might endanger that territory and subject him to censure. This was a valid excuse, though there is reason to believe that it was not the only one. It is in evidence that he was influenced by his distrust of the Missourians, and their officers, and justly enough, he hesitated about risking a battle so long as the army was subject to a divided command. Suspecting the cause of his unwillingness to move, Price waived his rank and proposed to take a secondary position, though he reserved the right of resuming the command of his own troops whenever he should think proper to do so. Being now at the head of both armies, and having been informed of the entry of the Confederates into southeast Missouri, McCulloch agreed to attack Lyon; and accordingly he marched at midnight of Sunday the 4th, so as to have his men in position by daybreak the next morning. Soon after starting he learned that Lyon had retreated and was now beyond his reach, but he did not allow this to check his advance. He still pushed on, and that night he camped at Moody's Spring, twelve miles from Springfield. The next morning, he moved two miles further and took a position on Wilson's Creek, near some fields of corn then in the "roasting ear" stage, as "that was to be his main dependence for food during the next few days" and until his trains could arrive.

Here the disputes between the Confederate commanders were renewed, Price still urging an advance, whilst McCulloch was determined not to make a blind attack, as he called it, upon Springfield. According to his own account the Missourians failed to furnish him with reliable information as to the strength and position of the enemy and the character of the defenses in and around Springfield, as he expected them to do, though "to urge them he declared that he would lead the whole army back to Cassville rather than bring on an engagement with an unknown enemy." At length on the 8th, Price learned, upon what he considered good authority, that Lyon was preparing to abandon Springfield, as Peckham says he intended doing up to the day before the battle. Communicating this information to McCulloch, Price insisted so strenuously upon an advance that

McCulloch agreed to call a council of war. This was held at noon of the 9th, and after a stormy scene in which Price threatened to take the Missourians and with them alone give battle to Lyon, McCulloch yielded, and the army was ordered to march at nine o'clock that evening. Before that hour it began to rain, and as three fourths of the command were without cartridge boxes, and would consequently have found it difficult to keep their powder dry, the order was countermanded, though the men rested upon their arms preparatory to a forward movement in the morning.

Lyon was now sorely perplexed. No reinforcements had reached him, and if we may judge from his own dispatches and the testimony of his officers, he was at a loss whether to retreat or to hold his position until driven back. He was even undecided whether, in case of retreat, he should fall back upon Rolla, Missouri, or Fort Scott, Kansas. At last, being loth to give up the Southwest he decided to fight, in opposition, as his biographer tells us, to the opinion of his council. Having made up his mind to this, he lost no time in carrying out his design. On the morning of the 9th, after a consultation with Sigel, he adopted the hazardous plan of dividing his little army in the face of a numerically superior force. One of his columns, consisting of 1,200 men under Colonel Sigel, was to move to the left or eastward of the Cassville road and Wilson's Creek, for the purpose of turning the Confederate right; whilst he himself, with 4,200 men, including eight companies of regulars and ten pieces of artillery, was to attack the enemy's left, on the west side of the creek. Both of these movements were successful, as the Confederate pickets had been withdrawn during the night; and at dawn on the morning of the 10th, the Southern army lay between Sigel and Lyon and in blissful ignorance of their proximity. Almost the first intimation that the rebel generals had of the presence of an enemy was the roar of Lyon's guns as he came into position on the west side of the creek, followed immediately by the boom of Sigel's cannon, as it thundered forth a quick response from the other end of the line.

Breaking up the consultation which, early as it was, they were holding, McCulloch hastened to the east side of the creek, and put himself at the head of the troops that subsequently whipped Sigel and drove back Plummer; whilst Price, having ordered the Missourians to follow as rapidly as possible, hurried to the front where he met Cawthon's brigade which was falling back before Lyon, though still "resisting all that it could." By the time that he had steadied this brigade, and formed it anew under the brow of Bloody Hill and out of the range of Totten's cannon, the Missourians began to arrive on the field. In less than half an hour, 3,100 of them, including Guibor's battery of four guns, were in position; and soon afterwards, Churchill's regiment, 600 strong, of McCulloch's brigade, came up and took its place in the line of battle.

To attack this force Lyon now moved with about 1,900 men, the rest of his command, except four companies of regulars under Captain Plummer, being held in reserve. At this time the two armies were concealed from each other by the dense growth of underbrush with which the hill was covered, though they were so close to each other that the order to advance was distinctly heard within the Confederate lines. Holding their fire until the Union troops had come within easy range, Price's men opened upon them with shotguns and rifles, " while from opposing heights, Totten, who had but lately been stationed at Little Rock, where his family still resided, fought furiously against Woodruff's battery, which now turned against him the very guns that had been taken from him a few months before.

"The battle thus joined upon the hillside was waged for hours with intense earnestness. The lines would approach again and again within less than fifty yards of each other, and then, after delivering a deadly fire, each would fall back a few paces to reform and reload, only to advance again, and again renew this strange battle in the woods. Peculiar in all its aspects . . . the most remarkable of all its characteristics was the deep silence which now and then fell upon the smoking field . . . while the two armies, unseen of each other, lay but a few yards apart, gathering strength to grapple again in the death struggle for Missouri." [1]

By ten o'clock the Confederate regiments that were on the east side of the creek, having defeated Sigel and driven back Plummer and his regulars, began to cross over and hasten to the assistance of Price. Seeing the approach of these fresh troops, some of whom had not been under fire, Lyon at once ordered forward every available battalion. "The engagement," so the Federal reports tell us, "now became general, and almost inconceivably fierce along the entire line, the enemy appearing in front often in three or four ranks, lying down, kneeling, and standing, the lines often approaching within thirty or forty yards of each other as the enemy would charge upon Captain Totten's battery and be driven back." For an hour and more this bloody work

[1] *The Fight for Missouri*, p. 275.

continued, and it was at this stage of the battle that Lyon, while leading a charge, was killed. Soon after his fall, there came a lull in the fight, during which Sturgis, who succeeded to the command, summoned the principal officers to a consultation. The question, we are told, with most of them was whether retreat was possible, and so doubtful did it then appear, that even while the discussion was going on, the Federals were called upon to resist an attack in which the Confederates charged within twenty feet of Totten's guns. Fortunately for the cause of the Union, the attack was repulsed, and before it was renewed, the Federals, unable to hold their ground against the increasing force of the enemy, abandoned the field and began a retreat which only ended at Rolla.

This closed the battle. It had lasted about six hours, and considering the number of men engaged, and the fact that but few of them had ever been under fire, and that a large proportion of them were armed with nothing but shotguns and hunting rifles, it was one of the bloodiest, as it was one of the most memorable, conflicts of modern times; of the 5,400 Union men that took part in the fight over 1,000 were killed or wounded, whilst of the 10,000 Confederates that were actually engaged over 1,200 suffered. If to these numbers we add the 186 Federals, chiefly of Sigel's command, that were missing, it will give a total of 2,547 killed, wounded, and missing, out of 15,000 actual combatants, or about sixteen per cent. But if we limit ourselves to the contest on Bloody Hill, which was to all intents a separate battle, it will be found that of the 3,500 Federals and 4,200 Confederates that were there pitted against each other, the former lost 892 and the latter 988 men; or taking both together it will be seen that of the 7,700 men engaged, 1,880, or about twenty-five per cent., were killed or wounded, and this, be it remembered, among troops but few of whom had ever fired a shot in anger, and almost one half of whom were insufficiently armed. Of the Confederates who fought on Bloody Hill, 3,100 were Missourians and 1,100 Arkansians, and their respective losses were 680 and 308. On the side of the Federals, the first Missouri, Blair's regiment, and Osterhaus' battalion bore themselves with equal gallantry. Out of 925 men belonging to these two commands, 91 were killed, 248 wounded, and 11 missing, making a total of 350, or about thirty-seven per cent. The Iowa and Kansas troops, too, fought equally well; but of the German regiments under Sigel, the same cannot be said. When brigaded with other troops the Germans made fairly good soldiers, but left to themselves they were never able to stand before an equal number of Confederates, and in this case they were expected to attack a superior force.

As soon as it was known that the Federals were leaving the field, McCulloch was urged to pursue them vigorously, but this he refused to do, as many of his men had fired their last cartridge in the battle, and were consequently without ammunition. That night, the Federal troops evacuated Springfield, and on the 17th they arrived at Rolla, a somewhat disorganized mass of fugitives, but with their large and valuable train of three hundred and seventy wagons safe.

A few days after the battle, General Price called on McCulloch and proposed to him to coöperate in a march to the Missouri River. This McCulloch declined, alleging first his orders, which made the defense of the Indian Nation his primary consideration; secondly, the scarcity

of ammunition ; and thirdly, the fact that the force intended for the invasion of southeast Missouri had been
obliged to fall back, and consequently he could not
reckon upon a diversion in that quarter. To a Confederate officer, as McCulloch was, the first of these reasons
was, of course, sufficient ; and accordingly he led his
brigade back to their camp in the Indian country, whilst
the Arkansas State troops, under General Pearce, returned homeward. Price, however, was not to be de-
terred from his expedition to the Missouri, and on the
25th of August he set out from Springfield on the campaign which resulted in the capture of Lexington.

Proceeding northward as far as Bolivar, Polk County,
he turned sharply to the west, for the purpose, as he tells
us, of " chastising " Senator General James H. Lane and
his brigade of freebooters, who had already begun that
career of robbery, arson, and murder, which converted
Lawrence, Kansas, into a mere fence-house for stolen
property, and led, in August, 1863, to the sack of that
town, and the massacre of 183 of its inhabitants by
Quantrell's band of guerrillas.

Having driven Lane and his doughty warriors out of
the State and away from Fort Scott, and thus secured his
flank from attack, Price continued his march northward,
and on the 13th of September, he sat down before Lexington with his advance guard of mounted men. By the
18th, his ammunition wagons and the rest of his forces
arrived, and he then began the attack on the place in
earnest. After fifty-two hours of firing it was surrendered, the garrison having been cut off from their supply
of water. The loss on either side was trifling, owing to
the fact that the Union troops were entrenched, whilst
the Confederates made movable breastworks of bales

of hemp, under shelter of which they approached the enemy's works with comparative impunity.

According to General Price, the fruits of this almost bloodless victory consisted of 3,500 prisoners, 5 pieces of artillery, over 3,000 stand of arms, 750 horses, about $100,000 worth of commissary stores and a large amount of other property. He also obtained the restoration of $900,000 in money which had been taken from the bank, and he recovered the great seal of the State and the public records, which are said to have been stolen from their proper custodian.

During the two weeks and more that Price was at Lexington, his force was considerably augmented by recruits, many of whom were from the north side of the river, though the increase was nothing like as great as was reported. Instead of 60,000, there were probably never more than from 15,000 to 18,000 men in and about his camp, including hundreds who had come to see the fight, just as they would have gone to a country fair. Of this number, 11,000 may have started with him when he began his retreat; but so numerous were the desertions during the next ten days, that it is doubtful whether, at any time after crossing the Osage, he could have mustered 7,000 men for duty. As this force was never materially increased, there is no reason to believe that during the year and more that the Missouri state guard was in existence, it was ever stronger than at Wilson's Creek; and there, as we have seen, it numbered 7,000 men, 2,000 of whom were unarmed. After crossing the Osage, Price, no longer in fear of pursuit, moved leisurely southward and took up a position in the southwestern portion of the State, where he was in easy communication with McCulloch, and could, at the same time, protect the

General Assembly which had been summoned by Governor Jackson to meet in extra session at Neosho, on the 21st of October.

Of the proceedings of this body it is unnecessary to speak in detail. It was a mere rump, — not a quorum of either house being present, — and consequently its acts were irregular and of no legal force. Moreover, it had relinquished the power of legislating upon the subject of secession to the convention, which was still in session, though this fact was conveniently ignored, and an act was passed which purported to dissolve the ties existing between the State of Missouri and the United States of America. For purposes of its own, the Confederate government saw proper to regard this action as valid, and on the 28th of November Missouri was formally admitted into the Confederacy, though it was now too late to make the fight for her with any prospect of success. In fact, it was whilst the few members, present at this meeting of the General Assembly, were playing at legislation that Fremont, whose pursuit of Price had been delayed by the want of transportation, arrived at Springfield with a well-appointed army of forty thousand men. His purpose, so it was stated, was to force the Confederates to a battle, and in case of success, of which he had no doubt, he then proposed to sweep down upon Little Rock, Memphis, and ultimately New Orleans. Unable to stand before this overwhelming force, McCulloch was preparing for a retreat into Arkansas, when on the 2d of November Fremont was relieved from the command of the army which he may be said to have created. A few days afterwards, in obedience to a suggestion from President Lincoln, General Hunter, who had succeeded to the command, fell back upon Rolla and Sedalia.

Of course this retrograde movement again uncovered the entire Southwest, and Price and his half-clothed and half-fed Missourians were not slow to avail themselves of the opportunity of returning. For a few months, now, they lived at their ease. Their quarters were comfortable, forage was abundant, their food was plentiful and of the best, and money, such as it was — state "scrip" and Confederate notes — circulated freely and apparently without any fears as to its future value. A Confederate veteran, to whose account of the state guard I have repeatedly had occasion to refer, tells us that often during the years 1863–64, when on duty in South Carolina, and living on rice, molasses, and sweet potatoes, "which were served with commendable regularity twenty-one times per week," his mind would revert to the "flush times" at Springfield, and he would long for the scraps that then fell from his table.

These halcyon days were not to last. On the 13th of February, General Curtis, with twelve thousand men, was so near Springfield that Price, who had delayed evacuating the place in the hope that McCulloch would come to his assistance and enable him to risk a battle, was obliged to beat a hurried retreat into Arkansas. Shortly after passing the state line, the Confederates were met coming to the rescue; and the meeting was made memorable by the fact that the 3d Louisiana had a Confederate battle-flag, the first that the Missouri troops had seen. Although the combined force of Price and McCulloch was fully as numerous as that which was pursuing them, yet they continued to fall back until they reached Cove Creek, in the Boston Mountains, twenty miles beyond Fayetteville. Here they halted, and here they were on the 2d of March when Van Dorn arrived and took the command.

Including Pike's brigade of Indians and half-breeds, the Confederates now numbered about fourteen thousand available men, and with this force Van Dorn turned on Curtis, who occupied a fortified position on Pea Ridge, near the Elkhorn tavern, with ten thousand five hundred men. After a conflict which lasted through portions of the 6th, 7th, and 8th of the month, the Confederate attack was repulsed and the Union army was left in possession of the field. In this contest the Missourians, including those who had entered the Confederate service as well as the state guard, numbered about six thousand eight hundred men, six thousand of whom were actively engaged. They formed the left wing of the army, and are said to have borne the brunt of the battle. From the first shot to the last, according to Van Dorn's official report, " they continually pushed on, never yielded an inch they had won, and when at last they received the order to fall back " — an order made necessary by the deaths of McCulloch and McIntosh, the capture of Hébert, and the defeat of the Confederate right wing — " they retired steadily and with cheers," thinking it only a change of position.

After some two weeks given to rest and reorganization, Van Dorn moved with the Missourians and a large part of his other troops to Des Arc, a town on White River in the eastern portion of the State, where he arrived on the 7th of April. The next day, General Price published an order, in which he bade farewell to the state guard. Shortly after, he was transferred to the other side of the Mississippi, with about five thousand of the Missouri troops, who had followed him into the Confederate service. On their arrival at Beauregard's headquarters near Corinth, Mississippi, they were joined by a number of their fellow-citizens, and together they organized the famous 1st and 2d Missouri Confederate brigades. Including the six batteries that had crossed the river with them, and allowing to each regiment and battery its full complement, they may have numbered ten thousand men. This is an outside estimate; and as these brigades were never in a position to increase their strength, it is not probable that the Missouri Confederates, serving on the east side of the Mississippi, ever exceeded the number here given. Of the subsequent career of this gallant band it is not my province to speak, though the story of their courage, their endurance, and their devotion to the cause of the South has been well told, and the record is one of which every Missourian may feel proud. Let it suffice to say that on the 5th of July, 1861, they had fought their first battle at Carthage, Missouri, and on the 9th of April, 1865, the very day on which Lee surrendered, these brigades, now consolidated and reduced to a mere skeleton scarcely four hundred strong, fired their last gun at Fort Blakeley on the shores of the Gulf of Mexico.

With the admission of Missouri into the Confederacy and the transfer of so many of her troops to that service, the organization of the state guard virtually came to an end. Thereafter, the Missourians who " went South " and entered the Confederate army, were known as Confederates not as state troops, and to this extent lost their individuality, though in their regimental and brigade organizations they were still credited to the State. Of the number who, during the next three years, left their homes and in the face of grave dangers made their way to the Confederate army, it is impossible to speak with certainty. According to an estimate furnished by General James Harding, they did not exceed six regiments of infantry, ten of cavalry, and eight batteries. Allowing to each regiment its full complement of one thousand men, and to each battery one hundred, it would give sixteen thousand eight hundred as the total number of Missourians on the west side of the river; or, making every allowance for subsequent increase by recruiting, they may have amounted to twenty thousand. This is a liberal estimate, and if we add to it the ten thousand that were east of the river, it will swell the grand total to thirty thousand, and this, it is believed, will cover all the men that Missouri contributed to the Confederate service.

Contrasted with the magnificent array of one hundred and nine thousand men, including eight thousand colored troops, whom she sent into the Union army, the Southern contingent is small; but if we consider it with reference to the Breckinridge vote in the autumn of 1860, or if we compare it with the secession vote for members of the convention in February, 1861, it will be found to amount, practically, to a levy *en masse.* Moreover, it was composed of the best material in the State, consisting in good part of men who served without other hope of reward than that which comes from the conscientious discharge of a duty, and of others, and they were not a few, who were driven into the rebel ranks by outrages perpetrated upon them by the military authorities. Under the lead of Price, Marmaduke, and Shelby, these men were always ready for a raid into the State, and though they were never able to reëstablish themselves upon her soil, yet such was their activity that they succeeded in keeping much of the region south of the Missouri in a constant state of turmoil and excitement. In the end they shared the fate of the Confederacy, and of the army of which they formed a part. Step by step they were driven back, until, at the close of the rebellion, they were massed upon the line of Red River, and not in the Ozark Mountains and upon the Arkansas.

CHAPTER XVI.

FROM THE EVACUATION OF THE STATE TO THE END OF THE WAR.

ALTHOUGH the Confederates were never able to recover the ground which they lost in the early part of 1862, when they were driven from Springfield and forced to evacuate New Madrid, it would be a mistake to suppose that the advance of the Federals and the military rule which they established were followed by a restoration of peace and order. So far were they from it, that, probably, but few months elapsed during the four years that the war lasted, in which there was not an outbreak of some sort in some part of the State. According to the official records, between the 20th of April, 1861, the date of the capture of the Federal arsenal at Liberty, Missouri, and the 20th of November, 1862, — a period of nineteen months, — over three hundred battles and skirmishes were fought within the limits of the State. Of the number that took place during the last two years of the war it is not possible to speak with accuracy, but it is probable that there were half as many more ; and it may be said of them that they were relatively more destructive of life, as by this time the contest had degenerated into a disgraceful internecine struggle. In many, perhaps a large majority, of these skirmishes, especially those that occurred in the northern half of the State, the combatants on the side of the Confederates were regularly enlisted soldiers, who were endeavoring to make their way south. Theoretically, this ought to have been impossible, for all this region was within the Federal lines, but practically there never was a time when, in spite of martial law and the formidable barrier which the Missouri offered to those going south, a rebel recruiting officer could not have been found on the north side of the river by any one who was anxious to do so. In the last great raid into the State, the one led by Price in person in the autumn of 1864, he is said to have been joined by over five thousand recruits.

Facts like these indicate a deep-seated spirit of discontent ; and to account for it we shall have to trust to other influences than those that sprung from sympathy with the people of the South and the cause for which they fought. Unquestionably this sympathy, founded upon political considerations and strengthened by ties of blood, was chiefly instrumental in sending into the Southern army the men who followed Price and Jackson at the outset of the war. It will not, however, explain the outbreak which took place in the summer of 1862, nor will it account for the fact that as late as the autumn of 1864, Missouri, though still overwhelmingly true to the Union, was in as unsettled a condition as she had been at any time since the capture of Camp Jackson.

Probably, the one measure which, more than all others, contributed to the above-mentioned outbreak, was the order of Governor Gamble enrolling the entire fighting population of the State, and authorizing General Schofield to call such portion of it into active service as might be deemed necessary to put down all marauders and preserve the peace. The order was somewhat indefinite ; it was generally supposed to be preliminary to a draft, and it was looked upon by the Southern sympathizers as betraying an intention on the part of the state and federal authorities to force them into the army and make them fight against their friends and relatives in the South. They also regarded it as a violation by the State of the implied bargain which had been entered into when they were disarmed and obliged, under penalty of arrest and imprisonment, to take an oath not to bear arms against the United States or the provisional government of Missouri, and to give a bond for the faithful observance of the oath. They held, and with some measure of justice, that in exacting this bond, as had been generally done throughout the State, the government had recognized them as non-combatants; and they resolved that if they must take a part in the war, they would choose the side upon which they were to fight. Hence, as General Schofield admits, the first effect of this measure was to cause every rebel who could possess himself of a weapon to spring to arms, "whilst thousands of others ran to the brush to avoid the required enrollment."

Another measure of more or less influence in moulding public opinion was the Emancipation Proclamation of January 1, 1863; not that it applied directly to Missouri, or that it can be said to have weakened the Union sentiment among the great mass of the people, but for the reason that it gave rise to serious differences among the Union men, and, in the opinion of not a few, it removed the contest from the high plane upon which it had hitherto been conducted, and reduced it to the level of mere party politics. To understand this, it is necessary to bear in mind that the proclamation, or rather the overthrow of slavery which it brought about, was in direct violation of the assurances upon which the federal government had thus far carried on the contest ; and whilst as a war measure it was clearly justifiable, it was looked upon as introducing new and different issues into the struggle, and as involving the exercise of a power for which there was no warrant in the Constitution. From this point of view it was open to criticism, and that it was so considered by President Lincoln himself is evident from the answer he returned to a delegation of Missouri radicals who visited Washington for the purpose, among others, of insisting upon the immediate abolition of slavery in the State, in preference to the scheme of gradual emancipation which the convention had recently adopted. Speaking of the political situation in Missouri at this time, Lincoln said that it was a " perplexing compound " of Union and slavery, " even among those who were for the Union, to say nothing of those who were against it." Thus there were "those who were for the Union *with* but not *without* slavery ; those for it *without* but not *with ;* those for it *with* or *without*, but prefer it *with ;* and those who are for it *with* or *without*, but prefer it *without*. Among these, again, is a subdivision of those who are for *gradual* but not for *immediate*, and those who are for *immediate* but not for *gradual*, extinction of slavery." These different opinions, he continued, might be honestly entertained by loyal men, and this would, of course, give rise to different ideas as to the proper way of sustaining the Union. For this reason, then, he declined to accede to the changes upon which the radical delegation thought proper to insist, and in so doing he preserved to the people of the State the small remnant of self-government which had been left them. In concluding his answer, and apparently by way of emphasizing his position, he says in his terse and pointed way : " The radicals and conservatives each agree with me in some things and disagree in others. I could wish both to agree with me in all things ;. for then they would agree with each other, and would be too strong for any foe from any quarter. They, however, choose to do otherwise, and I do not question their right. I, too, shall do what seems to be my duty. I hold whoever commands in Missouri or elsewhere responsible to me, and not to either radicals or conservatives."

Potent as this measure may have been in separating men of conservative views from sympathy with the national administration, its influence was but slight when compared with that exerted by the constant interference of the military with unoffending citizens, especially with those who were suspected of rebel tendencies. To enumerate all the different shapes which this interference took were an idle task. Even after leaving out those cases that affected the entire community, and confining ourselves to those that involved crimes against a class or against individuals, they will be found to run through the entire gamut, — ranging from the arbitrary arrest and imprisonment of men and women for mere opinion's sake, to the murder of prisoners ; from the illegal requisition for unnecessary supplies by irresponsible parties, to robbery, pillage, and arson.

To a great extent these lawless proceedings were in violation of orders, and it would therefore be unjust to hold the department commanders or the administration at Washington responsible for them. They were the acts of subordinates, and it is but fair to add, that, as a rule, they resulted from ignorance and an excess of zeal, rather than from a spirit of wantonness or the desire of personal gain. By some curious process, the average military officials, especially those from other States, appeared to have satisfied themselves that Missouri was disloyal; and acting upon this conviction, and ignorant, perhaps, of the fact that there was such a thing as military law, they not unfrequently conducted themselves in a manner that would hardly have been justifiable in an enemy's country. Instead of discharging the delicate duties of their office in such a way as to give as little offense as possible, they acted as if it were the policy to exasperate the people among whom they were stationed, and drive them into the rebel army, or, worse still, into some wild and predatory band of guerrillas. In this, unfortunately for the peace of the State, they were too often successful.

But whilst it is easy to acquit the ruling authorities, civil as well as military, of complicity in outrages committed in defiance of orders, and of which they had no knowledge, it is not possible to absolve them from blame for those which they themselves perpetrated, or which were committed with their knowledge, and presumably with their approval. Take, for example, the outrages on the western frontier of the State, — those perpetrated by Union troops and Kansas Red-Legs upon Missourians, as well as those committed by guerrillas and outlawed Missourians upon the people of Kansas, — and, either as sins of omission or commission, they can be traced directly to mismanagement on the part of the Federal authorities.

Without stopping to enlarge upon the crimes of Lane and his brigade, to which reference has already been made, it is sufficient to say that in 1861 they burned the

town of Osceola, " an enterprise in which large amounts
of property and a score of lives were sacrificed ; " that
they " cleaned out " the villages of Butler and Park-
ville ; and, in a word, that they began in Missouri the
work of robbery and murder which resulted in depopu-
lating a large part of the western border.   Following in
the wake of this brigade of " thieves and marauders," as
Governor Robinson is said to have called them, came the
bands of robbers known as Red-Legs, whose custom
it was " at intervals to dash into Missouri, seize horses
and cattle, — not omitting other and worse outrages on
occasion, — then to repair with their booty to Lawrence,
where it was defiantly sold at auction."   These depredations were well known to the authorities.   In December, 1861, General Halleck, who seems to have been
powerless to remedy the evil, wrote to McClellan that
" the conduct of our troops during Frémont's campaign,
and especially the course pursued by those under Lane
and Jennison, has turned against us many thousands who
were formerly Union men ; " and on another occasion,
when speaking of the rumor that Lane had been made a
brigadier-general in the Federal army, he added that such
an appointment " is offering a premium for rascality
and robbing generally," and that " it will take twenty
thousand men to counteract its effect in the State."
This letter was seen by President Lincoln, who did nothing to bring about a different state of affairs on the border, though he signified his regret that Halleck should
have entertained such an unfavorable opinion of Lane.

If, now, we reverse the shield, we shall find that the
outrages of Lane and the Red-Legs not only sent a number of men into the Southern army, but that they also
drove others into adopting the lawless mode of life

known as "bushwhacking." The number of those who thus outlawed themselves was never large, certainly not a tenth of the force that might at any moment have been brought against them, and yet such was the inefficiency of the Federal authorities that these guerrillas, aided by certain hangers-on to the Confederate army, are said to have carried on a savage and, we may add, a seemingly successful predatory war with the Union troops, as well as with their freebooting neighbors over the border. This result was clearly foreseen by Governor Charles Robinson of Kansas. As early as September, 1861, he warned Frémont that there was danger that " Lane's brigade will get up a war by going over the line, committing depredations, and then returning into our State." In such an event the secessionists, he said, will be forced to retaliation, " and in this they will be joined by nearly all the Union men of Missouri." In the same letter in which he utters this warning he bears testimony to the peaceful disposition then prevailing among the Missourians. " There are," said he, " small parties of secessionists among them, but we have good reason to know that they do not intend to molest Kansas. . . . Indeed, a short time since, when a guerrilla party came over and stole some property from our citizens, the officers in command of the Confederates compelled a return of the property, and offered to give up the leader of the gang to our people for punishment. . . . If you will remove the supplies at Fort Scott to the interior," he adds, " and relieve us of the Lane brigade, I will guarantee Kansas from invasion . . . until Jackson shall drive you from St. Louis."

Unfortunately for the peace of the border, neither the protests of Robinson and Halleck, nor the example of the Confederates in offering to give up a guerrilla, were of any avail. The Kansas marauders were permitted to continue their depredations without any serious effort on the part of the Federal authorities to put a stop to them, and this course, as had been foretold, led to savage reprisals. In August, 1863, a band of outlawed Missourians, maddened by the atrocities that were committed on their people, made a descent upon Lawrence, Kansas, burned the town, and slaughtered one hundred and eighty-three of its inhabitants. "Jennison has laid waste our homes," was the declaration of more than one Missourian on the day of the massacre, "and the Red-Legs have perpetrated unheard-of crimes. Houses have been plundered and burned, defenseless men shot down, and women outraged. We are here for revenge — and we have got it." [1]

This savage butchery, indefensible even upon the score of retaliation, aroused the military authorities to a sense of their shortcomings ; and on the 25th of August, only four days after the massacre, General Thomas Ewing issued an order, which may have been intended to put an end to the disgraceful warfare that had grown up in this district, but which, considered as a military measure, was, fortunately, without a parallel in Missouri. Instead of obliging the Kansas robbers to stay on their own side of the border, and using the troops at his command to drive out or exterminate the "bushwhackers," as there is reason to believe he might have done, and as certainly would have been done by any one who really desired to give peace to the border, General Ewing issued an order, in the execution of which, those of the inhabitants of Jackson, Bates, Cass, and a part of Ver

[1] Spring's Kansas, p. 287.

non counties, who were so unfortunate as to live outside of certain limits, were driven from their homes, their dwellings burned, their farms laid waste, and the great bulk of their movable property handed over, without let or hindrance, to the Kansas " jayhawkers." It was a brutal order, ruthlessly enforced, and so far from expelling or exterminating the guerrillas, it simply handed this whole district over to them. Indeed, we are assured by one who was on the ground, that from this time until the end of the war, no one wearing the Federal uniform dared risk his life within the devastated region.

The only people whom the enforcement of the order did injure were some thousands of those whom it was Ewing's duty to protect. They were ruined ; and if possible the enormity of the outrage upon them was increased by the fact that, fourteen years later, General Schofield, who had approved of the order, justified his action on the ground that they were mere furnishers of supplies to the guerrillas, when in point of fact, tried by any known standard, they were as loyal to the Union as were their neighbors in Kansas. They had voted against secession ; they had not only, thus far, kept their quota in the Union army full, and that without draft or bounty, but they continued to do so ; and if they did not protect themselves against the outrages alike of Confederate bushwhackers and Union jayhawkers, it was because early in the war they had been disarmed by Federal authority, and were consequently without the means of defense. But it is unnecessary to pursue this subject further. Considered as a military measure, the only light in which we are privileged to regard it, this order was, as General Blair truly said, an act of imbecility — a confession on the part of the Federal commander that he was unwilling or unable to put down the bushwhackers — which should have cost him his command ; and neither General Schofield's nor President Lincoln's approval of the measure can change its character, though it may divide the odium.

A wholesale spoliation of this character was hardly calculated to make many converts among the secessionists proper, and as it did not commend itself to the great mass of the Union people, and utterly failed to give peace to the district in which it was tried, it was not repeated elsewhere. There were, however, other methods of confiscation, less brutal, perhaps, but equally unjust, that were practiced, and always with the same evil result. Among them, the favorite seems to have been to assess the Southern sympathizers for damage done by bushwhackers and Confederate raiders, or for the purpose of raising a fund to be used in the support of Union refugees and for other purposes. Of the injustice of such a proceeding it is needless to speak. The people who were thus called upon to make good these losses, or contribute to the charities which the government should have maintained, were in no manner responsible for the injuries which they were called upon to repair. Even if they had known of them, they could not have prevented them ; and yet so popular was this method of raising money, that, in August, 1862, the Southern sympathizers in St. Louis County were ordered to be assessed in the sum of five hundred thousand dollars for the purpose of arming the state militia and supporting the families of such militiamen and United States volunteers as might be left destitute. As if to add absurdity to injustice, it was furthermore proposed

to grade this assessment not only according to the wealth
of the individual, but according to the supposed degree
of his sympathy with the South. In other words, it was
proposed, in a community in which all shades of opinion
existed, to establish a dividing line between loyalty and
disloyalty, and to fix the rates of payment of those
who fell below the standard ; and this was to be done
not by an open trial, and the examination of witnesses
under oath, but by a board sitting in secret session and
obliged, from the nature of the case, to rest its decisions upon vague rumors, hearsay evidence, and general
impressions. That such a proposition could have been
seriously entertained, or that worthy citizens could have
been found who were willing to undertake the duties of
this office, is almost incredible at this late day ; but it
illustrates very clearly the spirit that then ruled in some
of the border States. Fortunately for the good name of
the State, the Rev. Dr. William G. Eliot, a loyal clergyman of St. Louis, called President Lincoln's attention
to the injustice and iniquity of this measure, and it
was countermanded. The disapproval of this particular
order of assessment, however, did not put an end to the
evil. It continued to flourish, and so serious did it
finally become that Governor Gamble, in December,
1862, forbade the militia of the State to aid in carrying
out any of these assessments, thus depriving the pro-
vost marshals of the services of these troops, and to
some extent putting an end to the practice.

Amongst the other and more general forms in which
this interference of military with the civil administration
manifested itself, may be mentioned the restrictions that
were placed upon trade and commerce, and the presence
of soldiers at the polls. With the first of these measures

we need not concern ourselves. It was a serious inconvenience to the people of the State, loyal as well as disloyal, and a positive injury to many; but it was regarded
as a necessary precaution, and hence it was willingly
borne even by those who suffered most from its enforcement.

The second of these measures cannot be dismissed
in this summary fashion. The presence of soldiers at
the polls is never a pleasant sight to a people accustomed to self-government, and in the present instance
it was made more objectionable by the fact that the
reason assigned for it was not sufficient, and because
it involved an unnecessary display of force for the purpose of carrying out an unnecessary and, so far as it partook of the nature of an *ex post facto* law, an illegal
ordinance. There were never any grounds for supposing that those who were disfranchised by the ordinance
of June, 1862, would attempt to vote; and even if they
had been allowed to do so, there was not the slightest
probability of their carrying the election. To intimate,
then, that the soldiers were permitted at the polls for the
purpose of preserving order and preventing intimidation,
is to assert that the loyal voters of the State, although
they outnumbered the disloyal in the proportion of two
or three to one, would not preserve order, and could be
so far intimidated as to prevent their voting. Such a
thing might have been possible at some outlying pre-
cinct, or in some guerrilla-infested neighborhood; but to
admit it of the State at large is to cast a reflection upon
the Union men which is certainly undeserved. Nevertheless it is the explanation which the order, relating to
the election of November, 1862, was made to give of
itself; and whilst it would hardly be fair, for the reason

just given, to characterize it as untrue, it would be obviously unsafe to accept it as the whole truth. This will be found in the evident determination of the authorities to enforce the ordinance of the convention, which made an oath of loyalty to the United States and the provisional government of Missouri a condition precedent to voting. In other words, soldiers were encouraged to be at the polls not so much for the purpose of preventing any person from being intimidated, as of intimidating any one who might attempt to vote without having taken the prescribed oath. In the language of the order, they were " to see that no person is either kept from the polls by intimidation, or in any way interfered with in voting at the polls for whatever candidate he may choose," though in a previous clause they were virtually instructed that no person was to be allowed to vote who did not pledge himself to vote in a particular way.

In view of the predominance of Union men in the State, this course was unnecessary. Indeed, the provisional authorities themselves soon saw it, and at the next election — the one held in November, 1863 — they so far rectified the mistake as to require the soldiers to vote in their camps. This was a step in the right direction, but it did not go far enough. The test oath for voters and candidates, which had been adopted as a safeguard against the possibility of having a disloyal government, was retained ; and although there was never any occasion for testing its utility from this point of view, yet in theory at least it was assumed to have effected the purpose for which it was designed. In practice it did much more, for it led to results that were not generally contemplated. By disfranchising those who, whilst not being secessionists, would not pledge them-

selves not to aid those of their friends and relatives who
were, it virtually handed the State over to the radical
Republicans; and what was far worse, it furnished them
with a precedent for the long list of outrages which for
some years made an election in Missouri such a sorrow-
ful travesty.   From 1862 to 1872 there was not an
election held in the State that could be called either full,
fair, or free; and this result, so foreign to the spirit of
our institutions, would hardly have been possible but for
the precedent furnished by the adoption of this ordinance and the methods taken to enforce it.

These were a few of the ills which grew out of this
interference of the military with the civil authority, and
to which the people of Missouri were subjected.   In the
North, where there was, substantially, no difference of
opinion, the evil was but little felt; but in the border
States, where every shade of sentiment existed, it was
very real, and there can be no question as to the influence it exerted.   Grievous as it was, and numerous as
were the individual cases of oppression to which it gave
rise, it did not affect the action of the Union men of the
State upon the one great issue of the war.   Upon this
point their conduct was uniformly consistent, and whatever may have been their differences of opinion as to
the means employed to restore the Union, they never
wavered in their fidelity to it.   In fact, so determined
were their efforts in this direction that they not only
succeeded in establishing order over the greater part of
the State, especially in those regions in which they were
not hampered by Federal interference, but they answered every demand made upon them by the national
authorities for men, without a draft, and with but a relatively small expenditure for bounties.

Notwithstanding the heavy contingent which the State sent into the Confederate service, she furnished to the Union army 109,000 men, about one eleventh of her entire population, or forty-seven per cent. of the number available for military purposes. The extent of this drain will be better understood if we compare it with the number of men furnished by the other States. According to the official reports, the percentage of troops to population in the Western States and Territories was 13.6 per cent., and in the New England States twelve per cent. ; whilst in Missouri, if we add to her quota the 30,000 men who went into the Southern army, it was fourteen per cent., or sixty per cent. of those who were subject to military duty. These are instructive figures, and they become more so when taken in connection with the fact that at the presidential election of 1860, Lincoln had but a tenth of the vote cast in the State.

Of the loss of life among the Missouri troops, Confederate as well as Federal, it is impossible to speak with accuracy, as there is no record of the mortality of those who went South. In the Union army, the deaths are put down at 13,885 — a fraction over twelve per cent. of all the men furnished by the State, — of which number 3,317 were either killed, or died of wounds received in battle. These are the official figures, and they are no doubt correct as far as they go, though it is doubtful whether they include the number of deaths among the state troops, who were never in the service of the United States. Of the mortality among the Confederates we are, as has been said, without any official record ; and the facts upon which we have to depend are of such a character that any attempt to fix the number of deaths among them must be but the merest guess-work. It is probable, however, that the ratio among them, especially in the cases of deaths from disease, was much greater than among the Union troops, owing to the unwonted hardships they were called upon to endure, and the want of medicines and suitable hospital accommodations for the sick and wounded. Taking these facts into consideration, and bearing in mind the privations to which they were unavoidably subjected in the way of an insufficiency of food and clothing, it is believed that an estimate, placing the total number of their deaths at forty per cent., would be within the bounds of reason. This would carry their loss up to 12,000 men, and adding this number to the deaths that occurred in the Federal service, it will swell the aggregate mortality in the two armies to 25,885. This estimate does not cover those who were killed in the skirmishes that took place between the home guards and the guerrillas; nor does it include those who were not in either army, but who were shot down by "bushwhackers" and "bushwhacking" Federal soldiers. Of these latter there is no record, though there were but few sections of the State in which such scenes were not more or less frequent. Assuming the deaths from these two sources to have been 1,200, and summing up the results, it will be found that the number of Missourians who were killed in the war and died from disease during their term of service amounted to not less than 27,000 men.

Heavy as was this loss of life, that of property was relatively quite as great. Leaving out of consideration the value of the slaves, which may be roughly estimated at $40,000,000, the other elements of wealth exhibit a marked decrease during the war and after. As late as 1868, after two years of prosperity, the taxable wealth of the State was rated at only $454,000,000, or $46,000,000 less than the amount returned in 1860. In many portions of the State, especially in the southern and western borders, whole counties had been devastated. The houses were burned, the fences destroyed, and the farms laid waste. Much of the livestock of the State had disappeared ; and everywhere, even in those sections that were comparatively quiet and peaceful, the quantity of land in cultivation was much less than it had been at the outbreak of the war. Added to these sources of decline, and in some measure a cause of them, was the considerable emigration from the State which now took place, and particularly from those regions that lay in the pathway of the armies, or from those neighborhoods that were given over to the " bushwhackers." The amount of loss from these different sources cannot be accurately gauged, but some idea may be formed of it, and of the unsettled condition of affairs, from the fact that only 41 out of the 113 counties in the State receipted for the tax books for 1861 ; and in these counties, only $250,000 out of the $600,000 charged against them were collected. In the last two years of the war, the collections in portions of the State are said to have been better, though they were still far from satisfactory ; and yet, notwithstanding these unfavorable conditions, the State expended over $7,000,000 in fitting out and maintaining her troops. The bulk of this sum was afterwards returned to her by the general government, and as it was used in paying the indebtedness which she had failed to meet during the war, it enabled her to reëstablish her credit upon the favorable basis upon which it now rests.

Of the numerous and daring raids that were made into the State we have not thought it necessary to speak, as they had no appreciable influence upon the result, either in Missouri or upon the country at large. Even when intended to mask some important movement, or to prevent reinforcements from being sent to a threatened point, they can hardly be considered as successful, since, as a rule, after the spring of 1862, the state troops and the enrolled militia could be depended upon to give a satisfactory account of these most unwelcome visitors. Such, though, was not always the case, and notably so in the raid led by Price in September, 1864. Entering the southeastern portion of the State at the head of 12,000 men, this gallant officer came within forty miles of St. Louis, passed in sight of Jefferson City, and moving up the Missouri, captured Lexington and Independence. Here he was confronted by troops from Kansas, and being closely followed by General Pleasanton with a large force of cavalry, he turned southward and made his escape into Arkansas, but not without heavy loss in men and material. In the course of the raid he marched 1,434 miles, fought forty-three battles and skirmishes, and according to his own calculation destroyed upwards of " ten million dollars worth of property," a fair share of which belonged to his own friends.

Considered with reference to the number of men, the distance marched, the battles fought, and the amount of property destroyed, this was one of the most memorable raids of the war ; and yet it is difficult to see what the Confederate authorities expected to gain by the movement. Price was not strong enough to maintain himself in the State against the overwhelming odds that could be concentrated against him, and without some such prospect his expedition was a predestined failure. As matters turned out, it did not prevent reinforcements from being sent to Thomas at Nashville, nor did it exert any perceptible influence upon the presidential election of that year. The property destroyed, at least that part of it which belonged to the federal government, was never missed; and it is probable that, after making due allowance for the exaggerations on both sides, Price lost, in men and material, quite as much as he gained.

This was the last effort made to carry the war into Missouri. In the following spring Grant and Lee closed in the death struggle around Richmond, and in the presence of this battle of giants all minor combats were dwarfed. When at last, on the 9th of April, it was known that the Confederate army, reduced to a mere handful but still ready for duty, had surrendered, the news brought a universal feeling of relief. By a proclamation of Governor Fletcher the 15th was set apart as a day of thanksgiving for " this hope of peace," and there were but few Missourians, Union men or secessionists, who did not join in the glad acclaim.

In due time the Confederate forces on the west side of the Mississippi laid down their arms, and in June some eight thousand of them arrived in St. Louis. Speaking of this event, the " Republican " of that city held the following language, which, *mutatis mutandis*, may with equal justice be applied to the gallant men who followed the flag of the Union. " In a few days all that portion of the rebel army which was recruited in Missouri, with the exception of a few who prefer to remain in the South, . . . will have returned to their farms, or their former places of labor or business throughout the State, and their character, habits and feeling as soldiers will disappear as they resume their old habits as citizens."

These pleasing anticipations were soon realized, though in certain portions of the State, especially along the southern and western borders, the guerrillas and marauders of all kinds showed an unwillingness to give up their freebooting habits and return to an orderly mode of life. The state authorities, however, proved equal to the occasion. Governor Fletcher ordered a large force into the disturbed districts, and this, taken in connection with the summary action of the people in certain counties, soon stamped out the evil. The turbulent spirits bred by the war, federal as well as rebel, were soon made to understand that the civil authority was again supreme, and that crime, no matter of what character or by whom committed, could no longer be cloaked under the guise of military necessity. In these disturbances the old soldiers, the men who had faced each other in the battle-field, were not arrayed on opposite sides, but they stood together for the maintenance of law and order. In the hard school of the war they had learned to respect each other, and as they had put away all feelings of hatred and uncharitableness when they laid aside their muskets, they found no difficulty in working together for the suppression of crime, the restoration of order, and the good of the State.

CHAPTER XVII.

TURNING now to the political history of these years we find that although the Emancipation Proclamation of President Lincoln did not apply to Missouri, yet the question of the abolition of slavery in the State entered largely into the local politics of the day. At the election held in November, 1862, for members of the General Assembly, a majority of emancipationists were returned, though they were unable to take any definite action in the matter, owing to the exhausted condition of the state treasury, and to the constitutional provision, which forbade the emancipation of slaves without the consent of the owners, or the payment of a full equivalent for the slaves so freed. Satisfied that the people of the State were in favor of doing away with slavery, the legislature indicated it so plainly that Governor Gamble summoned the convention to meet on the 15th of June, 1863, for the purpose of acting upon the question. After a prolonged debate, an ordinance was adopted which provided for gradual emancipation, and the convention then adjourned *sine die*.

The plan as adopted was as just and fair as any measure of confiscation can be said to be, but it did not satisfy the radical Republicans of the State. They wanted to have the slaves made free at once, and to effect this, they sent a committee to Washington for the purpose of inducing President Lincoln to extend the area within which his proclamation was operative, so as to include Missouri. Failing in the object of their visit, they returned home, and at once began their preparations for the election of November, 1864. Upon the direct issue of immediate and unconditional emancipation they carried the State by a majority of 30,000, though the total vote was but little more than half what it had been four years before. It was the first election for state officers that had been held since the beginning of the war, Provisional Governor Gamble having been appointed by the convention, as was Lieutenant Governor W. P. Hall, who became governor upon the death of Gamble in January, 1864.

The proposition to hold another convention having been carried, the delegates chosen to that body met at St. Louis on the 6th of January, 1865. Divided according to their nativities, it will be seen that thirty-five of them were born in the slave States, twenty-one in the free States, nine in Europe, and one is not given. Politically speaking, they were, as a rule, new men. But few of them were known outside of their immediate neighborhood, and it is but fair to add, in view of the specimen of political handiwork which they turned out, that still fewer of them were ever heard of again. The constitution which they framed, despite certain good provisions, evinced such a spirit of political intolerance, showed so clearly that its authors were unfit for statesmanlike work, that they were speedily relegated to the obscurity from which they should never have been taken. Unquestionably much of the bitter feeling displayed in this instrument can be ascribed to the excitement of the hour, and it would no doubt be pleasant if it could all be assigned to this cause. Unfortunately for this theory, the course of the radicals in carrying out these invidious restrictions, after the necessity for them had passed away, affords ground for the belief that their object in adopting them was not so much to punish the rebels, as it was to give the control of the State to the wing of the Republican party to which they belonged.

The first measure upon which, under the terms of the call, the convention was expected to act, was the one for the abolition of slavery. This was soon settled. On the 11th of January George P. Strong, of St. Louis, reported " AN ORDINANCE ABOLISHING SLAVERY IN MISSOURI," and recommended its passage. Various attempts were made to amend it, but they were voted down, and the ordinance, as reported, was passed by a practically unanimous vote, there being sixty for it, to four against it, whilst two were absent. A copy of the Ordinance, duly signed and attested, was forwarded by special messenger to Governor Fletcher, and in accordance with the request of the convention he issued a proclamation, declaring " that henceforth and forever, no person within the jurisdiction of the State shall be subject to any abridgment of liberty, except such as the law shall prescribe for the common good, or know any master but God."

At this time there were probably a hundred and fourteen thousand negroes in the State, worth for purposes of taxation forty millions of dollars. Ostensibly they were slaves, but practically they were not, for it was clearly understood, even by the slaveholders, that the institution in Missouri was dead, and that all that remained to be done was to see that it was decently and legally buried. The opportunity to do this was afforded by the convention ; and in promptly availing themselves of it, the people of Missouri may justly claim for her the credit of being the only one of the slave States which voluntarily and of its own accord abolished slavery. As we have repeatedly had occasion to declare, the people of the State had never been enamored of the institution, had in fact tolerated it from an unwillingness to interfere with vested rights ; and in striking it down they not only gave abundant proof of this fact, and at a cost, to the State, of a portion of the revenue of which she was sorely in need, but they again served notice upon the Confederate authorities that Missouri was in the Union and proposed to stay there.

Having disposed of this question in a satisfactory manner, the convention might well have adjourned, as the disfranchisement of the rebels, the one other matter upon which it was expected that action would be taken, had been accomplished by the convention which met in June, 1862, so far as it was possible to effect that purpose by a constitutional enactment. This action was by no means satisfactory to the members of the present convention. From the first they had fallen under the control of a few extremists, who were determined to be satisfied with nothing less than a thorough remodeling of the constitution ; and under their lead it was complacently resolved that the people " intended and expected " not only that slavery should be abolished and disloyalists disfranchised, but that the constitution should be so amended as to bring it into harmony with the change that had taken place in the industrial and political condition of the State. Doubtful as this measure was from a legal point of view, the members of the convention thought proper to regard it as tantamount to a removal of the restrictions imposed upon them by the call under which they met; and they proceeded to frame an entirely new constitution. This was submitted to the people, for ratification, in June, 1865, and was accepted by a majority of eighteen hundred in a total vote of eighty-five thousand.

In some of its articles, notably in those that related to education and to banks and corporations, the new constitution was a decided improvement upon the one adopted in 1820, and still in force; but in the article on the right of suffrage, especially in the clause which established a test oath for voters, there were features that were so outrageous as to outweigh the good that might have come from those provisions that were clearly of a beneficent character. Without stopping to enumerate the objections that might be urged against this particular clause, it will be sufficient to say that the oath as established was so comprehensive in its scope, and covered such a wide field of conduct past and future, that it is doubtful whether there was a prominent man in the State who could truthfully have taken it. Including subdivisions, there were over forty-five different offenses which the applicant for registration must swear he had never committed; and unless he could do so, he was not to be allowed to vote, or hold any state, county, or municipal office, or act as a teacher in any school, or preach, or solemnize marriage, or practice law, or serve as juror. He could not even hold any real estate, or other property, in trust for the use of any church, religious society, or congregation.

In the attempt to enforce this iniquitous ordinance,

much trouble occurred. The judges of the supreme court, satisfied that it was null and void, refused to vacate their offices, and were forcibly ousted. Ministers of the gospel, Catholic priests, and sisters of charity engaged in teaching were arrested, and in some cases fined and imprisoned. Prominent lawyers like Samuel T. Glover, a member of the Union safety committee in 1861, refused to abide by the law and challenged indictment; and when in November, 1865, that gallant soldier General Frank Blair refused to take the oath and brought suit against the judges of the election for declining to receive his vote, it was felt, even by those who had approved the ordinance, that the time had come when its enforcement was no longer possible. At the meeting of the legislature, in January, 1867, Governor Fletcher, who had opposed the adoption of the constitution, recommended that the 9th section of the 2d article should be stricken out for the reason that it had not prevented disloyal persons from being lawyers and school-teachers, and because " bishops, priests, and ministers teach and pray without taking the prescribed oath," thereby setting an example of disobedience to law, which may ultimately lead to anarchy. Before the legislature could act upon his recommendation, the supreme court of the United States, in January, 1867, decided that the test oath was unconstitutional.

The announcement of this decision gave a measure of relief to the people of the State, though the reign of intolerance was not yet over. The test oath and the methods taken to enforce it had brought a number of exceedingly small men to the front; and as they were naturally desirous of prolonging their lease of power, they adopted, in January, 1868, another registry law

which was even more stringent than the one it superseded. Under it, the governor, by and with the advice
and consent of the Senate, was authorized, at every
general election, to appoint a superintendent of registration in each senatorial district. These superintendents
appointed a board of registration for each county, to
whom was committed the whole electoral machinery of
the State, with power to purge the voting lists at their
own sweet will. In the hands of facile officials it was
easy, under this law, to produce any given result, and
there can be no doubt as to the unflinching manner in
which this privilege of purgation was exercised in some
portions of the State. At the election in November,
1868, the radicals were successful, J. W. McClurg their
candidate being chosen governor by a majority of over
19,000, though the aggregate vote was only 145,000,
20,000 less than it had been in 1860.

Efficacious as this law had proved to be when judged
from a party point of view, it did not enable the radicals to retain control of the State. The liberal Republicans as they were called, under the lead of B. Gratz
Brown and Carl Schurz, had long been restive under
this harsh legislation, and they now took issue with the
radical wing of their party upon the question of universal amnesty and universal enfranchisement. With
the aid of such Democrats as were allowed to vote, they
swept the State at the election held in the autumn of
1870. In justice, however, to Governor McClurg and
the General Assembly it must be said that, in point of
liberality, they showed themselves to be in advance of
their party. In his inaugural message the governor
had called attention to the policy of removing the dis-
abilities that had been imposed upon those who were

upon the side of the South during the war; and at a special meeting of the legislature in January, 1870, it was resolved to submit to the people, for ratification, certain proposed amendments to the constitution of the State, which virtually covered this ground. By one of these amendments the test oath for voters was abolished; another removed the disqualifications that had been imposed on account of former acts of disloyalty, and also those that were due to race, color, or previous condition of servitude; a third related to education; and there were still others that referred to the courts and to banks and corporations. All of these amendments were adopted, and at the same election B. Gratz Brown, the liberal candidate, was chosen governor by a majority of 41,000 in a total vote of 166,000. This, it will be observed, is only one thousand more than were cast ten years before, at the election of 1860, though the population of the State was now 1,728,000, or 540,000 greater than it then was.

The repeal of these disfranchising and disqualifying laws swept away the last vestige of the intolerant legislation that grew out of the war; and at the election of November, 1872, the Democratic party, composed largely of conservative Union men like Blair, Broadhead, Phelps, and others, carried the State by a majority of 35,000 in a total poll of 278,000. Compared with the vote of 1870, it will be observed that the increase in two years amounted to 112,000. This is too large to be attributed to natural causes; and whilst it would be manifestly unjust to assert that it represents the number of persons who were disfranchised, yet it gives good ground for the conclusion that the number of those who were affected by this measure was much larger than is usually supposed.

With the success of the Democrats at this election, the control of the State passed into the hands of those who were entitled to it by virtue of their numbers; and they still retain it. Of their management of affairs it is not my purpose to speak. Neither does it come within the limits of this work to treat of the rapid recovery of the State from the wounds of the civil war; of her phenomenal increase in wealth and population during the five years immediately succeeding the return of peace, or of the liberality which she has displayed in advancing the negro to all the privileges of citizenship. Facts upon these points are accessible to all, and as they contain within themselves the germs of actions whose results have yet to be worked out, their discussion belongs to the political economist, and would be out of place at this time and in this connection. The career of Missouri, or rather that portion of it which belongs to the domain of history, may be said to have been ended with the abolition of slavery. For fifty years and more this had been the issue upon which parties, in their struggle for power, had been aligned; and during all this period, through no desire of their own, but in opposition to their wishes as it was to their interests, it had furnished the people of the State with the motive for much of their political action. With its removal from the field of contention, the motive also disappeared; but in its place we have new interests, and these will give rise to new issues, around which parties will form. This will again bring on the struggle for power which in some shape has been going on since the formation of society, and will continue as long as human nature remains unchanged.

INDEX.

44